Ethical Dilemmas in Educational Research

Ethical Dilemmas in Educational Research

Dr Carol Brown and Professor Mary Wild

Open University Press

Open University Press
McGraw Hill
Unit 4
Foundation Park
Roxborough Way
Maidenhead
SL6 3UD

email: emea_uk_ireland@mheducation.com
world wide web: www.mheducation.co.uk

Copyright © Open International Publishing Limited, 2023

All rights reserved. Except for the quotation of short passages for the purposes of criticism and review, no part of this publication may be reproduced, stored in a retrieval system, or transmitted, in any form or by any means, electronic, mechanical, photocopying, recording or otherwise, without the prior written permission of the publisher or a licence from the Copyright Licensing Agency Limited. Details of such licences (for reprographic reproduction) may be obtained from the Copyright Licensing Agency Ltd of Saffron House, 6–10 Kirby Street, London EC1N 8TS.

Executive Editor: Eleanor Christie
Editorial Assistant: Zoe Osman
Content Product Manager: Ali Davis

A catalogue record of this book is available from the British Library

ISBN-13: 9780335251322
ISBN-10: 0335251323
eISBN: 9780335251339

Library of Congress Cataloging-in-Publication Data
CIP data applied for

Typeset by Transforma Pvt. Ltd., Chennai, India

Fictitious names of companies, products, people, characters and/or data that may be used herein (in case studies or in examples) are not intended to represent any real individual, company, product or event but they are indeed based on real individuals in many examples in this book.

For my special friends Carol Hawkins, Jenny Bodinham and Ellen Cocking. I treasure your love, kindness, laughter, and prayers.
Carol

For my father, Thomas Vincent Dwyer, who sadly passed away as we began working on this book and for my mother, Patricia Margaret Dwyer, who is stronger than she will ever know.
Mary

Contents

List of Tables and Figures   ix

List of Contributors   x

Foreword: Ian Menter   xii

I. INTRODUCING ETHICAL DILEMMAS IN EDUCATIONAL RESEARCH   1
   Carol Brown

II. ETHICAL GUIDELINES IN EDUCATIONAL RESEARCH   9
   Carol Brown

III. RESEARCH ETHICS COMMITTEES IN EDUCATION RESEARCH: COMMON PURPOSE, MISUNDERSTANDINGS, CHALLENGES AND MOVING FORWARD   20
   Sarah Quinton

IV. ETHICAL DILEMMAS IN THE SUPERVISION OF UNDERGRADUATE EDUCATION STUDENTS CONDUCTING RESEARCH FOR DISSERTATIONS   32
   Victoria Pratt

V. ETHICAL DILEMMAS IN ACTION   49
   Catharine Gilson

VI. INVOLVING CHILDREN IN RESEARCH: ACTIVE PARTICIPATION AND ONGOING ASSENT   61
   Carmel Capewell

VII. ELICITING THE TEACHER'S AND PUPILS' PERSPECTIVES IN THE CREATIVE CLASSROOM: ISSUES OF AGENCY AND PRIVACY   76
   Sarah Frodsham and Deb McGregor

VIII. STATISTICALLY SPEAKING: ETHICAL DILEMMAS IN HANDLING NUMERICAL DATA   93
   Mary Wild and Sarah Frodsham

IX. STARTING WITH SELF: RESEARCHING AS AN INSIDER   111
   Jane Spiro

X. ETHICAL ISSUES FOR THE RESEARCHER   127
   Mary Wild and Carol Brown

XI. ETHICS IN EDUCATIONAL RESEARCH WITH INDIGENOUS
COMMUNITIES 142
Patrick Alexander

XII. JOLTS IN THE MARGINS: PROBING THE ETHICAL DIMENSIONS
OF POST-PARADIGMS IN EDUCATIONAL RESEARCH 154
Linda J Shaw

XIII. CONCLUSION: THE HIDDEN LIVES OF ETHICS: BEYOND
THE PRAGMATICS 173
Mary Wild

Index 184

List of Tables and Figures

Tables

Table 1: Features of CHAT to be captured with ethical values and principles in mind — 80

Table 2: Relating ethical concerns: the data required to evidence the nature of creativity in classrooms — 88

Table 3: A global snapshot of students' performance in reading, mathematics and science (OECD 2021a) — 98

Figures

Figure 1: A diagrammatic representation of [second generation] CHAT (after Roth and Lee 2007 and Thompson 2015) to provide context to the selected creative processes paid attention to for the purpose of this chapter — 78

Figure 2: Diagrammatic representation of CHAT to illustrate foregrounded features of the first moment (The Lighthouse Keeper's Son) — 85

Figure 3: Diagrammatic representation of CHAT to illustrate the third moment (creating a parallel series circuit) — 87

Figure 4: Averages for 15 years PISA a) Reading, b) Mathematics and c) Science scale by all students' participants for New Zealand and the United Kingdom in 2018 (OECD 2021a) — 101

List of Contributors

Patrick Alexander is a Reader in Education at Oxford Brookes University. He is an anthropologist of education with an interest in schooling and socialization. An ethnographer by training, Patrick's linked interests relate to youth transitions, how young people are socialized into futurity and modernity and how this is shaped by intersections of race, class and gender. Patrick also researches professional learning and teacher engagement with research.

Carol Brown is a Senior Lecturer in Psychology and Education and a Faculty Ethics Officer at Oxford Brookes University. Her academic background is in psychology and she is a mixed methods researcher with an interest in large-scale quantitative analyses. Her research focuses on the psychology of education, achievement motivation, identity, educational inequalities and outcomes, student wellbeing and educational assessment, primarily in A-level students as she was formerly an A-level psychology teacher.

Carmel Capewell is a Senior Lecturer in Child Development at Oxford Brookes University focused on researching with children/young people; using visual methods; auditory processing difficulties (glue war/otitis media) and disability rights.

Sarah Frodsham is a Senior/Departmental Lecturer, STEAM research group co-convener, Research Associate, and Training and Development Officer. Research interests include STEM and STEAM with a specialism in creativity in science during all stages of formal and informal education. Her methodological interests include interpretivist approaches and visual methodologies.

Catharine Gilson is an Associate Lecturer in Early Childhood Education and Affiliate Lecturer with Oxford Brookes University and was previously Senior Lecturer in Early Childhood Education. Her research interests include the relational aspects of early childhood education and care, children's rights and children's voice, parental, voice and visual methodologies.

Deb McGregor is Professor in Education at Oxford Brookes University. She has worked across primary, secondary and tertiary education for over 25 years. She has taught across a range of subjects from thinking skills in primary and secondary schools to research methods and methodology in the UK and USA to masters and doctoral students. She is currently involved in various research projects related to science, creativity, learning in informal spaces, and school leadership and management. She has supervised doctoral students researching in each of these areas.

Ian Menter is an Emeritus Professor at the University of Oxford. Ian was former President of BERA, 2013–2015. He was Director of Professional Programmes at the University of Oxford and led the development of the Oxford Education Deanery.

Victoria Pratt is a Senior Lecturer in Education and Early Childhood at Oxford Brookes University and a PhD student at UCL. Her research interests focus on family diversity, single/solo motherhood, early childhood education and care provision; also, inclusive learning and learning in HE, focusing on undergraduate students' academic reading.

Sarah Quinton is an Associate Dean for Research and Knowledge Exchange and Reader in Digital Society and previous Chair of the University Research Ethics Committee, Oxford Brookes University. Sarah's particular research interests lie within exploring how the digital environment is shaping behaviour change across society, business, consumers and citizens, and the impact of digitalization on tools and perspectives within social science research methods and the ethical challenges in contemporary digital research.

Linda Shaw is a Senior Lecturer in Education and Early Childhood at Oxford Brookes University with an interest in social pedagogy, post-structural feminist perspectives on early childhood and play, intergenerational theory, and innovative spaces for play and learning. She has had an extensive career within the early years and primary sector.

Jane Spiro is a Professor in Education and TESOL at Oxford Brookes University. She is interested in creativity in language education, reflective writing and the role of narrative in qualitative research. Her publications include resources for creative reading and writing (*Creative Poetry Writing*, Oxford 2004; *Reflective Writing*, Palgrave Macmillan 2020), research into educational innovation (*Linguistic and Cultural Innovation in Schools* with Eowyn Crisfield, Palgrave 2018) and most recently, narrative research of the higher education experience (*Crossing Borders in University Learning and Teaching*, Routledge 2022).

Mary Wild is a Professor in Child Development and Education at Oxford Brookes University and was formerly Head of the School of Education at Oxford Brookes. Her research interests include professionalism in the early years, early childhood literacy, children's thinking and the use of ICT to support learning. Her previous publications include reflective texts for practitioners (Wild, M. (ed.) (2018) *Professional Dialogues in the Early Years: Re-discovering Early Years Pedagogy and Principles*. Critical Publishing; Wild, M. and Street, A. (eds) (2013) *Themes and Issues in Early Childhood*. Sage).

Foreword

Why an ethical perspective is crucial in educational research in the twenty-first century

Ian Menter
Emeritus Professor of Teacher Education, University of Oxford
BERA President, 2013–15

Ethical Dilemmas in Educational Research is a timely, much-needed volume. In Chapter II, Carol Brown suggests that:

> It goes without saying that it is a fundamental principle that researchers should not falsify, distort, suppress, selectively report or sensationalize their work.

Every chapter in this book can be aligned with this 'fundamental principle'. The reader is provided with numerous examples of how dilemmas may arise in the course of undertaking educational research, some of which may create tensions or even temptations towards compromising this principle, as well as many other important ethical positions that are discussed in detail. In the present neoliberal era of 'post-truth' and the promulgation of 'fake news', we have seen all too much evidence of ethical standards being eroded in many aspects of public life, including the film industry, churches, policing, sport, energy policy and, perhaps most notably, politics.

The populist politics that have emerged in many western societies in the twenty-first century (Eatwell and Goodwin 2018) have indubitably had some influence on educational research. There is pressure from the media, politicians and elsewhere for 'simple solutions', for panaceas to solve such issues, such as the persistent educational underachievement of children from disadvantaged backgrounds. Researchers, competing for-all-too scarce funds to support their research, may be tempted to overclaim for the effectiveness of their approaches (see Menter 2021). The present volume offers an invaluable set of insights that will help to prevent – or at least minimize – such distortions.

The approach taken in this book is based on a recognition that education and educational research are both processes – social processes involving human activity and decision-making. This is why both education itself and educational research are potentially unpredictable in their nature. Whilst teachers and researchers may plan on the basis of their values and their intentions, they can never be sure of what the impact and outcomes of their actions will be. There must therefore be an element of improvisation in these undertakings, and this is why the concept of 'adaptive expertise' has become so important in teaching and teacher education (Anthony et al. 2015). For underlying decisions and actions taken by teachers and by educational researchers there must be a set of values (Menter 2009). Research ethics and teachers' professional ethics may be seen as overlapping sets of values – they are not identical but there are at least two elements, both very apparent in the chapters which follow, that are common to both (see also Chapter IV in Menter et al. 2011). One is the need to respect and protect the rights of the learner in educational settings. Whatever the learner's or research subject's age, the teacher or researcher is likely to be the one with the greater power to influence what takes place. This power must not be abused. Secondly, both education and educational research are processes commonly underpinned by a deeply held commitment to betterment and improvement. In his BERA Presidential address of 2005, through playing with a possible distinction between *education* research on the one hand and *educational* research on the other, the late Geoff Whitty drew attention to the value position implied by the latter term and thus committed BERA itself to an explicit value and ethical position (see Whitty 2006). The ethical position is of course developed fully in BERA's Ethical Code, which is much referred to in this book (BERA 2018).

Another BERA initiative which is very relevant to the foregoing discussion is the investigation of the connections between research and the teaching profession carried out in 2013/14. The report which emerged from this inquiry urged that teachers' work and teacher education programmes should be imbued with a commitment to the development of 'research literacy' (BERA-RSA 2014). This concept is not only about teachers having the skills to undertake systematic enquiry and to make productive use of published research; it also suggests that as well as adhering to the professional ethics laid down by their professional bodies, they should be familiar with and aware of the significance of research ethics. The present book will be an invaluable source for the development of this aspect of research literacy for teachers and teacher educators.

The priority given to ethical matters in all social research – including educational research – has escalated dramatically over recent decades. In the early days of my own career, although as a neophyte educational researcher I was mindful of the possibilities of undertaking research which might do some damage to the young people who were taking part in an educational innovation, it was not a formal requirement that I should apply for permission to go ahead. The creation of research ethics committees across higher education institutions in the UK (as well as in other countries) created new challenges for researchers, at the same time as creating safeguards for them and for those taking part in the research. There are many chapters in this volume that demonstrate the nature of these challenges as well as showing the importance of such safeguards.

Among the many strengths of this collection of chapters is the awareness of a wide range of methods in educational research that are deployed, including not only qualitative but also quantitative approaches (see for example Chapters IX and VIII). Whatever research approach is taken, ethical issues will arise at all stages, from the inception of the research, the design of the study, the access to the field or the database, the selection of material for analysis and the ways in which the research is written up and then disseminated.

We also have evidence in this collection of the value of looking outwards, to broaden our perspective. Although the authors are based in England, they draw on much work from elsewhere, including studies undertaken in countries where ethical issues are seen in quite different ways. In Chapter XI, Patrick Alexander uses his anthropological perspective – a perspective all too rarely invoked in educational research – to challenge us to consider the ethical dimensions of our research within a critical postcolonial framework. This is helpfully followed by Linda Shaw's chapter (XII), in which she expands on these perspectives by exploring post-feminism, post-structuralism and their contribution towards understanding the complexity of 'intersectionality' in contemporary society and in educational settings.

Throughout the book, we are reminded of the responsibilities we carry as educational researchers, not only to those taking part in our research, but to the wider community and indeed to ourselves. As Carmel Capewell puts it in Chapter VI, where she is considering the involvement of children in research:

> The question is whether using one's moral compass (or even if one has one) could be a strong reason for ensuring that all researchers, and particularly those using qualitative methods in educational research, become reflexive researchers... This process needs to be an integral part of the research process so that even before ethics forms are filled in, researchers need to consider their own position in terms of values and their view of the research that they are undertaking.

Carol Brown, Mary Wild and their colleagues are to be commended for creating such a rich collection of experiences and analyses of ethical dilemmas in educational research. This volume will become an invaluable guide for educational researchers around the world, helping them to be reflexive and self-critical in order to make informed decisions and to develop research practices which are based on explicit humanistic values.

References

Anthony, G., Hunter, J. and Hunter, R. (2015) Prospective teachers' development of adaptive expertise, *Teaching and Teacher Education*, 49: 108–117.

British Educational Research Association (2018) *Ethical Guidelines for Educational Research*. British Educational Research Association (BERA). Available at: https://www.bera.ac.uk/publication/ethical-guidelines-for-educational-research-2018 (accessed 16 February 2022).

British Educational Research Association – Royal Society for the Encouragement of the Arts, Manufacture and Commerce (BERA-RSA) (2014) *Research and the Teaching Profession: Building the capacity for a self-improving education system.*

London: BERA. Available at www.bera.ac.uk/wp-content/uploads/2013/12/BERA-RSA-Research-Teaching-Profession-FULL-REPORT-for-web.pdf (accessed 28 June 2022).

Eatwell, R. and Goodwin, M. (2018) *National Populism: The Revolt Against Liberal Democracy*. London: Penguin.

Menter, I. (2009) Teachers for the future: what have we got and what do we need?, in S. Gewirtz, P. Mahony, I. Hextall and A. Cribb (eds) *Changing Teacher Professionalism: International Trends, Challenges and Ways Forward*. London: Routledge.

Menter, I. (2021) Snake oil or hard science?, in A. Ross (ed.) *Educational Research for Social Justice: Evidence and Practice from the UK*. Cham, Switzerland: Springer.

Menter, I., Elliot, D., Hulme, M., Lewin, J. et al. (2011) *A Guide to Practitioner Research in Education*. London: Sage.

Whitty, G. (2006) Education(al) research and education policymaking: is conflict inevitable? *British Educational Research Journal*, 32(2): 159–76.

Introducing Ethical Dilemmas in Educational Research

Carol Brown

Ethical dilemmas in educational research can pose interesting and challenging questions for researchers. A careful balance must be struck between the needs of participants, increasing regulatory guidelines and the academic freedom of the educational researcher. This text seeks to address an existing gap by going beyond the guidelines and focusing on the specific dilemmas that the educational researcher faces, illustrated with real-life anonymized and hypothetical examples, as well as published works. Research methods in the educational field have developed substantially in recent times, diversifying in their nature and application. This has generated a set of more complex ethical dilemmas for consideration. Educational researchers may therefore employ varying methodologies and assume differing ontological, epistemological and theoretical positions. This text seeks to acknowledge each of these possibilities rather than presupposing any one stance over another. It is also important to acknowledge that educational context extends beyond that of the traditional classroom and can encompass numerous environments including mainstream and special schools, residential units, hospital schools, pupil referral units, preschools, play centres, youth groups, alternative learning environments such as museums or outdoor centres, universities, organized social activity groups and workplaces, for instance. The ethical dilemmas, which are the focus of this text, assume that these can therefore arise in a range of contexts and are not limited to school settings.

The book has been developed due to the authors' experiences of processing ethics applications in a university ethics roles: from dilemmas raised when discussing and delivering ethics training sessions with educational researchers, from real-life experiences of conducting educational research and from their previously published work(s).

Firstly, the rationale for the book and its nature and focus will be outlined, starting with an overview of the ethical guidelines in educational research, the role of ethics committees with an emphasis on common purposes, and misunderstandings, challenges and dilemmas experienced by undergraduate students conducting dissertation research. This will set the context for discussion of the specific dilemmas that arise in educational research and relate them to real-life scenarios. Issues considered include ethical issues when using numerical data, researching self, ethical issues for the researcher, ethical dilemmas in action, involving children in research with an emphasis on issues of active participation, and ongoing assent, agency and privacy and ethical dimensions of research with indigenous communities and post-paradigms in educational research. The concluding chapter will then summarize and draw together the dilemmas facing educational researchers, highlight key emerging themes and provide suggestions for the way forward.

The next section of this introduction gives a more detailed overview of each of the chapters.

Overview

Chapter II: Ethical guidelines in educational research – Dr Carol Brown

In recent years there has been an increase in publication of ethical codes guiding educational research. These derive from professional bodies and research organizations, as well as universities themselves, and adherence to such guidelines may also be required by journals when seeking publication of studies. The rights of the child are central to these ethical recommendations (UNCRC 1989). This chapter aims to highlight the importance of ethical guidelines in educational research and provide an overview of the main issues that the educational researchers should be aware of. Commonly recognized principles, which underpin the codes, encompass not only minimizing harm, but also respecting autonomy and dignity, protecting privacy, ensuring equality, inclusivity and diversity, and demonstrating social responsibility (BERA 2018 p. 4; ESRC 2019). The costs and benefits must always be equally considered.

Chapter III: Research ethics committees in education research: common purpose, misunderstandings, challenges and moving forward – Dr Sarah Quinton

Whilst the changing legislative landscape surrounds all researchers and the rise in multi-modal opportunities through new technologies impacts many others, there are specific ethical sensitivities associated with educational research. These sensitivities result in greater ethical complexity, for example: context, dependency issues, participants' rights, children as a 'vulnerable' group and insider research. These particular aspects of educational research, amongst others, require detailed consideration. Such consideration is commonly provided by ethics committees within institutions which review and approve, or reject, research projects. This chapter will discuss and expose the misunderstandings regarding the role of research ethics committees. It aims to identify principles of good practice, using illustrative exemplars, as a way to move forward for both committees reviewing educational research projects and individuals undertaking such research. Progressing scholarship within educational research is a shared priority, and research ethics committees can play a positive role as a moderator in this.

Chapter IV: Ethical dilemmas in the supervision of undergraduate education students conducting research for dissertations – Victoria Pratt

This chapter will explore the ethical dilemmas experienced by educational researchers supervising final-year undergraduate research projects. Although undergraduate dissertations are typically small-scale and unlikely to involve contentious areas of research, ethical issues may still arise for several reasons. Students are required to complete their projects within a short timescale and for the specific purpose of attaining an honours degree – these pressures may create a conflict of interest between researcher and participant. At the same time, undergraduate-specific supervision training is uncommon and supervisors often have limited time in which to make judgements about ethical issues in students' research. The particular ethical sensitivities related to the field of educational research must also be addressed by students and supervisors as they negotiate the dissertation process. This chapter seeks to support researcher colleagues in this undertaking by offering a detailed exploration of undergraduate research ethics and by suggesting some ways to resolve the issues that arise.

Chapter V: Ethical dilemmas in action – Dr Catharine Gilson

This chapter focuses on the in-the-moment dilemmas that can occur for educational researchers when in the process of carrying out fieldwork. The gap between these ethical dilemmas in action, often termed 'situated ethics', and procedural ethics is explored, highlighting the complexity of the fieldwork context and the often unpredictable nature of undertaking empirical research. The chapter explores a range of issues (such as the disclosure of sensitive information when the topic is not contentious, the impact of the methods and/or methodology on the ethical issues that may arise, cultural differences, the power dynamic at play in educational settings between gatekeeper, participants and researcher), all of which can disrupt the smooth running of the study and require an immediate response. The issues are explored through examples of ethical encounters taken from two qualitative studies, which were conducted with practitioners, parents and students training to be teachers in a higher education institution. The chapter focuses predominantly on interviews as a method, including conventional semi-structured interviews and film elicitation interviews. Practical suggestions for the dilemmas discussed are offered and an informed, ethically aware and reflexive approach advocated.

Chapter VI: Involving children in research: active participation and ongoing assent – Dr Carmel Capewell

This chapter is set in the context of the UNCRC (1989), particularly Articles 12 and 25. It explores the ways in which children and young people can be supported to have an active role in all aspects of research from design to analysis and conclusions. It includes the ways in which young people with disabilities can actively be included in research in the UK and internationally. There is a discussion of the different perspectives of the competency of children and young people (CYP) both socially and by university research ethics committees. The perceived need to protect children from harm is at the heart of whether or not ethical approval is gained for research with children. Adults are seen as the guardians of children, even when those adults are being cared for by their children. This can lead to situations whereby CYP are excluded from expressing opinions about services provided for them or when parents/carers are absent from their lives. Equally, there is recognition that there are times when adults agree to CYP participation in research without the full assent of the CYP themselves.

Capewell produces examples from her research, and those from international settings, about strategies that have been successful in encouraging children to explain their experiences and how CYP can take an active role in research. These take account of the need to reconsider and develop traditional research methods to ensure that they are CYP appropriate. Such novel approaches can make ethics committees uncomfortable but the need for researchers to develop a personal moral compass to ensure active and full participation by CYP is argued.

Chapter VII: Eliciting both the teacher's and pupils' perspectives in the creative classroom: Issues of agency and privacy – Dr Sarah Frodsham and Professor Deb McGregor

Creativity is a contested entity, and teachers, researchers and learners each make contrasting assumptions about how, where and when it arises (or is even observable) in classrooms. Capturing key elements of activities that influence and support the development of creativity in educational settings involves collecting various forms of evidence. Deciding whether the focus for research is centred on teachers' creativity, students' originality or indeed should be evidenced through interactions determines the nature of research instruments required to collect the relevant data. Endeavouring to evidence the creative process as demonstrated through dialogic and actionable exchanges, for example, requires digital technology to capture visual and audio data through video cameras or dictaphones. This, however, presents ethical dilemmas regarding participants' (primarily teacher and learners') agency and privacy. Eliciting this kind of data can expose individual's thinking and processes of meaning-making that may evidence misinterpretations, outlandish or even distinctly incorrect conceptual ideas. Applying a cultural and historical activity theory (CHAT) theoretical framework to analyse emergent dialogue, inter-actions, use of artefacts, etc., in a classroom, therefore, should ensure all participants (including parents of minors) are fully informed and voluntarily consent to participate. Researchers consequently need to provide reassurance whilst also placing recording equipment in unobtrusive locations to elicit good quality, *authentic* visual and verbal data.

Chapter VIII: Statistically Speaking: Ethical dilemmas in handling numerical data – Professor Mary Wild and Dr Sarah Frodsham

This chapter considers the ethical dilemmas in analysing and drawing conclusions based upon extant databases, drawn from large-scale quantitative studies in education, including international and nationally comparative data sets. Making use of such extant databases may seem to preclude some of the traditional and more tangible ethical dilemmas related to the direct engagement of participants. However, the analysis and reporting of seemingly neutral numerical data raises further ethical challenges, especially when statistically-based findings can be overly reified and easily misrepresented or misunderstood. Behind the data, there are also multiple individual and contextual accounts that underpin the data that can be obscured or inappropriately aggregated. The ethical duty to present findings in a way that is contextually nuanced and socially sensitive is therefore crucial.

In this chapter, ethical conundrums inherent in underlying philosophies of education that underpin research are explored through a neoliberal lens, which arguably prioritizes measurable output over educational processes, with consequent implications for the form and conduct of research. This agenda also applies to the professional context that the academic researcher experiences, in which the research status of socially aware researchers and of more formally organized institutions is increasingly evaluated by metrics of research output and research impact. We will therefore argue that this metrification of research raises further ethical dilemmas at the personal and professional level for researchers of educational practice.

Chapter IX: Starting with self: Researching as an insider – Professor Jane Spiro

This chapter aims to interrogate the ethical issues connected with making oneself, one's practice or one's practice environment the focus of research. Approaches in which the researcher is explicit within the research are numerous, but all share the position that the insider perspective is a contribution to, rather than a threat to, the validity of the research. Such approaches have been legitimated in the past two decades – they have been published in recognized academic journals, received high quality research ratings and have been showcased by highly regarded scholarly publishers. Yet the potential differences in approach to self and bias, between these approaches and positivist or scientific approaches, remains contentious. Core ethical principles can be construed in several different ways, which at face value appear contradictory. This chapter grapples with these apparent contradictions for researcher-focused researchers and explores the challenge of negotiating core principles so these are meaningful in different kinds of research. Section One looks at core ethical values and the potential conflicts for the insider-researcher. Section Two involves the voices of researchers-of-the-self, discussing their responses to ethical questions about their research. Section Three looks at examples of insider research projects as they arrive at solutions to the difficult fit between insider research and the varied received interpretations of ethical core values. Section Four makes recommendations for building bridges between insider researchers and ethics committees as they work towards a shared community of practice that allows researchers across paradigms to learn from one another.

Chapter X: Researcher reflexivity, wellbeing and ethical safety – Professor Mary Wild and Dr Carol Brown

Often the focus in ethical research is on protecting the rights of participants and less attention is given to the effects of the process on the researcher themselves. This chapter will consider researcher wellbeing and the issues that may arise. It presents the ethical guidelines on researcher wellbeing and identifies potential risks, including those in the field or workplace. The researcher may, for example, find themselves unexpectedly dealing with sensitive issues and be consciously or unconsciously exposed to secondary trauma as they research topics within education. The importance of researcher reflexivity is highlighted. Often researchers, particularly the novice or student researcher, may not have been prepared, be aware or want to disclose that the research process is affecting their wellbeing. Ways that this problem can be mitigated or addressed are explored as preparedness for researcher wellbeing is considered. Whilst sensitive areas can be avoided this, in itself, may not be ethical, and this chapter discusses the implications and suggestions for ways forward when conducting sensitive research that may be potentially distressing.

Chapter XI: Ethics in educational research with Indigenous communities – Dr Patrick Alexander

This chapter proposes a series of points of contention that derive from an engagement with the ethics of educational research conducted with Indigenous communities. Whilst there are specific issues and concerns that must be addressed in educational research with Indigenous communities, the concerted involvement of Indigenous actors in the process of research also raises some foundational concerns about the ethics of educational research in general. This argument first takes into consideration the history of educational research and its relationship to Indigenous communities, particularly in the context of mass education and education policy that has focused largely on the assimilation of Indigenous communities into the wider architecture of colonization and the modern nation-state. Second, the chapter explores how educational research frequently privileges the school as a site of learning that is unproblematic in its benefits for Indigenous communities. In doing this, the chapter critiques the extent to which the forms of knowledge represented in mainstream educational research and in schooling are commensurate with championing Indigenous forms of knowledge. Finally, the chapter contends that in order to conduct ethical research with Indigenous communities it is important to reconsider what the purpose and outcome of educational research is in general. Where research continues to adopt an extractive approach to 'data collection', and where the ultimate outcome of educational research is to reproduce an essentially colonialist framing of what 'research' is for, the ethics of educational research remain contested and in need of continued decolonization, not least when applied to marginal populations, including many Indigenous communities. Doing so presents a profound opportunity to expand the horizons of what educational research might constitute in the future.

Chapter XII: Jolts in the margins: probing the ethical dimensions of post-paradigms in educational research – Dr Linda Shaw

Research methodologies that draw on post-structural theories often have a stated aim of addressing an identified social injustice or human rights issue. This chapter will consider the ethical dilemmas which form an integral element in paradigms such as post-feminist and post-colonial research when applied to the field of education. Such research aspires to reflect the complexities of lived experience in order to expose inequalities. In so doing it must tackle ethical issues around knowledge and power – the relative positions of researcher, and researched, within the investigation – and ethical identities such as those of adult or child, teacher or parent, pupil or young person and so forth. This is in addition to, and not a replacement for, rigorous research methods and design which take account of ethical procedures. The chapter draws on primary research and experience of early years education and care, playwork and teaching human rights and social justice to Education Studies and Early Childhood Studies students in higher education.

Chapter XIII: Conclusion - The hidden lives of ethics: beyond the pragmatics – Professor Mary Wild

The concluding chapter will synthesize the ethical issues and understandings shared by our contributing authors. It will do so in a spirit of dialogue and debate that reaches beyond the pragmatics of ethical dilemmas. It will acknowledge the differing research perspectives that each author brings to the consideration of ethical dilemmas, highlighting the complexity and multidimensional nature of research in education and the consequent ethical dilemmas that arise. The conclusion does not arbitrate between differing research traditions, nor does it seek to provide ready 'solutions' to ethical dilemmas as that would detract from the philosophical tensions that underpin contested assumptions about the nature and purpose of educational research. Instead, the conclusion will foreground the value of offering a range of personal insights and reflections on ethics in educational research and will reprise some of the resolutions to ethical dilemma that our authors have proffered. Three unifying principles will be invoked. Firstly, that researchers must always engage with ethical principles and guidance. Secondly, there is a recognition that a careful balance must be struck between the needs of participants, increasing regulatory guidelines and the academic freedom of the educational researcher. Finally, it is proposed that ethical dilemmas do not exist in isolation and can be best resolved as part of a community of researchers.

There are a number of features that make this book distinctive, including the following additions to the field:

- It is written by several academics from differing theoretical and methodological perspectives and disciplines across the spectrum of educational research. For these reasons, each chapter is written in the author's own voice and style rather than editing to ensure uniformity – this is a deliberate, ethical editorial choice.
- Alongside the informational problems on ethical issues in educational research, this text seeks to present some specific dilemmas encountered in practice with real life, anonymized examples provided.
- It focuses on *resolution* of ethical dilemmas in educational research and not just the dilemmas themselves.
- It discusses dilemmas that apply across the age range of ethical consideration when working with children – not just young children.
- There is inclusion of a worldwide perspective.
- It considers ways of conducting ethical research which has the potential to give marginalized participants a voice.

We hope it will be a useful resource for all of those involved in the ethical dilemmas that arise in the context of educational research.

References

British Educational Research Association (2018) *Ethical Guidelines for Educational Research*. British Educational Research Association (BERA). Available at: https://www.bera.ac.uk/publication/ethical-guidelines-for-educational-research-2018 (accessed 10 July 2019).

Economic and Social Research Council (2019) *Our Core Principles*. Available at: https://esrc.ukri.org/funding/guidance-for-applicants/research-ethics/our-core-principles/ (accessed 2 August 2019).

United Nations Convention on the Rights of the Child (UNCRC) (1989) *United Nations Convention on the Rights of the Child*. Available at: https://www.unicef.org.uk/what-we-do/un-convention-child-rights/ (accessed 20 July 2019).

 # Ethical Guidelines in Educational Research

Carol Brown

It is not the purpose of this text to provide an in-depth outline of the extensive ethical guidelines that govern educational research across the globe, but instead to engage with the ethical dilemmas that are posed for educational researchers. Nevertheless, these dilemmas cannot always be separated from the reality of the context in which they are situated, as will become apparent throughout this text. Ethical guidelines govern educational research and at least some oversight of these is therefore necessary in order to set the background for this text. This chapter will therefore very briefly discuss the historical emergence of the guidelines as well as outlining some of the main frameworks which researchers would be expected to familiarize themselves with in the conduct of their work.

These regulations and guidelines derive from professional bodies and research organizations and adherence to such guidelines may also be required by journals when seeking publication of studies. The Rights of the Child are central to most of these ethical recommendations (UNCRC 1989). This chapter therefore aims to highlight the importance of ethical guidelines in educational research and give an overview of the main issues that educational researchers should be aware of. Of paramount importance is that the costs and benefits of conducting any research with children must always be equally considered.

A brief historical context

The historical pathway to the emergence of ethical guidelines in educational research is rooted in examples of wider societal practices where ethics were questionable, rather than within social sciences themselves. Seminal examples include the Nuremberg war crime trials (Mitscherliche and Mielke 1947) and the Tuskegee Study of Untreated Syphilis in the Negro Male (Jones 1981) as highlighted in Sikes and Piper (2010). The judgment by the war crimes tribunal at Nuremberg laid down 10 standards to which doctors needed to conform when carrying out medical experiments on human participants. This resulting Nuremberg Code in 1947 (*BMJ* 1996) was the first set of guidelines to establish the standards under which human participants could be used within such research, including what we would now recognize as the need for consent, avoidance of suffering, protection from harm and right to withdraw.

A later key turning point in the focal shift towards research ethics involving human participants was the publication of the Belmont Report in 1976 (DHEW 1979). This focused on the basic ethical principles and guidelines that were deemed necessary in the conduct of research involving human participants in both biomedical and behavioural research. The foundations of this report can be seen as underpinning much of what is written in the various ethical codes across nations and organizations today. The key three ethical principles issued were: respect for persons, beneficence and justice and three applications to include informed consent, assessment of risks and benefits and selection of participants (known then as 'subjects'). Its primary aim of protecting those in research was fundamental in the history of ethical guidelines.

It was not until much later that specific guidelines emerged in the social sciences in response to studies where participants were potentially subjected to harm in the pursuit of knowledge. Examples include the psychological studies conducted on the social processes of conformity and obedience by Stanley Milgram and Philip Zimbardo. These laboratory-based studies involved the delivery of (fake) electric shocks to confederates at the instruction of an authority figure (Milgram 1963) or the acquisition of prisoner and guard roles in a mock prison setting (Zimbardo 1973). Both arguably caused distress to participants who had been deceived about the true aim of the study and therefore been unable to fully consent to the conditions. Although subsequent follow-up by the psychologists determined that there had been no negative long-term effects, and participants did not regret their participation, such studies paved the way to ethical guidelines that sought to give greater protection to those engaging in social research. In 1990 the British Psychological Society (BPS) issued the first Ethical Principles for Conducting Research with Human Participants and in 1992 the British Educational Research Association (BERA) produced the first set specifically for educational researchers in the UK. Below, and later throughout this book, other international guidelines will also be highlighted. Finally, in this brief historical overview it is important to introduce another key historical event of importance in the development of guidelines in educational research. This was the publication of the United Nations Convention of the Rights of the Child (UNCRC), which will now be outlined before specific ethical guidelines are introduced.

United Nations Convention on the Rights of the Child (UNCRC 1989)

The rights of the child are central to the ethical recommendations guiding research and indeed many of the ethical dilemmas that will be discussed in this text. In this chapter we therefore begin by exploring the implications of the United Nations Convention on the Rights of the Child (UNCRC 1989), as this is a framework that affects education research across most countries. The importance of the UNCRC cannot be underestimated.

As UNICEF highlight on their webpage, the UNCRC is 'the most complete statement of children's rights ever produced and is the most widely-ratified international human rights treaty in history'. It contains 54 articles that address all aspects of a child's life including their civil, political, economic, social and cultural rights. It asserts that governments and adults must work together to ensure children enjoy their rights whatever their ethnicity, gender, religion, language or abilities. This has led to a rights-based approach to research, which, as will become evident, is reflected in the ethical guidelines adopted when researching children.

There are four 'general principles' that guide interpretation of the articles and play a fundamental role in realizing the rights of all children (UNICEF). These include non-discrimination (Article 2), the best interest of the child (Article 3), the right to life survival and development (Article 6) and the right to be heard (Article 12). It is also pertinent to highlight a number of specific articles that most notably underpin ethical issues and guidelines in educational research.

The age of the child (Article 1) is determined as anyone under the age of 18, who has all the rights in the Convention and applies to every child without discrimination (Article 2). The key underlying principles determine the need to ensure that the best interests of the child are the primary consideration, that they are respected and protected and fully involved in any research process. The best interests of the child must be a top priority in all decisions and actions that affect children (Article 3). This inevitably includes research activities.

According to UNICEF (2007) the concept of 'best interests' has been the subject of more academic analysis than any other concept in the UNCRC. The *Implementation Handbook for the Convention of the Rights of the Child* (UNICEF 2007) states that best interests must embrace both short- and long-term considerations for the child and that any interpretation of best interests must be consistent with the spirit of the entire Convention with an emphasis on the child as an individual with views and feelings of his or her own (p. 38). It also goes on to say that the best interests of the child will not always be the single, overriding factor to be considered because there may be competing or conflicting human rights interests, for example, between individual children, between different groups of children and between children and adults. What is essential, however, is that the child's interests must be the subject of active consideration and there must be demonstration that children's interests have been explored and taken into account as a primary consideration (p. 38).

Parents and carers have the right to provide guidance and direction to children to allow them to enjoy their rights commensurate with the child's own capacity to make choices (Article 5); this has implications for consent to participation in projects. Similarly, the Convention determines that every child should have the right to express their own views, feelings and wishes in all matters affecting them and to have their views considered and taken seriously, giving due weight to age and maturity (Article 12). They should be free to express their thoughts and opinions and to access information (Article 13). They also have the right to privacy (Article 16). UNICEF (2007) argue that Article 12, together with the child's right to freedom of expression (Article 13), and other civil rights to freedom of thought, conscience and religion (Article 14), and freedom of association (Article 15) underline children's status as individuals with fundamental human rights and views and feelings of their own (p. 149). Article 12 does not set any lower age limit on children's right to express views freely (p. 153).

The Convention also determines that governments must protect children from all forms of exploitation and specifies that this includes research (Article 36). Although the focus is on medical research, UNICEF recognize that there is a balance to be struck – by ensuring children are not exploited by researchers (for example by breaches of their privacy or requiring them to undertake tasks that breach their rights or human dignity) and not outlawing research which would otherwise offer hope, cure or research progress (p. 544). Governments must however ensure that children and adults know about the Convention (Article 42).

The next section of this chapter will go on to look at specific ethical guidelines that direct educational research. The links with the UNCRC are however explicit. The British Educational Research Association's (BERA 2018) ethical guidelines, for example, state that 'BERA endorses the UNCRC; the best interests of the child are the primary consideration, and children who are capable of forming their own views should be granted the right to express those views freely in all matters affecting them, commensurate with their age and maturity' (23, p. 15). The code of ethics goes on to say that 'research following the UNCRC will take account the rights and duties of those who have legal responsibility for children, such as those who act in guardianship as "responsible others"… this may involve gaining consent of those responsible for children' (24, p. 15).

Specific ethical guidelines used to govern educational research are now considered in more detail.

Ethical guidelines

Although specific ethical guidelines are discussed here, it is important to preface this by noting that there is no single set of international, multidisciplinary guidelines that govern the ethics of research with children across nations. Cultural variants can, in themselves, create ethical dilemmas and is a theme that will be addressed in some of the chapters in this text. As Brooks et al. (2014) highlight, not all countries have detailed guidelines and the implementation of codes varies between countries and even between institutions within countries and between disciplines.

To illustrate, even within the UK, there are ethical guidelines issued by various professional bodies with disciplinary differences, such as the British Sociological Association, British Psychological Association and the British Educational Research Association. Then there are also codes issued by funding bodies, for instance the Economic and Social Research Council (ESRC) or

Research Councils UK (RCUK). Despite these variations there are however commonly recognized principles which underpin the codes encompassing an emphasis on minimizing harm, respecting autonomy and dignity, protecting privacy, ensuring equality, inclusivity and diversity and demonstrating social responsibility (Hammersley and Traianou 2012; BERA 2018; ESRC 2019). Researchers generally accept the proposition that a focus on justice, beneficence, respect, research merit and integrity are an important guide for ethical decision making in research with children (Halse 2011).

British Educational Research Association (BERA) guidelines

Given the commonality in underlying emphasis, an introduction here is provided to just one set of specific guidelines. Whilst it is acknowledged that they cannot be entirely culturally representative, the Ethical Guidelines for Educational Research (2018) published by British Educational Research Association (BERA) have been chosen because they:

- are a detailed and specific set of guidelines that comprehensively reflect the core shared underlying ethical principles evident in many documents, including globally;
- are rooted in the rights-based UNCRC framework;
- are accompanied by supporting documents for researchers which aim to aid the ethical decision-making process within educational research (see Hammersley and Traianou, 2012);
- co-exist and are incorporated more widely into alternative ethical frameworks, such as those published by the ESRC, legislative requirements and best practice;
- recognize a diversity of approaches in educational research (BERA 2018 piii);
- represent best ethical practice that have served the educational research community well in the past and will in the future (BERA 2018 piii);
- take into account new developments in educational research, such as the use of social media, online mediums, legislative changes and the growing impact of educational research on internalization and globalization (BERA 2018 piii).

This latest set of guidelines was formed from several previous iterations. The first set of guidelines was originally published in 1992. The guidelines were subsequently updated in 2004 and 2011 (BERA 2018 p. 36–38).

The guidelines are divided into several sections:

- responsibilities to participants
- responsibilities to sponsors, clients and stakeholders in research

- responsibilities to community
- responsibility for publication and dissemination
- responsibilities for researchers' wellbeing and development.

The dilemmas that many of these pose will emerge as themes throughout the book. The aim of this chapter is to simply outline the guidance. Each of these will now therefore be considered in turn.

Responsibilities to participants

The opening to this code of ethics clearly states that BERA believes educational researchers should operate with respect for anyone involved in their research and that participants should be treated fairly, sensitively, with dignity and without prejudice. In terms of the focus on ethical dilemmas in educational research, it highlights how attention should be specifically paid to the ways in which inequalities affect children. Ultimately, BERA determine that researchers have a responsibility to maximize the benefits but minimize any risk of harm to participants, sponsors, educational researchers and educational professionals. These principles underlie many of the specific guidelines that follow in the rest of this chapter.

Consent

Voluntary informed and ongoing consent are a fundamental aspect of this code of ethics. Participants have the right to withdraw from research at any time without giving a reason. In order to provide consent, it is the researchers' duty to ensure participants clearly understand what is expected of them and what will happen to their information. An explicit link is made to the UNCRC in this section of the code where BERA clearly state that the principles of consent apply to children who should have the right to freely express their own views and that their best interests should be a primary consideration. Consent may be required from a parent or guardian and where vulnerable participants may be unable to fully consent then instead assent should be obtained.

Consent needs to be considered within a cultural context, with due sensitivity and adaptation as necessary, for example information should be translated and provided appropriately. Where applicable, gatekeeper consent should be sought and due attention given to institutional ethics approval and safeguarding. Opt-in and opt-out consent must also be considered in context and in line with local legislation.

Whilst consent may not be required for the use of overt publicly available data, it may be the case for some data sources, such as that derived from online communities, and researchers have a responsibility to consider this and seek consent where necessary and possible. Ownership and consent for use of secondary data similarly needs consideration. Within this code, specific issues around consent are discussed with regards to ethnographic and observational studies, random control trials, autoethnography and action research where tensions may arise (see also Spiro, Chapter IX).

Transparency

The importance of openness and honesty is emphasized in this section. Non-disclosure should be avoided unless it is a critical aspect of the research design and would need institutional ethics approval. If data is to be used more than once, or stored in a shared repository, then researchers must make this explicit to participants at the outset and inform them how the data will be used and how long it will be stored for. Such data should ideally be stored in an anonymized and disaggregated form to avoid subsequent participant identification. Sponsorship of research must be clearly specified and any work that would lead to commercial gain or have a conflict of interest should be avoided.

Right to withdraw

Participants should be able to withdraw from research at any time and without giving a reason. They must be informed of this right and the contact details of the researcher provided. Whilst researchers are encouraged to reflect on the participant's desire to withdraw in terms of their own practice, any decision on change of approach to encourage reengagement must be cautious to avoid coercion. An exception to the right to withdraw may be if the participant is contractually obliged to participate – the BERA code outlines employees facilitating an evaluation study as an example – where compliance may be requested from a third party by the researcher.

Incentives

Whilst this guideline suggests that payment for participation in educational research should be discouraged, if incentives are included then this must be reported and they should be used wisely and in such a way that they do not positively influence participation.

Harm arising from participation in research

Researchers have a duty of care to reduce potential risks to participants, minimize and manage distress and discomfort, and avoid making excessive demands on them including on their time, required effort and impact on lives of participants. These risks are especially important to consider in the case of vulnerable participants, for example children in the context of educational research. Any potential disadvantages or harm must be flagged to participants or addressed by the researcher if occurring unexpectedly in the course of the research. This includes any disadvantages occurring as part of the research design where one group may otherwise benefit from an intervention. In terms of harm, however, the rights of the individual must be balanced against the potential wider social benefits of any research.

Privacy and data storage

Confidentiality, privacy and anonymity are of paramount importance in research, although researchers should also recognize that participants may wish to seek recognition and waive their right to anonymity in some cases. It is acknowledged that anonymity is not necessarily the norm in some research approaches (for example when using historical, archival or autoethnographic data). Particular issues for consideration around anonymity are highlighted for research using digital contexts, visual methodologies and participatory methods including the need to balance the appropriateness of concealing identities and the importance of participant voice against any misuse of such data. Furthermore, this section of the code also recognizes that anonymity cannot always be guaranteed, for example, in small samples or if prominent institutions are used. However, it is the researcher's responsibility to ensure participants are aware of the consequence of identification.

Recent changes to UK Data Protection laws (GDPR 2018) also necessitate that individuals are informed about how and why their personal data is being stored, for what purposes and by whom, and researchers must comply with this legislation in their work. All data must be kept securely. The code suggests that for researchers working in an international context they must be aware of local customs for data protection and ensure data storage elsewhere if necessary.

Disclosure

Where research brings to light illegal behaviours or those that are harmful to self or others then researchers should disclose this to the relevant authorities and have a statutory duty to do so in some instances (e.g. in relation to abuse or acts of terror). Their intention and reasons for disclosure should be shared with the participant where possible. Notes should be kept on decisions made and reasons for them. All decisions about disclosure should however be situated with the cultural context (the example given in this section is where low-level corruption may be frequent and endemic in some cultures). Overall, the researcher is encouraged to carefully consider decisions to override the principles of confidentiality and anonymity and withdraw any data that is compromised by necessary disclosure.

Responsibilities to sponsors, clients and stakeholders in research

Contracts with sponsors, clients and stakeholders should consider open access to the results of any research and sponsors should be acknowledged in any publications. At the outset, responsibilities and entitlements should be agreed and if research is being conducted in the researcher's own workplace, they should seek consent from the stakeholder. This guideline highlights that researchers should think about how they position themselves and the design, analysis and interpretation of their work in relation to the interests of their sponsors, or stakeholders, and declare any conflicts of interest.

One of the important aspects of this code is the specific reference to methods and the clear assertion that the ethical guidelines are not intended to favour any one type of research approach or method. It states that researchers should have knowledge of several alternative approaches, consider these in any given work, be able to justify the choice and ensure the methods employed best fit the purposes of any particular research. Within any given approach, researchers must also ensure that methods, findings and inferences are robust and reflect quality and integrity.

Responsibilities to community of educational researchers

The educational community includes academic researchers, student researchers, independent researchers and others who conduct research within organizations such as universities, schools, government, charities and commercial bodies. Educational researchers are guided to conduct their research to the highest standards so that they protect the integrity and reputation of all educational researchers and engage in critical debate in a professional way in order to improve practice and enhance academic knowledge. A named person should be available to address issues or complaints where this is not the case, or where there are concerns about malpractice, and researchers have a duty to respond appropriately.

Plagiarism is also covered by this section of the guideline, with all researchers ensuring due recognition has been given to relevant sources. Anonymized data used in any research should be available for external analysis, and researchers have a duty to report not just positive, but also the negative results of their work.

Responsibility for publication and dissemination

This section emphasizes the ethical responsibility on researchers to ensure that their research findings are communicated publicly in an appropriate way for their audience, including the lay reader, and with due consideration to the relevant language. A recent development in some countries such as the UK is consideration of providing open access for publications so that there are no restrictions on access to knowledge. The guidelines on scope and format of publications therefore ties in with both this and the necessity to consider the needs and interests of the communities involved in the research. It goes without saying that it is a fundamental principle that researchers should not falsify, distort, suppress, selectively report or sensationalize their work.

Authorship is also addressed in this section. A central concept is that anyone who has made a substantive and identifiable contribution should be duly credited and acknowledged for doing so. Individual outputs based on collaborative research are not permissible without consent. The order of authorship must reflect the contributions made, including leadership contribution, or be determined alphabetically, but should not be based on professional seniority.

Responsibilities for researchers' wellbeing and development

This section of the guidelines is focused on safeguarding the wellbeing of researchers – both their physical and psychological wellbeing. BERA highlights that this may be particularly pertinent to researchers conducting qualitative fieldwork that may be hazardous and where there may be a need for risk assessment and ongoing monitoring of researcher safety. The code indicates that international, post-war settings and those with high risk of disease necessitate specialist training for the researcher. This is an issue that will only become more important in light of the Covid-19 pandemic and brings additional considerations for the ethical need to ensure researchers' wellbeing. These issues will be further discussed by Wild and Brown in Chapter X, which looks at researcher reflexivity, wellbeing and ethical safety.

The responsibility of employers to mitigate against exploitation of those in more precarious roles, such as fixed-term contracts and where there may be competing demands (e.g. in the case of student researchers) is also considered in this section.

Conclusion

This chapter has presented the historical need, process and framework for ethical guidelines in educational research. It has looked at the origins of guidelines, the emphasis on a rights-based approach and the specific regulations of the British Educational Research Association.

The concept of ethical guidelines is not however without critique. There may be conflicts between the principles, varying interpretations of them, especially cultural variations, and a situated need for judgement (Hammersley and Traianou 2012), for example, the tension of balancing the principles of do no harm versus the right of the vulnerable participant to make autonomous decisions if harm might then result (Hammersley and Traianou 2012). Decisions will always be made within a specific research environment and within the context of varying methodologies. These very conflicts will indeed underpin some of the dilemmas raised throughout this book.

There are also philosophical discussions and dilemmas around the implementation of guidelines and the extent to which they are even necessary. Although research inevitably involves an element of potential risk, especially when vulnerable participants such as children are included, there have been arguments that, in reality, there are no reported incidents of harm or potential harm caused by social science or educational researchers (Hammersley 2009; Parsell et al. 2014). Ethical regulation is, however, a necessary part of the process and the next chapter will therefore focus on the role of research ethics committees in educational research.

References

BMJ (1996) The Nuremberg Code, *British Medical Journal*, 313:1448. Available at: https://www.bmj.com/content/313/7070/1448.1 (accessed 19 July 2022).

British Educational Research Association (2018) *Ethical Guidelines for Educational Research*. British Educational Research Association (BERA). Available at: https://www.bera.ac.uk/publication/ethical-guidelines-for-educational-research-2018 (accessed 10 July 2019).

British Psychological Society (BPS) (1990) *Guidelines*. Available at: https://www.bps.org.uk/article-types/guidelines (accessed 28 June 2022).

Brooks, R., te Riele, K., and Maguire, M. (2014) *Ethics and Education Research*. London: Sage Publications Ltd.

DHEW (1979) National Commission for the Protection of Human Subjects of Biomedical and Behavioral Research (NCPHSBBR) *The Belmont Report*. Government Printing Office.

Economic and Social Research Council (2019) *Our Core Principles*. Available at: https://esrc.ukri.org/funding/guidance-for-applicants/research-ethics/our-core-principles/ (accessed 2 August 2019).

Halse, C. (2011) Confessions of an ethics committee chair, *Ethics and Education*, 6(3): 239–251.

Hammersley, M. (2009) Against the ethicists: on the evils of ethical regulation, *International Journal of Social Research Methodology*, 12(3): 211–225.

Hammersley, M. and Traianou, A. (2012) *Ethics and Educational Research*. British Educational Research Association. Available at: https://www.bera.ac.uk/publication/ethics-and-educational-research (accessed 10 July 2019).

GDPR (2018) *Guide to the General Data Protection Regulation (GDPR)*. Information Commissioner's Office. Available at: https://www.gov.uk/government/publications/guide-to-the-general-data-protection-regulation (accessed 28 June 2022).

Jones, J. (1981) *Bad Blood: The Tuskegee Syphilis Experiment*. Free Press.

Milgram, S. (1963) A behavioural study of obedience, *Journal of Abnormal and Social Psychology*, 67: 371–378.

Mitscherliche, A. and Mielke, F. (1947) *Doctors of Infamy: The Story of the Nazi Medical Crimes*. Schuman.

Parsell, M., Amblerb, T. and Jacenyik-Trawogerc, C. (2014) Ethics in higher education research, *Studies in Higher Education*, 39(1): 166–179.

Sikes, P. and Piper, H. (2010) Ethical research, academic freedom and the role of ethics committees and review procedures in educational research. *International Journal of Research and Method in Education*, 33(3): 205–213.

UNICEF (2007) *Implementation Handbook the Convention on the Rights of the Child*, United Nations Children's Fund.

United Nations Convention on the Rights of the Child (UNCRC) (1989) *United Nations Convention on the Rights of the Child*. Available at: https://www.unicef.org.uk/what-we-do/un-convention-child-rights/ (accessed 20 July 2019).

Zimbardo, P.G. (1973) On the ethics of intervention in human psychological research with special reference to the Stanford prison experiment, *Cognition*, 2: 243–256.

Research Ethics Committees in Education Research: Common Purpose, Misunderstandings, Challenges and Moving Forward

Sarah Quinton

Whilst the changing legislative landscape surrounds all researchers and the rise in multi-modal opportunities enabled by new technologies impacts many others, there are specific ethical sensitivities associated with education research which result in greater ethical complexity, for example context, dependency issues, participants' rights, children as a 'vulnerable' group and insider research. These particular aspects of education research require detailed consideration. Such consideration is commonly provided by ethics committees within institutions that review and approve or reject research projects. This chapter will discuss the roles and responsibilities of research ethics committees and expose the misunderstandings that may exist. The use of illustrative exemplars will be used to elaborate key issues, and suggestions for good practice will be provided as a way to move forward for both committees reviewing education research projects and individuals undertaking such research. Progressing scholarship within education research is a shared priority and research ethics committees can play a positive role as a moderator in this.

This chapter is derived from five years of observations as Chair of a British University's research ethics committee, interactions with both UK and non-UK based research ethics academics, and as a practising and experienced social science researcher. Many education research projects are carefully and sensitively conceptualized, designed and executed with consideration given not only to the relevant stakeholders and regulatory requirements, but also going beyond what is 'required' to engage in a more proactive ethical response. For example, the involvement of secondary school children as co-creators of research projects goes beyond what is required but can be taken as an example of good practice and moreover, an inclusive learning opportunity for young members of society to be 'part' of research not the 'subject' of research. However, exemplars also exist of very poor practice. To illustrate, there is the implementation of education research projects in developing economies which assume that consent of children is not necessary, as though these minors are somehow of lesser importance than children in the UK. This type of poor practice has been referred to as ethics 'dumping'. There is also the misguided justification seen in ethics applications that research going on in a UK school is the responsibility and under the control of the headteacher and no other permissions are necessary. Schools and educational settings are not autonomous islands and the same laws and regulations in relation to research ethics apply here as elsewhere.

Common purpose and misunderstandings

Research ethics in educational research should not be partisan with people aligned to opposing sides. Assuming that everyone, including the researcher and the ethics committee members, has a vested interest in rigorous, valuable educational research which will both inform scholarship and develop practice would be a sound starting point. This is the common purpose which may get 'lost in translation' between the education researcher and those who review applications for projects and determine ethics approvals. Ethics committees do have a role to play in potentially enhancing educational research through the critical reviewing of research proposals. Ethics committees can and should be viewed as a 'critical friend' to educational researchers and this could be embedded within educational researcher training.

University ethics committees and institutional review panels (also called IRBs) perform a multiplicity of roles and responsibilities which occasionally get overlooked by the individual education researcher or research team. First and foremost is the responsibility ethics committees have to potential participants, which sometimes results in researchers having to reconsider either their intended participants and/or their research design. For example, designing a battery of survey instruments to be completed by children may be detrimental to their wellbeing in terms of time needed, the repetition of these surveys and the subjects raised by the questions.

Ethics committees also have a responsibility to the wellbeing of the researcher to ensure that they are not likely to put themselves in harm's way when conducting their research. An illustration of this is if the research design suggests researchers visiting the homes of children, which may be relevant to the study, but which needs careful consideration and planning to ensure safety protocols are in place.

Responsibility for reporting on ethical compliance for externally funded education research projects also lies with research ethics committees. Charities, foundations or government departments may commission education research and these organizations expect certain codes of ethical research conduct to be enacted. Education researchers can overlook this compliance aspect in their enthusiasm for undertaking a research project and feel overburdened by paperwork. Yet it is the paperwork trail which is the mechanism through which ethics committees report research ethics compliance to funders.

As an institutional body, the ethics committee also has a responsibility to encourage good practices that will uphold the reputation of the institution, and this includes research ethics. Poorly conceived, designed and implemented research, particularly when it involves children, carries a high probability of impacting the institution's reputation through complaints and negative media coverage. The consequences may also be substantial for the settings involved in the research, the participants and their families and the researcher as well as the university.

In essence, when an ethics committee reviews an education research application it has to be mindful of the roles and responsibilities outlined above. The enhancement and support of rigorous research that benefits individuals and society and minimizes any type of harm is the core intent of these review panels.

Unfortunately, and to the detriment of both educational research and research ethics committees, the perceived lack of understanding between educational researchers and the research ethics policies of universities and institutions was agitated by authors such as Hammersley (2009) and Halse and Honey (2007), who positioned themselves as 'opposing' ethics committees. Quite frankly, this helped neither the researcher nor the institutions, nor society more broadly. Ethics committees, or their equivalent, are required at public institutions where research is undertaken. A more constructive approach has been suggested by authors such as McAreavey and Muir (2011) and Connolly and Reid (2007), who suggest working with the committees to improve dialogue and interactions and thus the likelihood of more positive outcomes for educational researchers.

The occasional feeling of 'lost in translation' between education researchers and ethics committees is, I believe, based on misperception rather than reality. Ethics committees do recognize the good intentions of educational researchers. Education research is important and necessary to progress the scholarship and inform practice and can play a transformative role in the development of our societies, and committees do appreciate this. On a more practical note, ethics review panels and committees do recognize the time constraint of certain projects around school and academic calendars and that these types of projects may require expedient attention from an ethics committee. However, those projects, whilst needing prompt reviewing, must be assessed carefully owing to the very nature of the research, the core of which is the child and the education setting – both of which have specific sensitivities.

A further practical aspect where misunderstandings arise can be seen in the language used in education research ethics applications. Whilst certainly not limited to education research, application documentation can be full of jargon, written by insiders for insiders, not for the public, not for school governors and certainly not for potential participants. The lack of making explicit what the safeguarding reporting procedures are for a sports club or the use of year group numbering as labels for groups of children are examples of this. The reviewing of a research proposal by a non-specialist ethics committee provides an opportunity to hone the clarity of a project. Clarity is important as it assists in the gaining of informed consent by potential participants, which is itself a requirement for good research ethics practice.

The outlined common purpose and the tensions arising from misunderstanding that have been outlined in this section are set within the evolving environment of research ethics and it is this I now turn to.

The dynamic landscape of research ethics

The rise and increasing ubiquity of digital tools used in research has created more multi-modal ways to capture and retain research data for all researchers, including researchers in education. Live streaming of in-class activity as a data set, digital photographs of children and the use of social media as a data source may all be relevant to certain research projects. However, the speed of technological advance, diversity of platforms and adoption of these by the public and the young in particular has resulted in ethics guidelines rarely maintaining currency. In addition, the 'right to be forgotten' and the option for children once grown to change their minds about what they once consented to, and request the removal or deletion of data held about them, adds another layer of complexity for educational researchers. For example, research video footage of a male child in school uniform in school which may appear uncontentious to many may be decided upon by that individual as not true to their self-identity and they may wish it to be deleted as that young person gets older and decides to transition.

The illustrations outlined above indicate the dynamic nature of the research environment in relation to, but also beyond, educational research. Aligned to this shapeshifting of research practice and thinking is the changing legislative landscape, which attempts to manage the enactments of developments in technology in order to safeguard society and its members. The focus of this chapter is not the argument about the competency of the legislative frameworks to manage ethical research practice, but rather that it is important for researchers to understand that they exist in a changing landscape. For example, the requirement for Privacy Notices in the UK which need to be provided to research participants detailing why their data is being collected and how it is collected, stored and disposed of (GDPR Privacy Notice, www.gov.uk). However, the changing legislative landscape is reactive rather than proactive to the adoption, use and possible misuse of information.

Combined with the reactive and evolving legislative frameworks within which education researchers must operate is the greater public scrutiny of institutions. Schools, universities research institutes and educational charities all face more scrutiny than was possible in the past. Digital technologies have enabled real time search, tracking and sharing of information across the internet and social media, which is both an opportunity but also a risk for institutions and individuals undertaking research. The public, quite rightly, have greater access to and immediacy of information, which has led to greater calls for transparency in research but also greater critiquing of research practices, sites and outputs of research as well as queries directly aimed at those institutions, such as universities, that endorse specific research projects.

Ethics Committee Chairs have to respond to queries and complaints from parents questioning the appropriateness of asking seven-year-old children about their preferred gender, to school governors critiquing poor grammar and punctuation on participant information sheets, to members of the public questioning the validity and purpose of a research study they have been asked to participate in. Whilst we should not deter anyone from making such enquiries, it is important that education researchers recognize the role played by research ethics committees in responding to such, more public, scrutiny.

Furthermore, there are no universal research ethics guidelines to refer to. Institutional and university research ethics processes and approvals differ across countries. For example, in the UK, USA, Scandinavia and the Commonwealth, processes are applied based on a compliance model. Documentation is required using formalized templates and, commonly, online tools with independent internal reviewers determining the ethical suitability of the project and methods. Revised documentation is frequently required and final official written approval has to be gained prior to the start of any research project involving human participants. In Europe and Asia there is less uniformity in approaches to research ethics approvals processes. To elaborate, in Japan since 2006 the Ministry of Education has required all universities to have research ethics codes of conduct, but this is not the case in China. In Spain and Italy, there is emphasis on research ethics policies within biomedical research but far less ethics guidance on social science or humanities research. Decisions are often made on a case by case basis with an in-subject peer or peer group making the decisions or by applying the norms for national subject areas such as the BERA policies in the UK (see Chapter II).

Specific sensitivities in education research

There are a number of specific ethical dilemmas for those involved with education research such as issues surrounding context, dependency, participants' rights and the role of insider research, as Zeni (2001), amongst others, has highlighted and the following discussion foregrounds these.

Context

The context within which educational research may take place can, and does, vary widely. From mainstream schools to secure residential units for highly traumatized children, from established extra curricula organizational settings such as The Scouts to beatbox music academies in deprived urban areas, these contexts add to the ethical complexities that an institutional ethics committee has to consider. For example, in residential settings there are often requirements for further permissions from health and wellbeing professionals before any research can be undertaken and/or significant limitations on the research methodologies that might be implemented.

Children and their parents/families may have a – not unreasonable – expectation of a certain level of privacy whilst children are in specific settings undertaking daily or regular activities, such as learning, exercise and/or socialization. Educational settings are not (in the UK and many other countries) public spaces and the use of these settings as a site of research needs to be sensitively managed. The perceptions about the appropriateness of a place as a site for research will vary widely. To illustrate, some children and/or parents/carers may consider the interruption to any formalized learning for a research project or, particularly with older children who may be studying towards external qualifications, the perceived 'loss of learning time' that a research project may involve as unethical.

The regional and/or national context may also influence ethics decisions (UNICEF.org, n.d.; Schenk and Williamson 2005); for example educational research on literacy in young children conducted in war-torn Yemen will require different considerations from a similar research project in Northern Europe. Attention will need to be paid not only to national regulatory frameworks but also, in the case of Yemen, local cultural norms and customs regarding the project itself, the methodology, the access and recruitment and so on. As education research becomes increasingly globalized, reflection on the appropriateness and the feasibility of the researcher's institutional research ethics policies becomes necessary. Education researchers working in an international context may find The Global Code of Conduct for Research in Resource Poor Settings (www.glocalcodeofconduct.org) insightful as a guide for responsible research practice.

Ethics committees need to and do consider the setting, national or international context of each education research project very carefully. What may seem normal practice in a given context to education researchers may warrant further clarification by an ethics committee which has many stakeholders to consider and most importantly the wellbeing of the potential participants.

Beyond the wellbeing of the participants of the research, ethics committees are also required to consider the wellbeing and safety of the researcher. Both the context and the subject may have the potential to cause psychological or physical harm to education researchers as further discussed by Wild and Brown in Chapter X. Researchers may be party to distressing or disturbing information during a research project and effort should be made to provide opportunities for debriefing and good ethics practice would suggest that these plans should be included in an ethics application.

The combination of education and children can be highly emotive issues for research participants and wider members of society. Physical threats and social media harassment of education researchers, though uncommon, are not unheard of and reviewers of research proposals need to determine if the benefit will outweigh the risks, including the risks to the researcher or research team.

In terms of social/religious context, there may be tensions created by these contexts for researchers. To elaborate, a project that investigates how teenagers learn practical life skills conducted within segregated societies, such as within Orthodox Jewish or Muslim communities, is likely to be challenging owing to the context within which these communities operate. Here, carefully managed access and communication will be necessary to develop sincere relationship building, particularly if the researcher is not an existing member of those communities (McAreavey and Das 2013). The use of specific communities as a context for education research, along with other types of research, should be considered carefully by ethics reviewers in order to avoid 'over-researching populations' without a well explained justification. Over-researching certain contexts can result in feelings of 'othering' by those communities (see Lahman 2008; Baak 2019). Thus, the sample or desired population may be questioned by an ethics review panel in terms of whether the sample indicated is core to the research question or whether suitable data could be gained from a different group or community.

Dependency Issues

Dependency issues are not unique to education research, however, the nature of the interwoven relationships between educators, children, parents/carers, peer friendship groups, senior and junior staff make dependency a multi-layered element in many educational research projects. Tensions may be felt between headteachers and junior staff when teaching staff are being asked to participate in school-based research or to facilitate research projects in their classroom, which adds to their workload. These staff may be fearful of being seen as uncooperative if they do not engage in a research project. School-based research projects have a tendency to assume the willing participation of classroom teachers in their design and this needs questioning by ethics committees to ensure fairness to any teaching staff.

The complexity of the parent/carer and child relationship and the obvious dependency within those relationships may also create greater ethical challenges for ethics committees. Children's participation in research is limited by the power wielded in adult decision-making, often but not always, for good reason. At what point and how competency is defined for children to participate in research remains unclear (Moran-Ellis and Tisdall 2019). The involvement of children in research can be viewed as part of embedding them into an inclusive and empowering culture. For example, at what age can a child be asked for consent to participate without the permission of their parents/carers? The encouragement of research in society necessitates increasing participation from relevant groups, and the acculturation of children to participation in research that may have positive impacts on their society may be seen as part of the educational process. Expressing informed autonomy by opting in to participate in research without parental consent may cause unease for some but can be seen by others as one aspect of becoming an independent thinker. Should young people aged 12 or 14 or 16 be able to consent to research studies independently of their parents?

Does it depend on the purpose of the research and its level of sensitivity? These are questions that ethics committees grapple with and which researchers in education need to acknowledge.

A further dependency-related situation may occur with regards to consent. For example, a research project looking at the impact of familial abuse on scholastic achievement may work with organizations supporting young survivors and the survivors themselves, as well as the school setting but may, legitimately, not necessarily gain consent from the parents. So, whilst the usual child/parent dependency and the rights and responsibilities of parents and carers are important in research ethics, within this situation not asking for parental/carer consent or involvement may be highly appropriate. In such a case, an ethics committee would weigh up the potential impact of any involvement by the parents, as even the mere act of asking parents for consent could be negative for the recovery of the child.

Participants' rights

Frequently, those involved in education research as participants (children teaching/support staff/ parents and carers) are not well informed and/or engaged with good research ethics practices, or even aware of current data protection regulations. This information asymmetry (Howe and Moses 1999) can have consequences for gaining informed consent and also for understanding how to withdraw themselves from a study and withdraw their own data.

Dependency between senior and junior staff has already been elaborated, but the extent of staff involvement in a research project can be an issue. Staff in education settings have the right not to be overly burdened by the requests of the researcher as they go about their busy daily professional activities. They also have the right not to participate and not to be penalized in any way for not participating. Facilitating alternative provision for some children, maintaining reflective diaries, being filmed whilst teaching, providing assessment information or being interviewed regarding educational policies and frameworks may be stressful and excessive requests. Ethics committees need to ensure that non-participation is made an explicit option for all potential participants, as well as determining what is a reasonable level of involvement in a research project for those who wish to participate.

Whilst much emphasis is given, correctly, to the participant in an education research project, the researcher should also be acknowledged as having rights that must be upheld. Here, the ethics committee needs to determine if debriefing for a researcher or regular consultations with other experienced academics may be valuable, for example if the research is focused around sensitive topics such as discrimination or deprivation. The researcher may have elicited relevant but difficult material, which they then need to process as part of the research project. Internalizing evidence about childhood deprivation, disadvantage or even disclosure of abuse will impact that researcher. Ethics committees do consider the rights and wellbeing of the researcher as central in their evaluation of any research project.

The education researcher may also have a statutory responsibility to disclose safeguarding and certain other issues to the relevant internal and external authorities, and ethics committees should be mindful to ensure a clear process is articulated for this in applications. Researchers should know what the safeguarding policy is for any setting they might be researching in, as well as who the designated safeguarding officers are.

Those who are not direct participants in a research project also have rights. The rights of third parties, including other children who may not be directly involved in the research, requires careful contemplation by an ethics committee. For example, other children who may be inadvertently recorded (via audio or video) during a research activity. Evaluating the rights of non-participants needs to be determined here by the ethics committee, as the material including these individuals might need to be excluded and deleted unless specific consent has been given for their inclusion. Exceptions to this might include recording of general playground activity or unidentifiable groupings of children moving on and off a bus, for example.

Children as a vulnerable group

A frequently heard default position is that children are a vulnerable group and must be protected. Whilst this is true and enshrined across disciplines and national and international policies (see, for example, institutional safeguarding policies, UNICEF policies on the rights of the child) it should also be remembered that empowering children through having their 'voice' heard in education research can be highly valuable – not just for the project but for the child themselves (see the special issue focusing on young people's voice in the *International Journal of Educational Research*, vol 104, 2020). As outlined in a previous section, the inclusion of children, not only as participants in research but also as co-creators of research, may create a better understanding by the young of how research operates and how it may impact society constructively. In addition, greater engagement with research based on actual experience of it as a child may result in more positive predisposition to research as an adult. Recently enabled through social media, children have found their voices to articulate and illustrate their thoughts, feelings and experiences connected with education, and beyond, into their everyday lives.

One specific area in research where children may be considered vulnerable and need protection is inadvertent identification. The use of digital technologies, particularly image-based, has largely been beneficial to social science researchers including those conducting education research. However, an unintentional consequence has been the ability to identify and trace the location of children and also their families. There will be children and their families who, for their own safety, should never be included in research that may identify them or their location. In such cases, image-based data in particular should be avoided.

Insider research

Insider research does present particular ethical challenges, not only for researchers in education, but for other subject areas where it is an established research approach, such as organizational research where, for example, employees might situate their research within their own firms. Arts-based researchers may research their own body of work as an extreme version of insider research by taking an auto-ethnographic approach. Supporters of insider research highlight the depth of insight that may be gained from such intimate knowledge of a context.

However, there are both advantages and weaknesses to insider research, the intricacies of which are beyond the parameters of this chapter (for further reading see Merton 1972 on this topic also Spiro Chapter XI of this book). However, there is a tendency for educational researchers to research settings with which they are familiar and, in some instances, where they may have taught and or have access connections. This privileged access to knowledge and the potential to lose researcher neutrality are elements of a complex set of interrelationships that require reflexivity and careful consideration (Mercer 2007).

Insider research projects in education can suffer from a set of biases built up by an education researcher. Biases in the perspective taken as an 'in-house expert' often developed from working with, or having close association with, a particular context or group. For example, doctoral students in education frequently design research around their own employment setting – one with which they are intimately familiar. Here, occasionally assumptions are made about the willingness of colleagues to collect data on someone's else's behalf. Or the assumption is made that there is a specific solution that requires some evidence to support the preferred, pre-chosen solution. Closeness to a subject and previous experience in that setting bring tacit knowledge, but questions should be asked about what that knowledge is built upon and how robust it is as a potential foundation for a research project.

Familiarity also can deny innovation in aspects such as research design, which can become an ethical issue if, for example, there are more appropriate ways in which to gather data but where the 'internal norms' are being followed. Learning from other subject areas and contexts can improve an education research project both in terms of methodology and also in terms of conceptualization of the research question. Insider research can limit more creative thinking. Research ethics committees may be considered to evaluate insider research harshly when compared to other research approaches. However, in reality, the ethics committees are more likely to surface questions that the researcher needs to give attention to which will enhance the project, rather than, as some might think, criticize the approach outright.

Good practice suggestions

To summarize this chapter, suggestions for good practice are now provided. To forge a more constructive working relationship, further training for both researchers and ethics panel members is suggested. Encouraging ongoing dialogue between education researchers and ethics committees will facilitate a sense of mutual and informed endeavour towards ethical excellence in research

(McAreavey and Muir 2011). The use of role play, in which the researcher becomes an ethics reviewer and vice versa, may add insight to the prevailing and established perspective that each 'side' is said to adopt. If a researcher was asked to respond to an illustrative complaint from a member of the public, their future ethics applications may be more detailed and less complacent. Similarly, if ethics panels gave more detailed guidance on completing the relevant documentation, and feedback that recognized that the documentation was not familiar to those applying for ethics approval, possibly less time would be spent by both parties.

In addition, a more explicit recognition by ethics committees that there is a wide diversity of research approaches and that within certain subject areas, such as education research, more ethically complex approaches such as insider research may be appropriate would help mitigate any alienation perceived by education researchers. Pursuant to this, if researchers could make explicit their recognition of the ethics challenges within insider research and provide plans for the mitigation of those challenges then both groups would be well served.

Avoiding the 'lost in translation' can be achieved by earlier interventions. From the researchers, this means asking for clarification of what is needed for ethics approval, ensuring documentation is in line with current legislative requirements and preparing applications in advance of deadlines. From the research ethics committees – giving very clear feedback that makes no assumptions about ethics knowledge, implementing processes that are simple to follow and emphasizing the 'friend' element of being a critical friend.

Moving away from defensive positions to more supportive and mutually beneficial relationships will facilitate, in the longer term, more robust and rigorous research within the education environment to the advantage of all.

References

Baak, M. (2019) Racism and othering for South Sudanese heritage students in Australian schools: is inclusion possible? *International Journal of Inclusive Education*, 23(2): 125–141.

Connolly, K. and Reid, A. (2007) Ethics review for qualitative inquiry: adopting a values-based, facilitative approach, *Qualitative Inquiry*, 13(7): 1031–1047.

GDPR (n.d.) Privacy Notices. Available at: https://www.gov.uk/government/publications/data-protection-and-privacy-privacy-notices

Halse, C. and Honey, A. (2007) Rethinking ethics review as institutional discourse, *Qualitative Inquiry*, 13(3): 336–352.

Hammersley, M. (2009) Against the ethicists: on the evils of ethical regulation, *International Journal of Social Research Methodology*, 12(3): 211–225.

Howe, K.R. and Moses, M.S. (1999) Chapter 2: Ethics in educational research, *Review of Research in Education*, 24(1): 21–59.

Lahman, M.K. (2008) Always othered: ethical research with children, *Journal of Early Childhood Research*, 6(3): 281–300.

McAreavey, R. and Das, C. (2013) A delicate balancing act: negotiating with gatekeepers for ethical research when researching minority communities, *International Journal of Qualitative Methods*, 12(1): 113–131.

McAreavey, R. and Muir, J. (2011) Research ethics committees: values and power in higher education, *International Journal of Social Research Methodology*, 14(5): 391–405.

Mercer, J. (2007) The challenges of insider research in educational institutions: wielding a double-edged sword and resolving delicate dilemmas, *Oxford Review of Education*, 33(1): 1–17.

Merton, R. (1972) Insiders and outsiders; a chapter in the sociology of knowledge, *American Journal of Sociology*, 78 (July), 9–4.

Moran-Ellis, J. and Tisdall, E.K.M. (2019) The relevance of 'competence' for enhancing or limiting children's participation: unpicking conceptual confusion, *Global Studies of Childhood*, 9(3): 212–223.

Schenk, K. and Williamson, J. (2005) *Ethical Approaches to Gathering Information from Children and Adolescents in International Settings: Guidelines and Resources*. Washington, DC: Population Council. Available at: https://www.popcouncil.org/uploads/pdfs/horizons/childrenethics.pdf (accessed 28 June 2022).

UNICEF (n.d.). *Research with Children*. Available at: https://www.unicef-irc.org/research/ethical-research-for-children (accessed 28 June 2022).

Zeni, J. (2001) *Ethical Issues in Practitioner Research*. New York: Teachers Collage Press.

IV Ethical Dilemmas in the Supervision of Undergraduate Education Students Conducting Research for Dissertations

Victoria Pratt

Introduction

This chapter will explore the ethical dilemmas experienced by educational researchers supervising final year undergraduate research projects. The supervision of these projects is often seen as a relatively low-stakes, routine undertaking and has received little attention in the literature on educational research (Ashwin et al. 2017; Roberts and Seaman 2018). However, closer examination suggests a range of ethical issues arise for both student and supervisor. Central to this is the fact that undergraduate students are usually novice researchers – they have no previous experience to guide them in negotiating the complex ethical landscape of educational research described elsewhere in this book. In addition, undergraduate students' primary purpose in conducting research is to secure a qualification. This differs from the intended aim of educational research given by the British Educational Research Association (BERA 2018: 3), which is 'to extend knowledge and understanding'. The pursuit of a good mark may pose a conflict of interest with ethical responsibilities, particularly regarding the treatment of participants (Hack 2012; Verrier and Day 2020). This possibility is exacerbated by a common assumption in the research community that undergraduate research is low risk by definition (Richman and Alexander 2006). Students often share this perception and may not expect to identify ethical issues in their research (Maguire et al. 2013).

Time pressure may further influence the ethical conduct of undergraduate dissertation projects. Students typically complete their research in one academic year, concurrently with other assessed modules and placements (Malcolm 2020); this leaves minimal time to accommodate setbacks or adaptations before the submission deadline. Supervisors, working within the same narrow timeframe, often have a large number of undergraduates to support. This may only allow for 'brief encounters' with each student (Rowley and Slack 2004), during which supervisors must make relatively rapid judgements about supervisees' research skills, including their understanding of ethics (Malcolm 2020). As Gallagher et al. (2014: 176) warn, this may lead students and supervisors to view ethical appraisal as no more than 'a bureaucratic hurdle which impedes the timely progression for the completion of a dissertation'. This time sensitivity, together with the presumption of low risk, means that undergraduate research projects are rarely scrutinized by University Research Ethics Committees (Tinker and Coomber 2004). Supervisors must make their own decisions about ethical guidance for students.

This chapter seeks to support researcher colleagues in this undertaking by offering a detailed exploration of undergraduate research ethics in the following stages. The first section will establish the context for why and how undergraduate education students are expected to conduct research for dissertations. The second section will examine the ethical dilemmas faced by students and their supervisors in relation to the five areas of responsibility defined in the British Educational Research Association's Ethical Guidelines for Education Research (BERA 2018). This set of guidelines has been chosen for the reasons outlined by Brown in Chapter II and it covers responsibilities to: participants, sponsors, clients and stakeholders in research; the community of educational researchers; publication and dissemination; and researchers' wellbeing and development. The final part of the chapter will offer suggestions for the resolution of these dilemmas.

Why and how are undergraduate education students expected to conduct research for dissertations?

Research-based dissertations are such a familiar feature of final-year undergraduate study that undertaking them is almost a 'cultural expectation' in the UK (Healey and Jenkins 2009). However, it is important to understand why this has come to be the case and to consider how students are expected to complete these demanding pieces of work. In this section, we will also consider the particular position of undergraduate education students and examine what ethics-related instruction is included in education degrees that may prepare students for the dissertation.

Advocacy of student research can be traced back to Humboldt's model of higher education in the early nineteenth century, although, historically, undergraduate research has more often been framed in opposition to academics' own research (Willison and O'Regan 2007). In the United States, the development of selective undergraduate research programmes in the 1970s and 1980s led to a wider pedagogical shift towards the integration of research and teaching. This was reflected in the revolutionary Boyer Commission (1998) which made 10 recommendations for undergraduate education. The eighth of these was that: 'the final semester(s) should focus on a major project and utilize to the fullest the research and communication skills learned in the previous semesters' (Boyer Commission 1998: 27).

In the UK, the completion of such extended projects had already begun to be associated with the award of honours degrees. In the 1980s, when most assessment was by examination, dissertations 'offered students the opportunity to demonstrate their "honour worthiness"' (Rowley and Slack 2004: 176). It is now the case that the majority of degrees in the UK are awarded 'with honours' and the Qualifications Framework explicitly links the honours level of qualification to the ability 'to initiate and carry out projects' (QAA 2014: 26). Although the requirements for honours degrees vary internationally (Healey et al. 2013; Roberts and Seaman 2018), the final-year research project has become a common endeavour in many countries. Whilst usually called 'dissertations' in the UK, the term 'capstone project' is used in the United States and Australasia (Healey et al. 2013); other terms include 'senior essays', 'extended essays' and 'projects by independent study' (Todd et al. 2006). These all typically involve 'the collection of primary data and/or the analysis of existing/secondary data' (Todd et al. 2004: 335) and are characterized as the 'pinnacle' (Ashwin et al. 2017), 'culmination' (Feather et al. 2014) or 'acid test' (Healey et al. 2013) of undergraduate education.

With such prestige attached to the dissertation, students are likely to approach it with the hope of doing well. It is also the most substantial piece of work undertaken during an undergraduate degree – usually 8,000 to 12,000 words in length and equivalent to two modules' credit (Healey et al. 2013). As such, the mark awarded is likely to influence students' final degree weighting (Derounian 2011). Success in the dissertation has also been linked to employability – it offers an opportunity for students to demonstrate 'work-ready' competencies such as self-direction (Todd et al. 2004), intellectual flexibility (Doyle and Buckley 2007) and discipline-specific research skills (Verrier and Day 2020). With both degree classification and future employability in the balance, students' experiences of completing dissertations within the short prescribed timeframe are likely to be intense. Further pressure may be created by the expectation that students work individually (Todd et al. 2004) and are given autonomy in choosing their research topic (Feather et al. 2014). These varied challenges considerably raise the stakes for undergraduate student researchers, which may not be conducive to the investment of time and effort into ethics processes.

However, for education students, a fundamental disciplinary interest in ethics might be expected to offset this risk. Education is commonly viewed as 'a moral enterprise' (Bullough 2011), in which values and beliefs are central to practice (Boon 2011). In the UK, just over 136,000 students enrolled in education and teaching courses in the academic years 2019/20 to 2020/21 (HESA 2022). This includes initial teacher training (ITT) students completing degrees in education, but also those studying education studies and early childhood studies. These are relatively new degree subjects that do not lead to qualified teacher status but have grown rapidly since their introduction in the 1990s (Bartlett and Burton 2006; Palaiologou 2010). They have subject benchmark statements, and in each of these, ethics is specifically mentioned in the 'defining principles' section. For education studies, there is an expectation that courses will 'draw on a wide range of...ethical perspectives' (QAA 2019a: 6). For early childhood studies, reference is made to 'an understanding of...ethical principles and children's rights' (QAA 2019b: 5). However, no research has been published on the extent to which these recommendations are reflected in ethics-related course content, or if this content is transferable to dissertation ethics.

Education degrees that lead to qualified teacher status do not have a benchmark statement, but providers must draw on the content of the ITT – core content framework (DfE 2019). In contrast to the education studies and early childhood studies benchmark statements, the framework makes no specific reference to ethics. This absence seems to be reflected in limited provision of ethics education in teacher training courses. In a narrative review of the literature, Maxwell and Schwimmer (2016: 355) suggest that mandatory ITT modules related to ethics are 'vanishingly rare' and that the topic as a whole is neglected. Similarly, Walters et al. (2018) found little information about the inclusion of ethics education in their comparative survey of ITT provision in five OECD countries (Canada, the United States, Australia, England and the Netherlands). Where information did exist, this indicated that, rather than discipline-based ethics content informing students' dissertation research, this worked the other way round. In England especially, the main (or only) way in which students learned about wider ethical issues in education was found to be by completing ethics processes for their own projects.

It may be that the practical dissertation context is the best location for education students to engage with ethics: Doyle and Buckley (2014: 156) argue that this 'affords them the opportunity to wrestle with ethical considerations in a real-world situation'. A recent study of education studies undergraduates' perspectives found that students also identified the dissertation as a key opportunity to learn about ethical issues (Donnelly et al.'s 2020). However, if the dissertation must serve this additional educational purpose, it is all the more important that undergraduate research supervisors have a good awareness of the ethical dilemmas that may arise.

What ethical dilemmas may be faced by undergraduate dissertation students and their supervisors?

This section will address the ethical dilemmas involved in undergraduate dissertation research using the five areas of responsibility set out in the British Educational Research Association's Ethical Guidelines for Education Research (BERA 2018). These cover responsibilities to participants; sponsors, clients and stakeholders in research; the community of educational researchers; publication and dissemination and researchers' own wellbeing and development. The relevance of these guidelines to undergraduate research is made explicit – BERA (2018) suggests that they are used for training in education degrees and states that 'the intended audience for these guidelines is anyone undertaking educational research ... (including studying for a qualification)' (BERA 2018: 1).

1 Responsibilities to Participants

As established in Chapter II of this book, the protection of those participating in research is at the heart of the historical development of ethical guidelines. This underpins BERA's (2018: 8) statement that to operate within an ethic of respect, 'researchers should not undertake work for which they are not competent'. This poses the first and most fundamental dilemma for supervisors of undergraduate research – do they assume this competence in students, or judge it and how do they respond if they consider it lacking? Given that the dissertation is usually a required course element, refusing to allow a student to conduct research would be problematic. This issue of competence is further complicated if undergraduate projects involve children – the UNCRC's (1989) influence has ensured particular emphasis on the protection of children in research. This is set out in UNICEF's report on Ethical Research Involving Children (ERIC), which argues that specialized skills and training are essential:

> Respecting the dignity, rights and well-being of children in research requires that researchers understand, and are adequately skilled, in implementing the increasing evidence about what constitutes ethical research. (Graham et al., 2013: 96)

Supervisors must therefore make a judgement about the adequacy of ethical understanding and skill possessed by student researchers who intend to conduct research with children. As Maguire et al. (2013) point out, students with existing childcare qualifications and experience may well possess these attributes, but an assessment of some kind needs to be made. At the very least, supervisors may be expected to ensure that students are familiar with their responsibilities towards research participants, whether children or adults and to discuss with them how these apply in the chosen dissertation context (Miller 2013).

BERA (2018) breaks down participant responsibilities into six further separate areas that are implied by an ethic of respect, and these will be considered next: consent, transparency, right to withdraw, incentives, harm arising, privacy/data storage and disclosure.

1.1 Consent

Securing voluntary, informed and ongoing consent is a key responsibility all researchers owe to participants. A key dilemma for undergraduate students is the short period of time in which this must be achieved – the need to secure participants quickly may undermine the ethical conduct of the process. One convenient way students may seek to recruit participants is by inviting undergraduate peers to take part in research. This raises issues of both coercion and over-testing, although students are likely to be well-informed about their rights as participants and so less vulnerable (Hack 2012). Students may also attempt to recruit participants from within their employment or placement settings, which again raises issues around voluntary consent (Doyle and Buckley 2014). In addition, this approach places students in a challenging 'dual role' (BERA 2018: 13) in which they may experience tensions around confidentiality and workplace power dynamics. Another easily accessed location for participant recruitment is family and friends. However, BERA (2018: 13) warns this situation is one where 'potential participants may not be in a social position vis a vis the researcher that enables them to easily give unrestrained informed consent'. In all these situations, supervisors may need to support students in balancing the demands of timely recruitment with ethical responsibility.

Undergraduate researchers have to commit additional time and effort to the consent process if they wish to recruit children as participants in research. As previously stated, BERA's (2018) endorsement of the UNCRC requires that students and supervisors take the best interest of the child as the primary consideration. In the Planning and Preparation section of UNICEF's Ethical Research Involving Children, Graham et al. (2013: 104) suggest that to do this, the first question to ask is 'does this research need to be done?' and then 'is this research important for children?'. These are challenging questions for undergraduate research and will be explored in the next section on 'transparency'. Assuming the research is seen as necessary and important, BERA (2018) raises a number of further issues around gaining consent for child participants, which are faced by all educational researchers. Preliminary gatekeeper consent may be required from schools or other educational settings, as well as permission from those who have legal responsibility for a child, in the form of parental or guardian consent. Children themselves should also have the opportunity to give informed consent, 'commensurate with their age and maturity' (BERA 2018: 15). This all requires time-consuming ethical engagement by students, who have limited time to spare.

Desk-based research may seem to offer an 'easy' alternative to the recruitment of human participants, whether adults or children, but students might not recognize that this approach still raises issues of consent. Secondary or archival data is likely to have been collected for an entirely different purpose than that intended by a student (Morrow et al. 2014). In addition, official data sets may include systematic bias or misrepresent participants (Miller 2013). Online or internet-based research is another approach where complex issues of consent arise that may not be immediately obvious to undergraduate researchers. These include the difficulty of ensuring participants understand what they are consenting to, establishing whether they are of an age or position to give informed consent and protecting the 'online identity' of participants (Maguire et al. 2013). In fact, Cohen et al. (2018) suggest consent for internet-based research may need to be negotiated several times over, if it is to be truly voluntary, informed and ongoing. Once again, this may create a conflict of interests between undergraduate students' responsibilities to participants and the timely completion of their dissertation research.

1.2 Transparency

The second area of responsibility to participants relates to transparency. The key dilemma for supervisors and students here is the recommendation that:

> Researchers should not undertake work in which they can be perceived to have a conflict of interest or in which self-interest…might compromise the objectivity of the research. (BERA 2018: 18)

As mentioned earlier, students' main interest in completing research for a dissertation is to develop research skills and to achieve a qualification (Hack 2012). The wider value of undergraduate dissertations is usually framed as 'a vehicle for learner development' (Malcolm 2020: 8) not as research at all. Indeed, undergraduate dissertations rarely create new knowledge or theory and are unlikely to be generalizable or produce statistically significant results (Rowley and Slack 2004; Hack 2012). These points lead Gallagher et al. (2014: 172) to argue that:

> If the primary benefit of research is to provide training for the students, a key ethical principle is breached: namely, that research should prioritize the well-being, safety, dignity and rights of those who participate in research, rather than those who conduct it.

A different risk-benefit position is proposed by Hack (2012). Whilst undergraduate dissertations may only make a small contribution to research, the societal benefits of students gaining research skills, including in ethics, are tangible. This argument may be all the more relevant in the field of initial teacher training, given the limited opportunities that students are given to engage with ethics in the curriculum. Healey and Jenkins (2009) make a similar point, suggesting that dissertation research creates transformational knowledge for students, even this is not 'new knowledge per se'. BERA (2018: 8) itself recognizes that:

> At times, some benefits to participants may be compromised in order to achieve other gains or goals, but these compromises should be justifiable and, where possible, explicitly accounted for.

The dilemma for undergraduate supervisors and students is how to ensure the true benefits and purposes of dissertation research are made transparent to participants, who may be unaware of the differences between levels of research (Doyle and Buckley 2014). It is worth remembering that participants may 'trust in the wider value of the research beyond the researcher's personal interests' (BERA 2018: 18), simply by its association with a university. This makes it all the more important that students avoid 'hyperclaiming' what their research will achieve and that supervisors ensure it is worthy of participants' time (Miller 2013).

1.3 Right to withdraw

Educational researchers must 'recognize the right of all participants to withdraw from the research for any or no reason, and at any time' (BERA 2018: 18). The potential dilemma this raises for students is again related to their need to complete research within a short timeframe. This may make it harder for students to support participants who wish to withdraw from research without applying any coercion or duress. Additional guidance from supervisors may be necessary in relation to this responsibility – one study of undergraduate students' comprehension of research ethics found that participant withdrawal was one of the most challenging issues to understand (Löfström 2012).

1.4 Incentives

The small-scale nature of undergraduate dissertation research means that incentives are not usually used, so no dilemma should arise in relation to this responsibility. However, supervisors may need to ensure students are aware that incentives are not required or if offered should be given equitably to all participants.

1.5 Harm arising from participation in research

BERA (2018: 19) states that:

> Researchers have a responsibility to think through their duty of care in order to recognize potential risks, and to prepare for and be in a position to minimize and manage any distress or discomfort that may arise.

As with incentives, the typically small scale and non-invasive nature of undergraduate research (Hack 2012) should ensure that this area of responsibility does not pose ethical dilemmas for students or supervisors. However, 'even seemingly innocuous projects may contain subtle risks' (Maguire et al. 2013: 123), and universities may face serious reputational and financial risks if students' projects do cause harm (Verrier and Day 2020; Doyle and Buckley 2014). There is potential for undergraduates' subjectivity or self-interest to lead them to overlook potential risks (Verrier and Day 2020), so supervisors' scrutiny of research designs is essential. This additional layer of risk assessment should offer protection for participants but also for student researchers themselves, who may lack the skills and experience to cope if harm does arise (Doyle and Buckley 2014).

1.6 Privacy/data storage

This area of responsibility to participants should be relatively low-risk for undergraduate researchers and seems to be one of the issues students find most straightforward to understand and explain (Löfström 2012). This may be because terminology around privacy and data storage is widely used in everyday contexts. However, this is one area in which the small-scale nature of undergraduate dissertation research may be problematic, as it may be more difficult to ensure data is anonymized effectively. The issue of 'deductive disclosure' of participants through gender, age or other details that may be identifying in an educational setting needs to be clearly communicated to students by supervisors (Maguire et al. 2013).

1.7 Disclosure

As with the risk of harm arising from participation in research, this is an area of responsibility to participants that students and supervisors should plan to avoid through research design. If an issue of disclosure does arise, BERA (2018: 26) gives clear guidance:

> Researchers should seek advice from a relevant responsible person before proceeding to disclosure if and when appropriate (students should seek advice from supervisors).

2 Sponsors, clients and stakeholders in research

Undergraduate students' responsibilities to this group are limited by the nature and purpose of dissertation research, which is not conducted on behalf of clients. However, universities and supervisors can be seen as stakeholders in undergraduate research, defined as 'any person or body who has a direct interest in its framing and success' (BERA 2018: 26). The individual nature of the supervisory process means supervisors are likely to have a strong interest in the success of 'their' dissertation students. Supervisors may even feel their own teaching and research skills may be judged in relation to supervisees' success or failure. This becomes ethically challenging when supervisors are responsible for first or second-marking dissertations that represent, to some extent, their own work. Malcolm (2020: 8) found that supervisors may attempt to resolve this ethical dilemma by reducing the level of support offered to students in the final stages of writing up the dissertation. This allows them 'to distance themselves from the product of their own guidance'. However, this staged strategy is not always made transparent to students, thereby undermining the intention to achieve a more ethical balance between the supervisors' dual role of stakeholder and marker. A further ethical dilemma raised by the marking process is that supervisors may subconsciously assess students' engagement with the supervisory process rather than the actual dissertation produced (Derounian 2011).

3 Community of educational researchers

Undergraduate researchers, like all researchers, should 'aim to protect the integrity and reputation of educational research by ensuring that they conduct their research to the highest standards' (BERA 2018: 29). If this responsibility is breached, public confidence in the research conducted by a particular university or by the wider research community may be damaged (Hack 2012). As Doyle and Buckley (2014) warn, poorly conducted undergraduate research may also dissuade local communities from engaging in valuable research led by more experienced educational researchers. Supervisors' own reputations may also be at stake, as they are usually the named 'appropriate contact' (BERA 2018: 29) on supervisees' participant information sheets. An ethical dilemma faced by supervisors here is the extent to which they can intervene in students' dissertation research without endangering students' autonomy (Vereijken et al. 2018). This tension around ownership runs throughout the supervision process, as students must 'simultaneously seek to learn research skills, operationalize their projects and do so under direction to ensure that research standards are adhered to' (Brydon and Flynn 2013: 368).

The area of responsibility towards the wider community of educational researchers set out by BERA (2018) also covers plagiarism. However, as with privacy and storage, undergraduate students seem to find this a relatively easy aspect of research ethics to negotiate (Löfström 2012). If supervisors do have concerns relating to plagiarism, these can be managed through existing university mechanisms for dealing with academic misconduct.

4 Publication and dissemination

In addressing this area of responsibility, BERA states that (2018: 32):

> Researchers have a responsibility to make the results of their research public for the benefit of educational professionals, policymakers and the wider public.

Indeed Gallagher et al. (2014) argue that the effective dissemination of findings from a research project should be a key factor in assessing its benefits. However, publication of undergraduate dissertation research is rare. Findings are generally only written up to be shared with, or read by, the supervisor, another marker and possibly an external examiner (Healey and Jenkins 2009). Feedback from this small group of readers is rarely used by students to revise or develop the research, which is more usually put aside and forgotten about (Walkington 2015). This outcome fails to meet either BERA's (2018) guidance or the Boyer Commission's (1998: 24) recommendation that, even for undergraduates, 'dissemination of results is an essential and integral part of the research process'. Students may struggle to identify dissemination of research as an ethical issue at all – in Löfström's (2012) research, less than a third were able to explain why it is important.

4.1 Authorship

Although unusual, it is possible that students may develop dissertation research for publication in an academic journal. Miller (2013) suggests that this raises ethical dilemmas around authorship, as supervisors play a key role in framing the research project and may expect to be given recognition for this. Taking a slightly different position, Brewer et al. (2012) suggest that supervisors may actively avoid co-authoring research with undergraduate students, out of concern this will be perceived as exploitative. Addressing this dilemma, BERA (2018: 34) suggests that 'consensual agreement on authorship should be gained as early as possible in the writing process' and should not be decided by academic status or seniority.

4.2 Scope and format

A final aspect of the researchers' responsibility for publication and dissemination is the format in which this is achieved. BERA states that this 'should take into account the needs and interests of the communities that were involved in the research' (2018: 35) and the chosen format should share findings as fully as possible. Given that most dissertation research is only presented in one format, as a formal written document for submission, it is difficult for undergraduate researchers to meet this responsibility unless they spend time creating alternative materials for sharing with participants. However, the dilemma here is that such efforts are unlikely to be rewarded with additional marks unless completed in advance of (and made visible in) the dissertation submission.

5 Researchers' wellbeing and development

The final area of responsibility covered by BERA (2018: 35) is perhaps the most significant for undergraduate research:

> Safeguarding the physical and psychological wellbeing of researchers is part of the ethical responsibility of employing institutions and sponsors, as well as of researchers themselves.

In addition to this overarching principle, the moral duty of institutions towards both staff and students is highlighted, as well as the potential for exploitation of differences in the role of student researchers. The ethical dilemmas this responsibility raises for students will be considered first, before turning to the dilemmas that supervisors may experience in addition to those of their supervisees.

Perhaps the first ethical dilemma is whether students' wellbeing and 'personal and professional career development' (BERA 2018: 36) are promoted by the completion of a dissertation. Research suggests that undergraduates feel 'cast adrift' in a stressful, fraught and arduous undertaking (Derounian 2011) and they find it 'a very difficult challenge' (Donnelly et al. 2020), akin to climbing a mountain (Wisker 2009). Healey et al. (2013) suggest that the very nature of dissertations may need questioning in a changing world. Only a small number of the growing and increasingly diverse student population will go on into careers in academia, and different forms of assessment may better prepare and support students for the future. Research itself is changing, with a wider range of activities 'counting'. Within the field of education there is a greater focus on interdisciplinary and real-world community-based projects. Healey et al. (2013) argue that the development of different forms of final year projects may be needed to meet these changes.

As well as raising questions around the developmental value of dissertations, ethical dilemmas in this area relate to students' wellbeing within the intensive supervisory relationship. This may be vulnerable to ethical misconduct because of the different power relations between the two parties (Shadforth and Harvey 2004). Role conflicts may exacerbate this, for example the supervisor's objectivity and professional judgement may be affected by holding multiple roles in relation to the student. Students' development and wellbeing may also be compromised by inadequate supervision or the intrusion of supervisors' views and values on the autonomy of students' research (Miller 2013). The pedagogical skill and research expertise of supervisors may vary (Verrier and Day 2020), raising questions of equity between students. Students may also be adversely affected by 'eleventh-hour' supervision, where a new supervisor has to be recruited due to ill-health or other reasons (Derounian 2011).

Whilst recognizing the potential ethical impact of these issues facing their supervisees, supervisors must also take responsibility for their own development and wellbeing. Undergraduate supervision is often the first supervisory experience academic staff have (Roberts and Seaman 2018) – as it rarely results in publishable work, the role is often delegated to early career or less active researchers (Brydon and Flynn 2013; Verrier and Day 2020). However, training and guidance for supervisors is typically focused on postgraduate supervision. Students' free choice of topic can be particularly challenging for inexperienced supervisors, who may feel compelled to adopt an 'expert' role in an unfamiliar area of research (Todd et al. 2006). All supervisors, however experienced, face significant time pressures that may lead them to adopt a functionalist approach (Malcolm 2020) which may not match or meet students' expectations. Indeed, making time for good quality undergraduate supervision may represent 'an almost altruistic commitment' by supervisors in the current academic climate (Del Río et al. 2018: 169). In this context, meeting BERA's (2018) ethical guidelines on responsibilities to researcher development and wellbeing represents a final challenge for both students and supervisors as they negotiate the inherently 'dilemmatic space' (Vereijken et al. 2018: 536) of undergraduate dissertation supervision.

How might students, supervisors and universities resolve these dilemmas?

This chapter has suggested that the supervision and conduct of undergraduate dissertations raises a range of ethical dilemmas that have not always received the attention they warrant in the literature on educational research ethics. However, this does not mean students should be prevented from undertaking any research that requires ethical approval – this outcome would serve students, researchers and society poorly (Hack 2012). Rather, it can be argued that students should be given first-hand opportunities to grapple with ethics, to enable universities 'to develop ethically sensitive individuals who use principled reasoning when facing dilemmas' (Doyle and Buckley 2014: 156). This is especially pertinent within the field of education, where students may go on to enter teaching and other related professions that are often seen as essentially moral in purpose (Walters et al. 2013). For students of any discipline, opportunities to develop essential graduate skills of critical thinking and creativity may also be undermined by 'squeezing out riskiness' (Wisker 2018: 5). It seems that a balance between caution and risk must be found that mitigates the ethical issues identified in dissertation research without rendering it educationally ineffective.

The first and most obvious way of achieving this is for universities to ensure supervisors receive specific training in good quality undergraduate supervision. This could address many of the dilemmas raised, particularly in relation to researcher wellbeing and development (Simpson and Wilson-Smith 2017). Vereijken et al. (2018) suggest that training should include opportunities for explicit reflection on supervisory practices, for example by using video recordings. Todd et al. (2006) suggest the creation of supervisor networks as a valuable and informal source of additional support. Verrier and Day (2020) argue that equity and consistency of supervision can be promoted through the use of supplementary group workshops to teach research methods, including ethics. Workshops reduce both duplication and workload for supervisors and they also offer a solution for less experienced supervisors, who may not feel comfortable taking an 'expert' role in all aspects of research (Todd et al. 2006). Taking this communal approach a step further, group dissertation supervision sessions have been trialled within the fields of social work (Akister et al. 2009) and nursing (Baker et al. 2014). In both cases, these had no detrimental effect on students' dissertation results and had positive outcomes in relation to students' motivation, time-keeping and decreased sense of isolation. A group supervision approach may also dilute the 'inherently fraught' supervisor–supervisee relationship, reducing the potential for tension (Derounian 2011: 92).

A further adaptation that may be combined with group supervision is for supervisors to offer students a range of set dissertation titles within their own research area (Abdulai and Owusu-Ansah 2014). Students can then develop these individually, with all parties having confidence in the academic merit and ethical design of the project from the outset (Verrier and Day 2020). However, this heavily scaffolded solution may be seen as ethically problematic itself. Whilst acknowledging the difficulty students face in producing researchable questions, Todd et al. (2004) argue that such 'tutor-led' research undermines autonomous learning; as an alternative, supervisors can share a wide range of examples of previous dissertations. In addition, Hack (2012) suggests providing students with tools to support the development of dissertation projects, including checklists for low-risk projects and approved recruitment methods.

Further solutions may lie outside the supervisory relationship, in the form of earlier and more rigorous preparation of students for the dissertation. Indeed, embedding the teaching of ethics from the very start of undergraduate courses could address many of the dilemmas identified in the final-year dissertation process. Interestingly, there is no standard pedagogical approach to the teaching of research methods in the social sciences, least of all ethics (Wagner et al. 2011). Löfström (2012: 359) suggests the value of simulations and role play, arguing that 'the importance of providing students with a good working model from the beginning of their studies and facilitating their commitment to sound professional norms and values cannot be stressed enough'. To best achieve this, the dissertation could be framed as one of many research activities to be undertaken by students throughout the three-year degree course. This is in line with the original Boyer Commission (1998) recommendations, which envisioned student research encompassing far more than a single project.

This 'students as researchers' pedagogical approach is increasingly well-recognized internationally (Walkington 2015), and offers further solutions to the ethical dilemmas raised by undergraduate dissertations. In particular, this pedagogy promotes wider opportunities for undergraduate research publication, which could address the issues raised by traditionally poor dissemination of dissertation findings. This includes an increasing number of undergraduate research journals, such as *Reinvention*, e-journals, and initiatives such as Oxford Brookes' Student Research Launch Pad, based on the Get Published! project. In the field of education specifically, the Early Childhood Studies Degree Network (ECSDN) has published undergraduate research regularly since 2017. Undergraduate research conferences offer further opportunities for the dissemination of research, led by the Council for Undergraduate Research (CUR) in the US; the British Conference of Undergraduate Research (BCUR) was established in 2010, the Australasian Conference on Undergraduate Research (ACUR) in 2012 and the International Conference of Undergraduate Research (ICUR) in 2013. Other strategies for disseminating undergraduate research include the use of blogs, podcast and wikis (Walkington 2015).

Conclusion

The undergraduate dissertation offers students a unique opportunity to acquire intellectual skills and a 'hallmark of graduateness' (Derounian 2011: 91) that is of particular value in an uncertain and rapidly changing knowledge environment (Malcolm 2020). However, as the UK Economic and Social Research Council (ESRC 2021) makes clear, 'the same principles should apply to student research as to all other research'. This means that the particular ethical dilemmas raised by student dissertation research must be recognized and mitigated, not only to protect participants, but also students, supervisors and the wider research community. Key factors are the time constraints within which dissertation research must be conducted, its inherently self-interested purpose and the inexperience of the researcher. This relative lack of experience may be shared by supervisors, who are unlikely to receive direct undergraduate supervision training. Some solutions to the resulting dilemmas faced in the supervision process have been suggested in this chapter. The most radical of these is to reframe the dissertation within a broader student research pedagogy – this would support the development of undergraduate research skills, including in ethics, throughout the degree and not only in its closing months. However, such an approach is necessarily university-led. For the solitary supervisor, recognition that undergraduate dissertation research is more ethically complex than it might first appear offers a simpler starting point.

References

Abdulai, R. and Owusu-Ansah, A. (2014) Essential ingredients of a good research proposal for undergraduate and postgraduate students in the social sciences, *SAGE Open*, 4(3): 1–15.

Akister, J., Williams, I. and Maynard, A. (2009) Using group supervision for undergraduate dissertations: a preliminary enquiry into the student experience, *Practice and Evidence of the Scholarship of Teaching and Learning in Higher Education*, 4(2): 77–94.

Ashwin, P., Abbas, A. and McLean, M. (2017) How does completing a dissertation transform undergraduate students' understanding of disciplinary knowledge? *Assessment and Evaluation in Higher Education*, 42(4): 517–530.

Baker, M.J., Cluett, E. L. Ireland, S. et al. (2014) Supervising undergraduate research: a collective approach utilising groupwork and support, *Nurse Education Today*, 34: 637–642.

Barlett, S. and Burton, D. (2006) The evolution of education studies in higher education in England, *Curriculum Journal*, 17(4): 383–396.

BERA (2018) *Ethical Guidelines for Educational Research* (4th edn). [Online]. Available at: https://www.bera.ac.uk/publication/ethical-guidelines-for-educational-research-2018 (accessed 29 June 2022).

Boon, H. (2011) Raising the bar: ethics education for quality teachers, *Australian Journal of Teacher Education*, 36(7): 76–93.

Boyer Commission (1998) *Reinventing Undergraduate Education: A Blueprint for America's Research Universities*. Stony Brook, New York: Carnegie Foundation for the Advancement of Teaching.

Brewer, G., Dewhurst, A.M. and Doran, D. (2012) Undergraduate research projects: practice and perceptions, *Psychology, Learning and Teaching*, 11(2): 208–217.

Brydon, K. and Flynn, C. (2013) Expert companions? Constructing a pedagogy for supervising honours students, *Social Work Education*, 33: 365–380.

Bullough, R.V. Jr (2011) Ethical and moral matters in teaching and teacher education', *Teaching and Teacher Education*, 27(1): 21–28.

Cohen, L., Manion, L. and Morrison, K. (2018) *Research Methods in Education*. Abingdon and New York: Routledge.

Department of Education (DfE) (2019) *Initial teacher training (ITT): Core Content Framework*. [Online]. Available at: https://www.gov.uk/government/publications/initial-teacher-training-itt-core-content-framework (accessed 29 June 2022).

Del Río, M., Díaz-Vázquez, R. and Maside Sanfiz, J. (2018) Satisfaction with the supervision of undergraduate dissertations, *Active Learning in Higher Education*, 19(2): 159-172.

Derounian, J. (2011) "Shall we dance?" The importance of staff-student relationships to undergraduate dissertation preparation, *Active Learning in Higher Education* 12(2): 91–100.

Donnelly, R., Ui Choistealbha, J. and Fitzmaurice, M. (2020) The student experience of final year in an undergraduate degree programme in education studies, *All Ireland Journal of Teaching and Learning in Higher Education* (AISHE), 12(2).

Doyle, E. and Buckley, P. (2014) Research ethics in teaching and learning, *Innovations in Education and Teaching International*, 51(2): 153–163

ESRC (2021) *Student research and ethics review*. [Online]. Available at: https://esrc.ukri.org/funding/guidance-for-applicants/research-ethics/provision-of-training-and-resources/ (accesssed 29 June 2022).

Feather, D., Anchor, J.R. and Cowton, C.J. (2014) Supervisors' perceptions of the value of the undergraduate dissertation, *The International Journal of Management Education*, 12(1): 14–21.

Gallagher, C., McDonald, L. and McCormack, N. (2014) Undergraduate research involving human subjects should not be granted ethical approval unless it is likely to be of publishable quality, *HEC Forum* 26:169–180.

Graham, A., Powell, M., Taylor, N. et al. (2013) *Ethical Research Involving Children*. Florence: UNICEF Office of Research. Available at: https://childethics.com/ethical-guidance/ (accessed 29 June 2022).

Hack, C.J. (2012) Ethical review of undergraduate student research projects: a proportionate, transparent and efficient process? *Bioscience Education*, 19: 1–8.

Healey, M. J. and Jenkins, A. (2009) *Developing undergraduate research and inquiry*. York: Higher Education Academy.

Healey, M., Lannin, L., Stibbe, A. et al. (2013) *Developing and Enhancing Undergraduate Final Year Projects and Dissertations*. York: HE Academy. [Online]. Available at: https://www.advance-he.ac.uk/knowledge-hub/developing-and-enhancing-undergraduate-final-year-projects-and-dissertations

HESA (2022) 'What do HE students study? Types of subjects and courses' [Online]. Available at: https://www.hesa.ac.uk/data-and-analysis/students/what-study/courses

Löfström, E. (2012) Students' ethical awareness and conceptions of research ethics, *Ethics and Behaviour*, 22(5): 349–36.

Maguire, M., Delahunt, B. and Everitt-Reynolds, A. (2013) doing the right thing: undergraduate researchers, in R. Donnelly, J. Dallat and M. Fitzmaurice (eds.) *Supervising and Writing a Good Undergraduate Dissertation*. Sharjah, UAE: Bentham Science Publishers.

Malcolm, M. (2020) The challenge of achieving transparency in undergraduate honours-level dissertation supervision, *Teaching in Higher Education*. Available at: https://doi.org/10.1080/13562517.2020.1776246 (accessed 29 June 2022).

Maxwell, B. and Schwimmer, M. (2016) Professional ethics education for future teachers: a narrative review of the scholarly writings, *Journal of Moral Education*, 45(3): 354–371.

Miller, R. (2013) Ethical issues in supervising undergraduate dissertations, in R. Donnelly, J. Dallat and M. Fitzmaurice (eds) *Supervising and Writing a Good Undergraduate Dissertation*. Sharjah, UAE: Bentham Science Publishers.

Morrow, V., Boddy, J. and Lamb, R. (2014). 'The ethics of secondary data analysis: Learning from the experience of sharing qualitative data from young people and their families in an international study of childhood poverty'. *NOVELLA Working Paper: Narrative Research in Action*. Thomas Coram Research Unit and the Institute of Education: University of London.

Palaiologou, I. (2010) The death of a discipline or the birth of a transdiscipline: subverting questions of disciplinarity within Education Studies undergraduate courses, *Educational Studies*, 36(3): 269–282.

QAA (2014) *UK Quality Code for Higher Education Part A: Setting and Maintaining Academic Standards. The Frameworks for Higher Education Qualifications of UK Degree-Awarding Bodies*. Gloucester: QAA.

QAA (2019a) *Subject Benchmark Statement: Education Studies*. Gloucester: QAA.

QAA (2019b) *Subject Benchmark Statement: Early Childhood Studies*. Gloucester: QAA.

Richman, K.A and Alexander, L.B. (2006) Ethics and research with undergraduates, *Ethics and Education*, 1(2) 163–175.

Roberts, L.D. and Seaman, K. (2018) Good undergraduate dissertation supervision: perspectives of supervisors and dissertation coordinators, *International Journal for Academic Development*, 23(1), 28–4.

Rowley, J. and Slack, F. (2004) What is the future for undergraduate dissertations? *Education + Training*, 46(4): 176–181.

Shadforth, T. and Harvey, B. (2004). 'The Undergraduate Dissertation: Subject-centred or *Electronic Journal of Business Research Methods* 2(2) 145–152.

Simpson, K.L. and Wilson-Smith, K. (2017) Undergraduates' experience of preparedness for engaging with sensitive research topics using qualitative research, *Psychology Teaching Review*, 23(1): 30–40.

Tinker, A. and Coomber, V. (2004) *University Research Ethics Committees: Their Role, Remit and Conduct*. London: King's College London.

Todd, M., Bannister, P. and Clegg, S. (2004) Independent inquiry and the undergraduate dissertation: perceptions and experiences of final-year social science students, *Assessment and Evaluation in Higher Education*, 29(3): 335–355.

Todd M., Smith, K. and Bannister, P. (2006) Supervising a social science undergraduate dissertation: staff experiences and perceptions, *Teaching in Higher Education*, 11(2): 161–173.

Vereijken, M., Rijst, R., Driel, J. et al. (2018) Novice supervisors' practices and dilemmatic space in supervision of student research projects, *Teaching in Higher Education*, 23(4): 22–542.

Verrier, D. and Day, C. (2020) How can we improve the final year dissertation? A consideration of ethics, quality, and one-to-one supervision, *Journal of Perspectives in Applied Academic Practice*, 8(2): 90–96.

Wagner, C., Garner, M. and Kawulich, B. (2011) The state of the art of teaching research methods in the social sciences: towards a pedagogical culture, *Studies in Higher Education*, 36: 75–88.

Walkington, H. (2015) *Students as Researchers: Supporting Undergraduate Research in the Disciplines in Higher Education*. York: HEA.

Walters, S., Heilbronn, R. and Daly, C. (2018) Ethics education in initial teacher education: pre-service provision in England, *Professional Development in Education*, 44(3): 385–396.

Willison, J. and O'Regan, K. (2007) Commonly known, commonly not known, totally unknown: a framework for students becoming researchers, *Higher Education Research and Development: Journal of the Higher Education Research and Development Society of Australia*, 26(4): 393–409.

Wisker, G. (2009). *The Undergraduate Research Handbook*. New York, NY: Palgrave MacMillan.

Wisker, G. (2018) Frameworks and freedoms: supervising research learning and the undergraduate dissertation, *Journal of University Teaching and Learning Practice* 15(4): Article 2.

V Ethical Dilemmas in Action

Catharine Gilson

Introduction

The ethical process does not finish once permission to carry out the study is granted by the ethics committee of the institution where the study is being conducted. However, you could say that one stage, often called procedural ethics (Cohen et al. 2018), has been completed in that the researcher is then in a position to carry out the fieldwork. In the course of collecting the data, there are almost always a myriad of ethically informed decisions to make. These are context-specific and regularly occur unexpectedly (Oliver 2010). They often take a researcher by surprise as, having thought exhaustively about the ethical implications of the proposed research study in order to gain ethical approval for the study, it can be disconcerting to be faced with a problem that you had not even considered might arise. Unlike procedural ethics, which is a formal, clearly delineated process, ethics in the field is dynamic, messy and unpredictable. Tutenal et al. (2019) argue that the tension between formal ethical approval and ethics in the field is evident in the proliferation of terms used to describe the latter: relational ethics, ethics in the field, ethics in action and situated ethics, for example. In this chapter, I am going to use the term 'situated ethics' to explore the nature of the ethical dilemmas that may arise for the researcher when carrying out the fieldwork. Guillemin (2004) prefers to use the term 'ethically important moments' as they may not be full-scale moral dilemmas, but spur-of-the-moment decisions that have to be made in an ethically informed way. However, I prefer the term 'situated ethics' as the term denotes that the specific context is central to the decision-making process.

One of the tensions between procedural ethics and situated ethics, as Cohen et al. (2018:114) point out, is that in situated ethics, 'ethical principles inform but do not simplistically determine' the decisions that are made. In order to illustrate the nuanced and context-specific nature of the dilemmas that may arise, I am going to base the discussion in this chapter on a series of ethical dilemmas that arose in the course of conducting a small-scale qualitative study and preparatory pilot study. I draw out from the examples the ethical issues that had to be addressed and consider whether they were resolved satisfactorily or whether I would make different, more informed decisions another time with the benefit of hindsight.

The notion of situated ethics being 'ethics in action' aligns with Schön's notion of 'reflection in action' (Schön 1984). It is worth remembering that as Emmerich (2018) points out, there is not a dichotomy between reflection on action and reflection in action, rather they are part of a continuum. In the same way, I take the view in this chapter that procedural ethics and situated ethics are not opposed to each other, despite the tensions that may exist between them. Instead, they are different phases of the process of conducting an ethical research study, even if the two phases require different approaches. Ethical issues arise throughout the research process and reflexivity is required at all stages of the research process, particularly in qualitative research where researcher subjectivity is acknowledged (Cohen et al. 2018).

Traianou (2018) points out that ethical dilemmas occur in the field most commonly, though not exclusively, in qualitative empirical studies where the environment is not controlled by the researcher. In educational research, researchers may be in a location that requires access to be granted by a gatekeeper. They will be guests in the setting and may not be able to control the noise volume in the room, the interruptions, the timings of the visit to collect data, whether that is an interview, an observation or an intervention. All these interventions, particularly the interview or observation, are essentially open-ended, in that the way the interview or observation will unfold is unpredictable. Thus Traianou (2018) argues that methodological and ethical judgements are intertwined and judgements will almost certainly have to be made about what is more and what is less important in the moment that the dilemmas arise (Flewitt 2005). The examples I refer to in this chapter are drawn from research interviews using two different methods that formed part of a small-scale qualitative study exploring parental and practitioner perceptions of their children's nursery education and care. Two in-depth interviews were conducted with each of the nine participants – a conventional semi-structured interview followed by an interview using film elicitation as a prompt for discussion. The methods were trialled extensively in a pilot study, which is also included in the discussion here as the findings shaped my ethical decisions, which in turn shaped the final methodological approach of the study.

Ethical issues of the interview as a method

Using interviews as a research method raises many ethical considerations. The power dynamic between the interviewer and the interviewee is recognized as a key ethical issue (Brooks et al. 2014), particularly in educational research where there may be a stark imbalance between adults and children. Such an imbalance can also occur between adults, for example, within the hierarchy of a school where the headteacher as the gatekeeper has given permission for the research to take place even though teachers themselves may be less enthusiastic to participate. As well as the obvious issues of adults interviewing children discussed in other chapters of this book (for example, by Capewell in Chapter VI), there is also the issue of insider researcher influence (Robson and McCartan

2016) where the researcher may be a current or former practitioner (see also Spiro, Chapter IX). Perhaps less commonly acknowledged is the dynamic of elite interviewing highlighted by Mason-Bish (2019), which can occur when the position or status of the interviewee is perceived to be much greater than that of the interviewer – a feature of one of the examples discussed below. The challenge of making sure that the principle of informed consent is adhered to is another ethical consideration highlighted, though as Malone (2003) points out, consent can never be fully informed when using a method that is essentially unpredictable as it deals with an encounter between two people. This too is an issue discussed below. However, the element that posed most challenge for me in the field was managing the emotionality of the interviews, which caught me unawares, particularly with the semi-structured interviews, and is an issue further discussed by Wild and Brown in Chapter X. I was better prepared for the film elicitation interviews as visual methodology is more widely recognized to raise ethical issues, as discussed below.

Discomfort or distress?

A key principle of ethical research is non-maleficence, in other words that it should not cause distress and harm to the participants (BERA 2018). This study did not set out to research a highly sensitive topic requiring participants to divulge personal information. However, the interview dynamic is charged with emotion, as Clarke and Hoggett (2009) point out, and it is easy to underestimate how apprehensive the interviewee may feel even when they are keen to participate. For example, one practitioner told me at the end of the first interview, after the voice recorder had been turned off, how much she had enjoyed talking to me and how anxious she had been beforehand. I wrote in my field notes that she looked flushed and almost tearful as she was speaking. However, she then went on to say that she had specifically asked via the headteacher to be included in the study as she was so keen to participate. It could be argued here that an interviewee can wish to participate in a study whilst also feeling anxious about the process beforehand, and so the discomfort generated by their apprehension is not necessarily experienced as harmful by them, as they want to take part. Nonetheless, whilst I would agree with Jones (1998) that people have a range of motives for participating in research, I do not support his view that the research interview can be regarded as therapeutic when discomfort is experienced and would not venture to suggest that this was the case in any of the examples discussed here. Equally, the interviewer has no control over the responses of the interviewees, who may choose to talk about topics that they find upsetting or may find themselves upset by what is intended to be an innocuous question. A case in point is that two practitioners (one male, one female) became tearful when asked to talk in the semi-structured interview about what they liked about teaching young children. They expressed surprise at themselves for doing so, but again, that response could not possibly have been foreseen by either the interviewer or the interviewee. I was concerned and disconcerted as the interviewer and was confronted with the dilemma of how to proceed when faced by an interviewee becoming tearful, particularly in an interview that was not designed to probe emotional or sensitive issues. My dilemma was whether to continue the interview or offer to pause or stop it. In the case of Matthew, the situation was defused by laughter:

Researcher: What is it that you like about working with young children?
Matthew: It's the playing, it's the joy of seeing children exploring and finding out, the same thing that you do every year, with the butterfly coming out of the chrysalis, but it's new for that child, and that is the joy, to see that, and to give them that opportunity to learn that. I'm going to cry now.
[Laughter]

I then went on to ask Matthew if he could talk about a child he had in his class at the moment who was enjoyable to teach, to ground the conversation in a concrete example, and the interview continued. The other teacher, Eleanor, also recovered her composure quickly, saying, 'I don't know why I feel emotional,' and so that interview also continued. However, the experience as a researcher made me aware of the unpredictability and the emotionality of the interview as a method, as well as highlighting the commitment and emotional investment of these teachers in their work with young children. It also made me aware of the need to consider possible mitigations even when the study is not investigating a sensitive topic, such as incorporating a debriefing time afterwards for the interviewee with the researcher, should they want it, and having a list of organizations to signpost them to for forward advice.

Film elicitation interviews

Visual methods are renowned for being fickle (Banks 2001; Rose 2016), so in many ways I was more prepared to encounter some ethically challenging moments in the fieldwork for the film elicitation interviews. And there were several – for example, the technology did not work for one of the pilot interviews, so I had to decide whether to continue with that interview or not. I made the ethical choice to proceed anyway so as not to waste the participant's time by rescheduling and used the data to compare with the data obtained using the film as a visual artefact, as it was notably different in content and emotional tone from the other four interviews in the pilot study.

Elicitation using visual images is a way of creating interest and engagement in the interview (Flewitt 2014) generating productive discussion that is often of a different nature from non-elicitation interviews in content and register (Rose 2016). Collier (1967), who pioneered visual methods in his anthropological research, noted that his photo elicitation interviews generated fuller, more detailed and specific responses than the non-elicitation interviews with the same participants. He also commented on the heightened emotional response elicited by the visual artefacts, an observation supported by Banks

(2001) and Rose (2007). Collier suggests that the visual image (in his study, a photograph) is an abstract form that represents an aspect of life such that it can be observed in a fresh and arresting way, provoking a different response from a non-elicitation interview and thus enriching the dataset if both kinds of interviews are used. Using film as an elicitation device in this study allowed fundamental issues in the pedagogic relationship between practitioner and children to be observed and then discussed in a way that was not possible in a conventional interview and could have been problematic in a direct observation of practice.

With the recent increase in the use of visual media in educational research has come an awareness of the ethical issues that may arise when using visual tools. Indeed, the proliferation and variety of visual methods is such that the International Visual Sociology Association (IVSA 2019) has produced a Code of Research Ethics that is recognized by the Economic and Social Research Council as a useful resource when undertaking research (https://www.ukri.org/councils/esrc/guidance-for-applicants/research-ethics-guidance/useful-resources/ 2021). With regard to photo (or film) elicitation, particular care should be taken to consider the potential impact of the image on the participant, given the emotional response that visual prompts often generate (Cohen et al. 2018). Several researchers have highlighted the need for the researcher to consider how provocative or disruptive the visual data is if it is found data rather than generated by the participants themselves. In particular, it is important to avoid harm by using data that generates intense negative memories (Barton 2015; Richard and Lahman 2015; Elliot et al. 2016). Perhaps the broader point here is that a researcher needs to be aware of the potential emotionality of visual methods and of the range of emotions they can generate, both positive, as indicated in this chapter, and negative.

I made the decision to use found data in the form of a five-minute clip from a French documentary, *Être et Avoir*, (Philibert 2002) in order to avoid the ethical challenges involved in generating data to be used as an elicitation tool in the interview. Not only would I have needed to obtain consent from the practitioners to be filmed, but also to use that data as the focus for discussion in an interview. To expose participants' practice to such scrutiny would have been much more of an imposition, in my view, than asking them to respond to an external focus. The film is a fly-on-the-wall documentary with no commentary, so the viewer sees episodes of a year in the life of a single-class, one-teacher primary school in rural France. It was a very successful film internationally, including in the UK at the time, which I hoped would go some way towards mitigating the ethical implications of using data from a different cultural context. The clip I used showed a maths lesson with the youngest children, including small group work and giving individual support to one of the youngest children, a little girl aged four. I was aware that by using a French film, I was offering a visual prompt that was likely to be outside the experience of my participants, and one that might have to be mediated by subtitles, but my decision to use this clip rather than one in which actors played the roles or a heavily rehearsed video with a commentary made for training purposes, was based on the desire to provide the most naturalistic observation possible and to maintain credibility with the participants, who were practitioners and parents.

I realized in the pilot study of the film clip, when deciding which clip to use, that participants had widely varying responses to the film clip. I actually chose it as an example of good practice, if somewhat old fashioned, that involved a range of teaching contexts that practitioners and parents could relate to (informal chat at the start of the day, small group work practising writing numbers and working one-to-one). For several participants, it triggered memories of their own schooling. For one participant, it triggered a negative memory – she said it reminded her of a music lesson when she was 14 and felt humiliated in front of the class as she could not tap out the rhythm she was asked to perform and burst into tears in front of her classmates. She clearly found it disconcerting to be reminded unexpectedly of this memory, which still had a strong emotional impact on her. As a result, in the final study, in order to mitigate the potential effect anticipated from the pilot study of generating negative memories (though these in research terms were interesting data) I conducted the semi-structured interview first in order to establish a rapport with the interviewees before the film elicitation interview. This strategy is an example of the intertwining of the methodological and ethical considerations – my decision resulted in participants not having childhood memories triggered by the film clip in the interview, which was desirable from an ethical standpoint. However, different methodological issues then emerged. Whilst I felt that the first semi-structured interview allowed me to establish a rapport with the participants (not least in that the participants agreed to come back for a second interview), the introduction of a third party in the form of a visual artefact had the effect of destabilizing the dyadic interview dynamic established in the first interviews. Some interviewees were quite happy about this and interested in the different approach of the film elicitation interview whilst others resisted it and initially kept trying to talk to me rather than watch the film, thus diluting the power of the clip as an elicitation method.

Ethical decisions are guided by principles, though of course these principles may vary from researcher to researcher, depending on what approach they take to the research. There are two main approaches, termed 'consequentialist' and 'non-consequentialist' by the ESRC (2008). A consequentialist approach regards ethical behaviour as that which generates the greatest good for the greatest number of people. A cost/benefit analysis may be involved, though ultimately what constitutes a cost and a benefit is a subjective decision (Cohen et al. 2018). An example of a consequentialist approach to ethics would be one of the early Head Start projects, where some participants received Head Start preschool programmes and others in the control group did not, but their parents could select from a menu of different childcare programmes (US Department of Health and Human Services 2010). My decisions above would seem to fall into the non-consequentialist approach to ethics, that is to say an approach guided by a principle of treating other people as you would like to be treated (Brooks et al. 2014). This is essentially a rights-based approach that considers participants to be ends in themselves rather than a means to an end. Within this category of non-consequentialist approaches to ethics, there is a sub-group which is variously termed 'ethics of care' or 'virtue ethics' which advocates a compassionate and relational approach to ethical decisions, such as that adopted in participatory research with young children, for example (Emmerich 2018). In their useful review of visual methodologies, the ESRC (2008) point out that there is a notable lack of consensus in research using visual methodologies on the principles that should guide ethical decisions. One reason for this might be the increasing variety of visual methodologies and methods now used in educational research, including approaches which see children and other participants as the generators of research and which raise a wide range of complex ethical issues.

Cultural context

Miltiades (2008) points out that the responses in an interview are shaped by the cultural influence of both the interviewee and also the interviewer. I had seen in the pilot study of the film elicitation interview that cultural background appeared to influence the responses of participants to the clip. In the pilot study, all five participants were female teacher-training students. Four were educated in the UK and one in China. It seems that the Chinese student had a markedly more positive reaction to the teacher in the film clip because firstly, the teacher was male and secondly, because he was relatively strict and formal and she saw those attributes as positive qualities. However, I had not anticipated the situation that occurred in the main study, where one participant declined to engage with the film clip at all. Yasmin was an experienced early years practitioner who worked as a manager in a private setting as her Kenyan teaching qualifications were not recognized in the UK. She had been recruited to the study by a colleague who had extended the invitation to students on a continuing professional development course at a higher education institution in south-east England. I was very grateful to her for participating and she was keen to tell me her story in the first semi-structured interview. In the second interview, Yasmin started talking as soon as she entered the room and I found it very difficult to stop her talking about her experiences and start the film. When, after 10 minutes, I did start the film clip with her agreement, she politely let the film spool through the five minutes then continued talking about what she had been speaking about before, despite my questions and prompts. After another five minutes, I managed to steer the conversation back to the film clip, where she dismissed the teacher saying, 'So I feel that this teacher was of his time and trying to do his best. Maybe theory at that time was not up to much.'

My dilemma was how firmly I should steer her back to talking about the film clip. In fact, I tried one more time and then gave up. The power dynamic between us influenced my decision as she was a mature woman probably similar in age to me. She commanded respect, and I had become aware during the course of the first interview that she was a very devout Muslim. Rather too late in the day, I realized that the fact the male teacher was teaching a mixed group of young children and working in very close proximity to a little girl might be culturally dissonant and make the clip difficult to relate to for her. In both the first and second interviews she stated her view that she thought women were more suited to teaching young children than men.

Yasmin: In the early years and Key Stage 1, I feel, yes, definitely, but then as they [the children] grow, they are OK, because I remember my daughter had a male teacher in year six but she was alright by then. But I think, initially, I think it's maybe the touch, or whatever, it's the male figure, or maybe I'm just culturally like that. Or maybe it's the caring nature, or the nurturing nature of the female, that I feel it is better to have.

The recurring theme of what Yasmin wanted to talk about in both interviews was the cultural insensitivity that she and her daughter had experienced coming to England and which as a result she was very keen to remedy in her teaching practice. I myself felt concerned subsequently that I had been insensitive in choosing this clip. However, in defence of my decision ethically, Yasmin did not appear upset by the clip as far as I could see, as she did not engage with it, either because she did not wish to or because it was too difficult for her to relate to. My experience in this study would seem to suggest that ethical dilemmas can often occur when there is a tension between different cultural backgrounds or contexts.

Film, like any visual artefact, privileges the visual and its effect is described by Rose thus:

> In particular, film is a powerful means of structuring looking, both the looks between the film's protagonists but also the looks between its protagonists and its spectators. (Rose 2007: 109)

However, it is important to recognize that visual media are not neutral and that people respond subjectively to the artefacts (Cohen et al. 2011). As Jacqueline Rose writes, 'We learn to see in particular ways, and this is process that is reiterated every time we look' (Rose 1983: 3). So, we learn to look within our cultural and societal norms and, equally, we learn not to look at areas that are prohibited or uncomfortable to contemplate. Inevitably, my cultural background influenced the choice of the clip, as well as the way in which I interpreted it. In terms of the ethical principles highlighted in the BERA guidelines (BERA 2018) I respected Yasmin's autonomy not to engage with the film and to choose what she talked about in response to my questions, thus I hope avoiding any maleficence.

The question of consent: the unexpected event

This section could also be called 'when the interview runs away from you'. I was nearing the end of the second interview with Rosa, a parent. I had given the participants the choice of where to conduct the interviews. Rosa asked for the interviews to be conducted in her home in the evening and was the only participant whose home I went into. In terms of the power dynamic, I was in awe of Rosa. Though considerably younger than me, she was a successful businesswoman with two very young children. She was also the chair of the PTA and volunteered in the gardening club of her daughter's school. She exuded efficiency and I was very concerned that there should not be technological hitches, as that would make me look unprofessional as a researcher. I was also aware that it was very generous of her to give her time at 8pm in the evening after a day's work and putting her children to bed. She was, as one might expect from the chair of the PTA, consistently supportive and very positive about her children's teachers. However, she then brought up the issue of feedback to parents, which was something that she was not happy about. At this point, she interrupted the interview to invite her husband to join the interview, calling to him to come in from watching the football in the next room as he had been present at one parent teacher interview when she had been travelling on business. Rosa's husband had recorded the interview on his mobile phone, so she was able to listen to the feedback later. They then both talked to me at length about this topic, as they were very disappointed with the lack of quantity and quality of the feedback they were given on their daughter's progress.

Whilst they were talking animatedly, various thoughts were going through my head. Firstly, the tape recorder was still running. Secondly, did her husband know the tape recorder was running and should I stop the interview immediately to ask him for his consent to be recorded or do so at the end of the interview? What should I do about the information sheet and consent form? What would I do if he did not consent? Would I have to lose the whole interview? In the end, I did not want to derail their conversation, and I decided not to ask him for his consent, but to use only what his wife, who had consented to the study, had said. By making this decision, it seemed to me that I was following as closely as I could the protocols set out in the formal permissions granted by the university research ethics committee of the higher education institution where the study was conducted. I lost some of the flavour of the interaction, but as they echoed each other, the content was there. In the write up of the findings, for transparency, I made it clear that Rosa's husband had joined the interview, invited by his wife. I made the spur of the moment judgement that the dynamic was too fragile to get out participant information sheets and consent forms to sign. Rosa's husband did not look overly pleased to be interrupted from watching his football game and I had the strong impression that, understandably, he would really like to be left in peace at nearly 9pm on a weekday evening. Also, the study was set up to be individual interviews not paired interviews and parity would be lost with the other interviewees. At the time they were speaking, and I was listening, I did not think the data would be relevant to the study when I wrote up the findings. In fact, Rosa's views turned out to be one of the most interesting tangential findings.

One could of course argue that I did not have consent to record Rosa's husband, and should not have done so at all, even though I did not use the data. By way of explanation rather than justification, I would add that it is hard to convey the speed with which the incident happened and the feeling I had of losing control of the interview. By the time I had decided what to do, five or ten minutes of recording had taken place. However, the tape recorder was visible in the middle of the table and a light showed it was recording. When I switched it off at the end of the interview, I told them that I would only be using what Rosa had said as she had consented to participate in the study, but her husband had not. They nodded as though this was an irrelevant detail. With hindsight, another time I would say that on tape, to have a record of the conversation and the verbal agreement. The question of consent was influenced here by an unexpected event and my wish to respect the autonomy of the interviewee to direct the conversation. Whilst the power dynamic was not that of an elite interview, it was notably different to the dynamic in the other interviews where I was interviewing practitioners and parents in a setting, not in their homes.

It is interesting to note that Rosa and her husband's lack of interest in what happened to the recording of the interview highlights another issue that is perhaps underplayed in educational research, namely the particularity of the research context and how much it may differ from the everyday context participants are used to operating in. For example, here, Rosa's husband thought nothing of recording the teacher at a parent–teacher interview. No consent form was signed and she had no control over what then happened to the data. The boundaries between what is custom and practice in an educational setting and what is acceptable ethically in a research study are more likely to be blurred when the researcher is an insider researcher, as they will be used to operating within the educational context, where, for example, it may be customary to video teachers as part of continuing professional development or indeed, performance management. However, it raises significant ethical dilemmas if a researcher wishes to use such an intrusive method in a research study. Another area where the discrepancy between the two contexts is very marked concerns the issue of informed consent and the right to withdraw at any time in the study, particularly where children are involved as participants. In educational settings and indeed more widely in society, it is customary for adults to expect children to do what they tell them to do, so it can be hard to persuade adults undertaking and participating in the research to adopt a different set of principles within the study.

Conclusion

The issues that have been raised here of informed consent, non-maleficence, beneficence and human dignity, respecting autonomy and being clear what constitutes ethically acceptable data are a sample of the many ethical dilemmas that can occur in the process of carrying out fieldwork. I am aware that in using examples from an empirical study, I am laying myself open to criticism for the ethical decisions I made. But as Helen Simons argues, 'Ethics is a situated practice and ethical principles are best discussed in concrete situations as there are a myriad of factors that can make a difference in particular contexts'

(Simons 2000: 53). It could be argued that until we can acknowledge the complexity and messiness of ethics in action, we will not be able to have constructive discussions about the ethical dilemmas we all face as researchers.

References

Banks, M. (2001) *Visual Methods in Social Research*. London: Sage.
Barton, K.C. (2015) Elicitation techniques: getting people to talk about ideas they don't usually talk about, *Theory and Research in Social Education*, 43(2): 179–205.
British Educational Research Association (2018) *Ethical Guidelines for Educational Research*. British Educational Research Association (BERA). Available at: https://www.bera.ac.uk/publication/ethical-guidelines-for-educational-research-2018 (accessed 27 October 2021).
Brooks, R., te Riele, K. and Maguire, M. (2014) *Ethics and Education Research*. London: Routledge Falmer.
Clarke, S. and Hoggett, P. (eds) (2009) *Researching Beneath the Surface: Psycho-Social Research Methods in Practice*. London: Karnac Books.
Cohen, L., Mannion, L. and Morrison, K. (2018) *Research Methods in Education*. 8th edn. London: Routledge.
Collier, J. (1967) Photography in anthropology, *American Anthropologist*, 59: 843–849.
Economic and Social Research Council National Centre for Research Methods (2008) *Visual Ethics: Ethical Issues in Visual Research*. NCRM/011. Swindon: Economic and Social Research Council.
Elliott, D.L., Reid, K. and Baumfeld, V. (2016) Capturing visual metaphors and tales: innovative or elusive? *International Journal of Research and Method in Education*. Available at: https://doi.org/10.1080/1743727X.2016.1181164 (accessed 27 October 2021).
Emmerich, N. (ed.) (2018) *Virtue Ethics in the Conduct and Governance of Social Science Research*. Bingley: Emerald.
Flewitt, R. (2005) Conducting research with young children: some ethical considerations, *Early Child Development and Care*, 175(6): 553–565.
Flewitt, R. (2014) Interviews in A. Clarke, R. Flewitt, M. Hammersley and M. Robb (eds) *Understanding Research with Children and Young People*. London: The Open University/Sage.
Guillemin, M. and Gillam, L. (2004) Ethics, reflexivity and 'ethically important moments' in research, *Qualitative Enquiry*, 10(2): 261–280.
IVSA (2019) International Visual Sociology Association: Code of Research Ethics and Guidelines. Available at: https://visualsociology.org/?page_id=405 (accessed 21 December 2021).
Jones, D.W. (1998) Distressing histories and unhappy interviewing, *Oral History*, 26(2): 49–56.
Malone, S. (2003) Ethics at home: informed consent in your own backyard, *International Journal of Qualitative Studies in Education*, 16(6): 797–815.
Mason-Bish, H. (2019) The elite delusion: reflexivity, identity and positionality in qualitative research, *Qualitative Research*, 19(3): 263–276.
Miltiades, H.B. (2008) Interview as a social event: cultural influences experiences while interviewing older adults in India, *International Journal of Social Research Methodology*, 11(4): 277–91.
Oliver, P. (2010) *The Student's Guide to Research Ethics*, 2nd edn. Maidenhead; New York: McGraw-Hill/Open University Press.

Philibert, N. (2002) *Être et Avoir*, France.

Richard, V.M. and Lahman, M.K.E. (2015) Photo-elicitation: reflexivity on method, analysis and graphic portraits, *International Journal of Research and Method in Education*, 38 (1): 3–22.

Robson, C. and McCartan, K. (2016) *Real World Research: A Resource for Users of Social Research Methods in Applied Settings*, 4th edn. Chichester: Wiley.

Rose, G. (2016) *Visual Methodologies: An Introduction to Researching with Visual Materials*, 4th edn. London: Sage.

Rose, J. (1983) *Sexuality in the Field of Vision*. London: Verso.

Schön, D.A. (1984) *The Reflective Practitioner: How Professionals Think in Action*. New York, NY: Basic Books.

Simons, H. (2000) Damned if you do, damned if you don't: ethical and political dilemmas in evaluation, in H. Simons and R. Usher (eds) (2000) *Situated Ethics in Educational Research*. London: Routledge Falmer.

Traianou, A. (2018) Ethical regulation of social research versus the cultivation of phronesis, in N. Emmerich (ed.) *Virtue Ethics in the Conduct and Governance of Social Science Research*. Bingley, UK: Emerald.

Tutenal, P., Ramaekers, S. and Heylighen, A. (2019) Conversations between procedural and situated ethics: learning from video research with children in a cancer care ward, in *EAD13 2019: Running with scissors:* 13th International Conference of the European Academy of Design, Dundee, 10–12 April 2019, edited by L. Valentine, J. Bletcher and L. Cruickshank.

U.S. Department of Health and Human Services, Administration for Children and Families (2010) *Head Start Impact Study. Final Report*. Washington, DC: U.S. Department of State.

VI Involving Children in Research: Active Participation and Ongoing Assent

Carmel Capewell

This chapter develops some of the ideas put forward by Brown in her chapter (II) relating to the United Nations Convention on the Rights of the Child (UNCRC 1989) with particular reference to Articles 12 (Right to provide their own views) and 23 (Rights of mentally or physically disabled child). It further explores the tension in educational research between the UNCRC's rights-based approach for children/young people (CYP) and how ethics committees' have a duty to ensure that participants are not 'harmed' by research (BERA 2018).

Alderson and Morrow (2011) explore the issues of risk, cost, harm and benefit by contrasting these terms when used in the context of health research and social research. The basis on which ethics committees are structured and review educational research is often through the lens of physical scientific research using a quantitative methodology (Alderson and Morrow 2011). Silverman (2010), and Ramcharan and Cutclife (2001) further identify that the issue for many ethics committees is that qualitative research methods are developing and so do not have the same familiarity of quantitative research. This is an underpinning context in which the issues identified in this chapter are reviewed and discussed. Although CYP are usually regarded to be under 18 years, I have extended the age range in this chapter based on the UK, SEND code of practice, which uses 0–25 years (Department for Education and Department of Health 2014). This chapter takes into account the rights of all disabled children to be included in expressing their views of how to best be supported in achieving their full potential. It draws upon research from across the world to illustrate how researchers need to balance the tensions of developing knowledge in educational contexts, gaining ethical approval, respecting the right of CYP to provide their own insights, whilst recognizing parents'/carers' duty of care for their children, along with the requirements/strictures of educational research funders. The latter always being the constraints of budget, time and publication.

This chapter begins with an exploration of the different perspectives on the competency of CYP and whether they are 'beings or becomings' (Qvortrup 1994; Mayall 2012; Tisdall and Punch 2012) along with the implications of that persepctive on all the stakeholders (Lewis et al. 2008) and the need to consider suitability of research methods (Bird et al. 2013). Closely associated with this is the interpretation of the capabilities of disabled CYP as to the level of their involvement and role in research (Carrington et al. 2007; Lewis et al. 2008; Kubiak et al. 2021). The way in which ethics committees see their role when CYP, and particularly those with disabilities, are active participants who are part of the research process rather than being researched upon is discussed (Harcourt and Quennerstedt 2014; Kubiak et al. 2021). There is the need to consider the role of parents/carers as gatekeepers, including their concerns and interpretations of the research, which may have implications whereby researchers may not gain access to CYP participants (O'Reilly et al. 2013; Klykken 2021). Researchers need to consider the appropriateness of research methods, especially those not designed with CYP in mind (Christensen and Prout 2002; Bird et al. 2013). This can include procedures, informed consent, ongoing assent and the accessibility of the language being used (Lawthom et al. 2012; Woolhouse et al. 2019). Finally, this chapter identifies the importance of areas where researchers should challenge themselves. These include: the assumptions they are making throughout the research process; the need to be responsive and reflexive about developing understanding of the participants' perceptions during the research process; monitoring and evaluating the methodology and methods being used; and how they are developing as ethical researchers (Etherington 2004; Chamberlain et al. 2021; Hanna 2021).

Beings or becomings

Our understanding of the difference between children as 'beings', who have the capacity to make adult-like, informed decisions and judgements, rather than being constructed as 'becomings', who are immature and lack the rational ability to make reasoned judgements, has developed through the active participation of CYP in research (Qvortup 1994).The distinction has been explored earlier than it was made explicit (Mayall 2012). This has become more theorized since the ratification of the UNCRC, but Tisdall and Punch (2012) look more critically at the assumption that all children are competent and wish to express their views, potentially questioning whether there is a more complex interaction between adults and children that needs to be explored. This is particularly so when considering the ethics of how adults can act on children's behalf and in the wider context of non-European settings.

Cunningham (2006), in his exploration of childhood within a Western European context, makes the point that there is a greater focus on the adult perspective of the abilities of children with limited exploration of their capabilities. This has led to situations that adult intentions, wellbeing as they may have been, have resulted in negative outcomes for children. An example of this is when children from the UK who came from 'poorer' backgrounds, be that social or economic, were sent to farm schools in Australia (Sherington 2012) without consultation and knowledge, leading to problematic outcomes. Similar situations (Morrow and Richards 2002; Harcourt and Quennerstadt 2014) can be seen in the decisions of ethics committees regarding whether or not it is appropriate for CYP to be part of educational research, under the perspective of protecting children from harm. Balen et al. (2006) outlined how an ethics committee initially rejected an ethics application for a research project to evaluate whether a programme met the needs of adolescents attending it. The programme was for adolescents whose parents had drug/alcohol dependencies. The CYP attended without the need for parental consent or even their knowledge. However, the ethics committee took a lot of persuading to accept that the young people were capable of making their own decision about whether or not to participate. Whilst the intentions may have been to protect participants during the research process, denying them their right to express their views would have been counterproductive. Situations can arise when ethics committees are overzealous in avoiding risk such that valuable research either does not take place, or the opinions and experience of CYP are omitted (Harcourt and Quennerstedt 2014).

In her study, based in South Africa, Pillay (2014) argues the case that educational researchers need to take a broader consideration of how children are perceived, moving from the perspective that adults' knowledge of children is greater than that of the children themselves. She proposes a rights-based approach, in line with the UNCRC, whereby children should be key contributors to educational research. She interviewed a small group of experts with strong formal ethics backgrounds in educational research with children on their views of the ethical issues involved. Although there was agreement about the need for children to participate in research, some experts felt that young children should be excluded from participating and that there should be no form of coercion regarding participation. The importance of ethics' committees was stressed with regard to protecting children from inappropriate methods (that may lead to upset/harm), the competence of the researcher (some were not in favour of novice recruiters researching with children) and the importance of taking the culture of the child into account. Her work, in the complex context of South Africa, has implications for researchers in the UK and other Western European situations. It emphasizes the value of having an ethics committee to provide an independent view on the research prior to starting a project, and ensuring that researchers think not only about the methods, but also about how the research will be disseminated and communicated to young participants.

Harcourt and Quennerstedt (2014) compare the role of ethics committees in Australia and Sweden. They review the perception of Australian ethics committees being about risk management and whether there needs to be a reshaping of practice when CYP are involved as active participants because they have special characteristics. In contrast, the Swedish view is that children are capable agents in their own lives. The Swedes encourage researchers to see ethics committees as providing a monitoring framework for researchers to develop their own ethical stance as part of their research practice. Their paper discusses how the different views of risk management, as portrayed in the Australian context, are contrasted with protecting participants within the context of researcher development in Sweden.

In Sweden, protecting participants, and especially children, from exploitation is managed by the requirement of adult consent for the CYP to participate, as well as agreement from the CYP that they wish to take part. The focus of ethical approval in Sweden is underpinned by two main principles – either the processing of 'sensitive personal data' or 'physical or mental harming' (Harcourt and Quennerstedt 2014: 3) or to develop reflective researchers who carefully consider all aspects of ethics in research. The outcome is that very few research proposals require formal ethical review (Harcourt and Quennerstedt 2014). The focus is on the researcher being subject to personal scrutiny and reflection in the context of review and participation in professional forums and practice. Apart from gaining the consents, the involvement of CYP in research is not treated substantially differently to that of any other human participant.

The Australian research ethics is guided by a national code, not a law (Australian Government 2018), which is required to be monitored by any institution undertaking or funding research. The code covers design, ethical review, and the conduct of the research (p.4). There is a separate section which considers the importance of children's capacity to both understand what the research is about and the expectations of them, and that they willingly agree to participate. In general, the Australian documents are underpinned by a view that CYP are more at risk from research than adults. The word 'risk' in relation to research with children is emphasized and used frequently in the documentation for gaining ethical approval. There is a requirement in Australia that all research involving CYP (under 18-year-olds) will go through a full review by the university ethics committee. Research that involves young children is especially scrutinized with a need to demonstrate clearly how their participation contributes to knowledge and why it is essential. This can lead to a lengthy review process, which takes a lot of time and can mean that either the experience and opinions of CYP are not included or that certain groups, deemed vulnerable, are excluded from the research process. In many ways this could reflect the process in the UK.

If there is an over-emphasis of risk avoidance with researchers being restricted in what they can do and meeting the procedural needs of the ethics committee, it is likely that researchers will not develop their ability to critically evaluate their own ethical stance. At the same time, there is a need to consider the ways in which CYP can meaningfully be involved in research that ensures that they can feel comfortable and confident about their participation. This includes CYP understanding the research process.

Consent of the adults but assent of the CYP

Although the UNCRC does not mention the right of CYP to participate in research, Article 12 does identify that, within the limitations of capability, their opinions need to be included. In part, the language of the UNCRC reflects a historic view of children that has changed since it was introduced. It may be that there would be different language used (Tisdall and Punch 2012) were the convention written now, potentially including participation in research. Similarly, Article 23 of the UNCRC, which is about disabled children, focuses more on resources and inclusion within the community rather than on them contributing their views. However, the statutory guidance for organizations in the UK working with disabled CYP or special educational needs (Department for Education and Department of Health 2014) makes it a requirement that CYP and their parents (and carers) are part of the conversation/action about their individual needs. This document recognizes the overlap between health and education. Although it does not specifically mention participating in research, it is fair to assume that this would be relevant in gaining understanding of their complex needs. There does appear to be more recognition of the relevance of including CYP in health research (Balen et al. 2006; Bird et al. 2013) than there has perhaps been in education (Lewis and Lindsay 2000).

Bourke and Loveridge (2014) review the research about how 'informed' and willing CYP are in participating in research. This is complicated by adults initially making the decision as to whether CYP are permitted to participate. They explore the difference between 'informed consent' and the usual good practice of trying to ensure that any CYP are aware of the procedures and requirements alongside the protective actions that researchers take (regarding anonymity, confidentiality and protecting privacy). The way in which the situation can become more problematic is when the school's procedures take precedence over the requirements set by the ethics committee and the intentions of the researchers (Bourke and Loveridge 2014). Bourke and Loveridge (2014) provide an example from one school where, rather than all children being given the opportunity to participate and parental consent gained through sending out the ethic's approved documents, teachers selected the children who they saw as being most skilled in responding in the interview situation. In such circumstances, researchers find themselves in an ethical dilemma as to how they should proceed.

There is also the issue of 'informed dissent' which is likely to occur when the adult (parent/teacher) has agreed for the CYP to participate, although this may not be the CYP's desire. Christensen and Prout (2002) tried to explore this through talking to the CYP involved in their research about some of the behaviours exhibited that may suggest less than active participation. This included yawning, looking away or saying 'don't know' in response to questions. Klykken (2021), in a Norwegian context, expresses concerns about whether CYP do assimilate the details of a research project and whether the researcher in qualitative research really understands the details of the process until the research actually begins. It may be that, in school settings, students are concerned about whether the comments from transcripts will have an impact upon their grades and/or relationship with their teachers, despite what researchers may say (Klykken 2021: 5).

I would argue that the insight gained from having the active involvement of CYP really is worth the effort. Parents/carers generally may have the best interests of their children at heart and believe they know their child well, but CYP are individuals with their own interpretations of experience. I have learned this from my own work (Capewell and Ralph 2015) in which a mother and child independently, and in separate discussions of their individual images and captions as part of a photovoice approach, related their different interpretation of an adjustment made by one of the teachers. In this example, the child was offered the opportunity to sit his tests in the staff room as he had difficulty blocking out the sounds of a 'silent' classroom, such as others scuffing their feet on the floor, turning pages and writing on their test papers. He found the staffroom much better than being in the classroom and his test result was much higher. On the other hand, his mother related that she thought he would be frightened, perhaps that he would be accused by other teachers of having done something wrong as he was sitting in the staff room. Although this may appear a minor difference in views, it acknowledges that children may have an alternative perspective. Additionally, if the mother's opinion had prevailed then something that the child found helpful would have not been implemented. This could have meant that a small adjustment which aided performance would have been denied if the child's view was omitted.

Issues around whether a CYP can give consent may become even more complicated when working with students with limited ability to verbalize. O'Síoráin (O'Síoráin et al. 2021) explained how ongoing assent was negotiated with children, such as one boy turning his back on her and returning to his seat to indicate that he did not wish to participate on that occasion. This sensitivity is often something that cannot be included in the original ethic's proposal but shows the need for researchers to demonstrate their own ethical values and responsiveness to participants.

In their study in Zimbabwe, Chamberlain et al. (2021) recognized that although there may be good reasons for exclusion criteria applied in advance of the research and approved by the ethics committee, situations in the field may require rethinking. It was only once the research was underway that they discovered one of their participants had additional needs, which had been an exclusion criterion for participating in the research. Chamberlain et al. explain that the contribution of this participant enriched the study as a whole and improved their skills as researchers. The researchers' concern, in advance of the fieldwork, was that they did not feel they had the resources and/or expertise to provide appropriate support to be able to include girls with special needs. But rather than turn the young woman away once in the research environment, she was included. The researchers made small adaptations, such as simplifying their language. They recognized that the young woman's involvement provided a deeper insight into the situation of why girls/young women were not in education.

The examples discussed in this section demonstrate that qualitative researchers may find themselves in the dilemma of having to adapt their research protocol outside their original ethics consent. This often has to be done in the moment rather than pausing the research to gain additional ethical approval.

Consulted or co-researcher

The active participation of CYP in research has seen a shift since the appearance of the UNCRC (United Nations 1989) from children being researched 'on' to researched 'with' (O'Reilly et al. 2013). In healthcare research, this has moved away from a situation whereby views of parents/carers provided information about young people to one where the young people themselves provided their perceptions and wishes (Bird et al. 2013).

In medical research the opportunity to consult CYP as part of a young people's advisory group (YPAG) is available to researchers. These groups can help researchers in the design, implementation and dissemination stages of research and have been part of the preparation for ethics applications (Sellars et al. 2021). In my own research (Capewell 2021), I had the opportunity to talk to a YPAG at the design stage of a research project. Although the YPAG members were older than the intended children in my research, they were able to offer valuable advice about the type of activities that may engage younger children, the way to approach them and gain their interest in the research. This included suggestions for the language to be used and some of the potential ethical issues that may arise. The group members had a lot of experience of different types of research methods and were supported by a dedicated youth worker. Although they were not going to participate in the research, they provided helpful insights. By recognizing their design input in my ethics application, the ethics committee commented that potential issues around their concerns about how the young children may react were answered as was the acceptability of the design.

Lewis et al. (2008) described weak and strong positions of involving disabled CYP in the research process. They use the 'weak' position to describe a method that has involvement by the disabled CYP and their families as active participants in data generation, but not as co-researchers (the strong position). Lewis et al. (2008) describes the three projects that the authors ran. In the first project by the University of Birmingham researchers, the aim was to understand the key concerns and priorities regarding their experiences in education. The methods used were surveys of the parents/carers, interviews with CYP, classroom observations and interviews with educational professionals and parents/carers. There was a further group who advised on the methods and acted as an advisory group. The data collected came from individuals with direct experience of the research focus. The second project, by researchers from the University of Bristol, involved 11 children with little or no verbal communication. The aim was to provide a resource pack for those working with similar children. In the research by the University of Cambridge, researchers had a reference group who were young people with learning difficulties used to working together to advocate their rights. The 'weak' position described in these projects was that the disabled CYP participated in the projects but were not instrumental as co-researchers. The involvement of disabled CYP relevant to the research aims potentially reassures ethics committees that there is appropriate support for the participants in the data gathering and that the reference and advisory groups would be able to provide researchers with insight into how to interact with participants and the importance of breaks and ways of communicating.

A more emancipatory (or strong) position is used by Kubiak et al. (2021) when six volunteer higher education students with intellectual disabilities attending a 2-year programme were invited to train as co-researchers and then interview their classmates about their experiences and suggestions for improving the way their course was taught. The students who were co-researchers underwent an 11-week training programme in which they kept reflective diaries about their experiences, skills development and self-esteem. They had input into the way in which the research was carried out, although not in the thematic data analysis of what was found. For ethical approval reasons their parents were asked for agreement for the students' involvement in the research. However, the active and ongoing willingness to participate was checked with the participants through regular discussions with the researchers and the opportunity to withdraw at any point in the research.

This section has looked at models of the role of CYP in research and how this can be done ethically and in a way in which the participants make a meaningful contribution. For the most part, traditional methods of data gathering were used. In the next section, the appropriateness of methods is considered in more detail and whether there is a need for different methods to be developed which are more acceptable to CYP.

Developing appropriate methods for researching with CYP or appropriating adult-focused research methods

This section considers the methodologies and methods that can achieve CYP's participation in ways that are meaningful to them and provide researchers with insight into the situations being researched. Research ethics committees rightly scrutinize research processes and procedures to ensure avoidance of exploitation or harm (Pillay 2014). MacDonald (2013) identifies the importance of how adults can view children, particularly young children, in research. She makes the point that if researchers approach a child as potentially incompetent and/or do not consider the appropriateness of a research methodology and methods, then there is likely to be confirmation of an unstated belief that children are not competent in expressing their views. Rather than asking children for their views, through interviews, surveys and focus groups, a variety of visual methods have been developed. These can help assuage some of the concerns of ethics committees as the CYP have more control over the production of the data.

If a framework of participatory action research underpins the methodology (Carrington et al. 2007), then the individual voices of CYP are inherent in both developing the research questions and their active role in data collection and interpretation lessens the opportunity for exploitation. This approach has been used by a number of researchers whereby the CYP themselves construct images in different ways (Carrington et al. 2007; MacDonald 2013; Capewell and Ralph 2015; Woolhouse et al. 2019) and interpret the meaning and implications of them in their lives. Although access to CYP to participate in educational research is usually through adult gatekeepers (parents/carers/schools), the above researchers recognize the importance of gaining both informed consent and ongoing assent from the young people themselves. However, the view of the adult gatekeeper prevails over the desire of the child regarding participation. This means that if an adult wishes the CYP to participate, then their individual right not to can be compromised. This can be overcome, either by additionally requiring the child's consent (MacDonald 2013), or through a data-gathering method that means that if the child does not produce any data this is accepted at face value (Capewell and Ralph 2015). There is equally the issue of when a CYP wishes to participate, but their parent/carer does not agree. In such cases, usual practice has been to include the CYP in the data gathering, but leave their data out when reporting the findings and in dissemination of the research (MacDonald 2013).

A further issue that raises concern in ethics committees is the use of images of people as part of the data-gathering and in dissemination activities. This is a problematic area in which practice is continuing to evolve. There appear to be international differences in practice with Carrington et al. (2007) paper from their work in Australia showing pictures of students, and in Miles' (2011) work in Africa when the images of one project involving children were shown to another group in a later project. However, in their UK research, Woolhouse et al. (2019) used software which 'cartoonized' the students in their research. Even when there has been permission by the students to have their images shared as part of a video, the need to go back to participants is important before those images are shared again. Lawthom et al. (2012) illustrate this regarding the situation of a young boy who had willingly participated previously in a research project that had produced a video. Fifteen months later when another project was proposed, the same video was shown. One of the researchers noted that the boy was visibly upset and embarrassed when the film was shown again in his community. Unfortunately, the researchers had not thought to go back to the participants in the video and ask them to re-consent to the video being shown, but rather assumed that this was part of dissemination material. This is not an easy situation for researchers or ethics committees and demonstrates the evolving nature of ethical issues. It does highlight the importance of researchers using their own moral compass to navigate situations as they appear. To some extent, by using ethical guidelines from an organization that promotes the methodology/method, Photovoice (2009) enables a researcher to both explore the ethical implications using the organization's expertise and to reassure ethics committees that the issues specific to that method have been considered in detail.

Photo elicitation, when researchers provide the photos, overcomes some of the issues that may arise when using participant generated images. It is good practice to provide the photos to be used as part of the ethical approval documents. This enables the ethics committee to understand which photos are being used and the rationale provided by the researcher for their use. Miles (2011) in her study in Zambia and Tanzania, identifies that photo elicitation had the advantage of enabling participants to minimize their use of written information, which is particularly important in countries with a tradition of oral communication and storytelling. By using captionless photos when reviewing what is going on in classrooms, the students raised the issue that the two students sitting on their own had perhaps been naughty (Miles 2011: 1096). This led to a conversation with their teachers, also present, about the extensive use of corporal punishment and its implications for child rights. As Miles (2011) suggests, the children felt empowered to raise this issue, which may not have happened without the use of image because of the potentially perceived power differentials between teachers and students. This method also provides a way through which students felt able to express their views, which may not have occurred through more traditional research methods.

The revision of ethical guidelines by BERA in 2018 seeks to take account of the way in which the internet has led to situations that once something is present in a digital form, there are limitations as to how the anonymity and confidentiality of participants can be protected. In the case of Lawthom et al. (2012), it seems that the sensible course of action is for researchers to revisit the permission and consent they had previously gained and for ethics committees to check whether the output of previous research will be re-used in new projects. However, perhaps the issue is really about researchers 'policing' themselves. This point is developed further in the next section.

Researchers' moral compass vs ethics committee requirements

This section returns (Harcourt and Quennerstedt 2014; Pillay 2014) to the different ways in which researchers develop a sense of being principled in carrying out research with human participants. In South Africa, Australia and, I would suggest, the UK, the emphasis is on external monitoring and risk avoidance. Whilst such an approach may lead to low-risk research and high compliance with guidelines, it may not encourage or give the time for researchers to develop their own moral compass through reflection and discussion. Additionally, it may mean that research involving children is deemed too difficult to gain ethical approval so does not take place or is more focused on adult's views. It seems that the situation described in Sweden (Harcourt and Quennerstedt 2014) places more emphasis on developing researchers who may think more deeply about the principles underpinning ethical research. The personal development of researchers in behaving ethically is important if the needs of CYP are to be included in research and if unexpected events during the research process can be handled morally and ethically by the researchers in real time.

Although all research projects are required to gain and comply with the approval of ethics committees, as has been identified earlier in this chapter and chapter V, there are times when situations occur in the field that are unexpected or outside the scope of the agreed ethics procedures. Unlike in quantitative research where there would be an expectation that the researchers would have identified all the aspects of the research in advance, this is not always the case with qualitative research. I define 'moral compass' as being those situations whereby a researcher could be within the ethical approval to continue with their research, but the situation may lead the researcher to question whether they should proceed. In many ways this is how research ethics develops beyond what ethics committees may give approval for. Sometimes such 'moral compass' moments do not occur until after the event. For example, when Hanna (2021) was exploring the experiences of migrant children in South Africa, she reflected that there were some responses that the children may give about their family situation that they may later regret disclosing. She came to understand that sometimes it was the moral course of action to move on rather than probe an answer. This sensitivity comes with experience, and maybe is why some respondents in Pillay's (2014) work suggest that novice researchers should not explore certain projects.

The question is whether using one's moral compass (or even if one has one) could be a strong reason for ensuring that all researchers, and particularly those using qualitative methods in educational research, become reflexive researchers (Etherington 2004). This needs to be an integral part of the research process so that even before ethics forms are filled in, researchers consider their own position in terms of values and their view of the research that they are undertaking. When ethical review processes are working well, alternative views to those of the researcher may help to avoid potential breaches of ethical approval. In some cases, it may have been envisaged to interview children without their parent or another person present, but the CYP wants someone with them. The researcher can be left with the dilemma that they may feel that the power dynamic between the child and parent may inhibit what the child says (O'Reilly et al. 2013). The researcher has the options of acceding to what the child wants, trying to build rapport with the child so that they feel confident to continue, or try to find ways that follow the ethically approved protocol. If the planned process is used, without reflection on the researcher's own stance and beliefs on the issue, I would suggest that this is a violation of the moral compass.

Ethics committees seem to pay less attention to what happens to CYP when the research study begins. Although there is the mechanism of 'chair's actions' for researchers to formally request changes in the methodology/ method as situations arise, it is problematic as to how often this is used. It could be that researchers are concerned about applying for chair's actions retrospectively, if they even apply at all. In most cases, if the researcher does not refer back to the ethics committee, they would be in breach of their ethical approval. To some extent, the researchers' actions are likely to be based on their perception of the ethics committee. If the process seems to be one of blocking and delay, or even adversarial, then additional approval may be less likely to occur.

Conclusions

Throughout this chapter, I have tried to balance the need to avoid exploitation of CYP when taking part in research and protecting them from harm, against the human rights perspective of providing them with the opportunity to express their opinions and experiences. As someone who does work with CYP in research projects, I have found that the unique insight they provide is not generally available other than by consulting them. The conclusions presented are a summary of the points raised in this chapter, which are for researchers to consider if they are acting ethically and respecting the contribution of CYP.

There is a need, however, to consider the way in which CYP are consulted. Using adult-designed methods are unlikely to be appropriate unless they are adapted for CYP. It is often the case that CYP are capable of expressing their opinions or analysing their experiences, but the way in which they are asked, including the type of language used, can inhibit their participation. It is likely that methods that are based on the construction of artefacts and images may help CYP to think about their experiences, thus giving them a basis upon which to verbalize and share their knowledge with researchers. Ensuring that CYP understand the aims of the research, the expectations of them and the relationship between them and researchers provides a good basis for effective research that is ethically sound.

The level of participation of CYP is an important consideration prior to the start of research. Researchers need to ask themselves what contribution CYP will make, not only to the data gathering and potentially the analysis, but even the research questions and methodology and methods. Input to the research can range from providing answers to questions pre-set by the researcher, to participating in a consultative role about the way the research takes place, through to being trained and developed as co-researchers involved in all levels of the research process.

Researchers do not act in a vacuum and the different roles of ethics committees are likely to impact the extent to which researchers are able to develop their own moral compass in conducting ethical research. When ethics committees take a risk-averse role, with a focus on preventing research with CYP, then it is likely that they will be viewed in an adversarial light by researchers. This can lead to researchers spending their thinking time on how to accommodate the requirements of the ethics committee and perceive them as a block. Alternatively, when ethics committees see their role as supporting the development of ethically focused researchers who are reflexive and concerned with how best to ensure participants gain a valuable experience from the research process, then it is likely that researchers will develop the expertise to be adaptable and skilled in dealing with potentially ethically compromising situations as they arise. The goal of researchers and ethics committees needs to be to cause no harm to anyone involved in the research process.

References

Alderson, P. and Morrow, V. (2011) *The Ethics of Research with Children and Young People: A Practical Handbook*. Sage: London.

Australian Government (2018) *Australian Code for the Responsible Conduct of Research*. Available at https://www.nhmrc.gov.au/about-us/publications/australian-code-responsible-conduct-research-2018 (accessed 10 December 2021).

Balen, R., Blyth, E., Calabretto, H. et al. (2006) Involving children in health and social research: 'human becomings' or 'active beings'? *Childhood*, 13(1): 29–48.

Bird, D., Culley, L. and Lakhanpaul, M. (2013) Why collaborate with children in health research: an analysis of risks and benefits of collaboration with children, *Archives of Diseases in Childhood, Education and Practice*, 98(2): 42–48.

Bourke, R. and Loveridge, J. (2014) Exploring informed consent and dissent through children's participation in educational research, *International Journal of Research and Methodology in Education*, 37(2): 151–165.

British Educational Research Association (2018) *Ethical Guidelines for Educational Research*. British Educational Research Association (BERA). Available at https://www.bera.ac.uk/publication/ethical-guidelines-for-educational-research-2018 (accessed 10 November 2021).

Capewell, C. (2021) Diaries and hearing maps from a diagnostic tool to a communication device between adults and 3–7 year old children with glue ear, in A. Fox., H. Busher and C. Capewell (eds) *Thinking Critically and Ethically about Research for Education*. Abingdon: Routledge.

Capewell, C. and Ralph, S. (2015) Living with glue ear: researching educational needs and listening to the voices of a mother and child, *The International Journal of Diverse Identities*, 15(1): 11–22.

Carrington, S., Allen, K and Osmolowski, D. (2007) Visual narrative: a technique to enhance secondary students' contribution to the development of inclusive, socially just school environment – lessons from a box of crayons, *Journal of Research in Special Educational Need*, 7(1): 8–15.

Chamberlain, L., Buckler, A. and Mkwananzi, F. (2021) Building a case for inclusive ways of knowing through a case study of a cross-cultural research project of out-of-school girls' aspirations in Zimbabwe: practitioners' perspectives, in A. Fox, H. Busher and Capewell, C. (eds) *Thinking Critically and Ethically about Research for Education*. Abingdon: Routledge.

Christensen, P. and A. Prout. (2002) Working with ethical symmetry in social research with children, *Childhood*, 9(4): 477–497.

Cunningham, H. (2006) *The Invention of Childhood*. London: BBC Books.

Department for Education and Department of Health (2014) *Special Education Needs and Disability Code of Practice: 0–25 years*. Available at: https://www.gov.uk/government/publications/send-code-of-practice-0-to-25 (accessed 21 November 2021).

Etherington, K. (2004) *Becoming a Reflexive Researcher Using Our Selves in Research*. London: Jessica Kingsley Publishers.

Hanna, H. (2021) Listening to silence in the quest to offer migrant learners a 'voice' through picturebook research in South Africa, in A. Fox, H. Busher and Capewell, C. (eds) *Thinking Critically and Ethically about Research for Education*. Abingdon: Routledge.

Harcourt, D. and Quennerstedt, A. (2014) Ethical guardrails when children participate in research: risk and practice in Sweden and Australia, *SAGE Open*, July-September, 1–8. Available at: https://doi.org/10.1177/2158244014543782 (accessed 29 June 2022).

Klykken, F. (2021) Implementing continuous consent in qualitative research, *Qualitative Research*, May 2021. Available at: doi:10.1177/14687941211014366 (accessed 29 June 2022).

Kubiak, J., Aston, D., Devitt, M. et al. (2021) University students with intellectual disabilities: empowerment through voice, *Education Sciences* May 2021(11) 571. Available at: https://doi.org/10.3390/educsci11100571 (accessed 29 June 2022).

Lawthom, R., Kagan, C., Richards, M. et al. (2012) Being creative around health: participative methodologies in critical community psychology, in C. Horrocks and S. Johnson (eds). *Advances in Health Psychology Critical Approaches*. Basingstoke: Palgrave Macmillan.

Lewis, A. and Lindsay, G. (eds) (2000) *Researching Children's Perspectives*. Maidenhead: Open University Press.

Lewis, A., Parsons, S., Robertson, C. et al. (2008) Reference, or advisory, groups involving disabled people: reflections from three contrasting research projects, *British Journal of Special Education*, 35(2): 78–84.

MacDonald, A. (2013) Researching with your children: considering issues of ethics and engagement, *Contemporary Issues in Early Childhood*, 14(3): 255–268.

Mayall, B. (2012) An afterword: some reflections on a seminar series, *Children's Geographies*, 10(3): 347–355.

Miles, S. (2011) Exploring understandings of inclusion in schools in Zambia and Tanzinia using reflective writing and photography, *International Journal of Inclusive Education*, 15(10): 1087–1102.

Morrow, V. and Richards, M. (2002) The ethics of social research with children: an overview, in K.W.M. Fulford, D.L. Dickenson and T.H. Murray (eds) *Healthcare Ethics and Human Values: An Introductory Text with Readings and Case Studies*. Malden, MA: Blackwell.

O'Reilly, M. Ronzoni, P. and Dogra, N. (2013) *Researching with Children: Theory and Practice*. London: Sage.

O'Síoráin, C-A., McGucking, C. and Carr-Fanning, C. (2021) Well that's another fine mess you got me into: the jargon of research (How do we translate this for the participant with additional needs?) in A. Fox, H. Busher and C. Capewell (eds) *Thinking Critically and Ethically about Research for Education*. Abingdon: Routledge.

Photovoice (2009) *Statement of Ethical Practice*. Available at: https://photovoice.org/about-us/photovoice-statement-of-ethical-practice/ (accessed 29 November 2021).

Pillay, J. (2014) Ethical considerations in educational research involving children: implications for educational researchers in South Africa, *South African Journal of Childhood Education*, 4(2): 194–212.

Qvortrup, J. (1994) Childhood matters: an introduction, in J. Qvortrup, M. Bardy, G. Sgritta and H. Wintersberger (eds) *Childhood Matters: Social Theory, Practice and Politics*. Aldershot: Avebury.

Ramcharan, P. and Cutcliffe, J. (2001) Judging the ethics of qualitative research: considering the 'ethics as process' model, *Health and Social Care in the Community*, 9(6): 358–366.

Sellars, E., Pararini, G., Michelson, D. et al. (2021) Young people's advisory groups in health resrach: scoping review and mapping of practices, *Archives of Disease in Childhood*, 106: 698–704.

Sherington, G. (2012) Contrasting narratives in the history of twentieth-century British child migration to Australia: an interpretive essay, *History Australia*, 9(2): 27–47.

Silverman, D. (2010) *Doing Qualitative Research: A Practical Handbook* (3rd edn) London: Sage.

Tisdall, K. and Punch, S. (2012) Not so 'new'? Looking critically at childhood studies, *Children's Georgraphies*, 10(3): 249–264.

United Nations Convention on the Rights of the Child (UNCRC (1989) *United Nations Convention on the Rights of the Child.* Available at: https://www.unicef.org.uk/what-we-do/un-convention-child-rights/ (accessed 19 November 2021).

Woolhouse, C., Kay, V., Hastings, C. et al. (2019) Developing creative communities to explore inclusion and exclusion with children, *Research Intelligence*, Summer: 27–28.

VII Eliciting the Teacher's and Pupils' Perspectives in the Creative Classroom: Issues of Agency and Privacy

Sarah Frodsham and Deb McGregor

Introduction

The aim of this chapter is to not only extend the debate regarding the nature and influences on creativity but to directly illustrate it through evidence from classroom interactions that require the use of digital technology, such as microphones, video and cameras. This digital means of illuminating creative processes, however, presents a number of ethical conundrums, which will also critically underpin this chapter. However, prior to exploring what these ethical dilemmas are, it is important to consider how views about creativity vary and the adoption of alternate frameworks or perspectives may that require more or less participant consideration in classroom settings.

Views about creativity in the classroom environment

Cremin and Chappell's (2021) review identified seven common features that typify creative practice within educational settings. They are: generating and exploring ideas; encouraging autonomy and agency; playfulness; problem-solving; risk-taking; co-constructing and collaborating; and teacher creativity (Cremin and Chappell 2021: 299). Whether these characteristics relate to the teacher's practices or learner's enactments and utterances within the classroom environment is not entirely clear. Davies and McGregor (2017) describe how teachers *know* when something is creative, but articulating the nature of it results in a plethora of definitions (Kind and KInd 2007; McGregor and Gaciu 2018). McGregor and Frodsham (2019) also demonstrate how assumptions about creativity in science education is often misunderstood or naively recognized. Alongside these debates, the Durham Commission (2019) aimed to identify the ways in which creativity is relevant in the lives of school age children both within, and beyond, the education system. They recommended defining creativity as 'the capacity to imagine, conceive, express or make something that was not there before'. However, when more recently examining teachers, enactments of their understanding and interpretations of creativity (Bell and McGregor et al. 2021), it became apparent that a singular view of creativity (McGregor and Frodsham 2019) was not sufficient to demonstrate how, when, where and why originality emerges in learning activity. These multiple understandings and interpretations have also been reflected in other academic writing too. For example, McGregor et al. 2022) suggest how it includes the way that learners mediate one anothers' development of thinking; how they engage in questioning and challenging each other; openly explaining and sharing their views or perspectives; discussing and contrasting alternate understandings to make sense of propositions; and constructing a joint solution to a problem that might otherwise remain untold and unknown. Evidencing these kinds of dynamic aspects of learning processes can expose a learner's lack of comprehension, understanding or even misinterpretations of curricular concepts. Grigorenko (2019) recognizes some of these common features of creativity, such as innovating, solving problems, being mentally flexible, imagining, etc., but she concludes in her paper that creativity remains 'a challenge for educational systems around the world' as it is 'something we would like to strive for, if we could only know what it is and how to teach [for] it effectively' (p.126). To add to the debate, Glaveanu (2018: 335) suggests that creativity can challenge 'old dichotomies between mind and body, individual and society' as it is very much a phenomenon that might be triggered by a thought or an action, emergent from solely one person or through the interaction between people. In considering this further, he suggested thinking about creativity through three ontological perspectives. They are: (i) associating creativity with the arts and emphasizing self-expression, originality and divergent thinking; (ii) connecting creativity with scientific discovery and problem solving; and (iii) post-modernity creativity, which invites the individual to reconsider the everyday from varying (and new) perspectives. These multiple and various ways of thinking about creativity can be problematical for the researcher endeavouring to evidence such an elusive entity that can be perceived and understood from such wide-ranging perspectives.

This chapter extends the above debates (McGregor and Frodsham 2019) regarding the nature and influences on creativity by directly illustrating, through analysis of transcribed video excerpts of a singular science lesson (a case). This will involve associated dialogue and aspects of teacher and learner interaction/s collected through the use of digital technology (microphones and cameras). It is through these portable technologies that we have endeavoured to clarify not only what creativity looks like (process and product), but also where and how it emerges. In this chapter we will consider the ethical issues related to recording visual and audio happenings in school classrooms to offer insights about creative processes, moments and outcomes. However, as stated earlier, this digital means of illuminating creative processes presents ethical conundrums, such as ensuring inclusivity, respecting participants' right to anonymity, confidentiality and dignity, maximizing benefits whilst minimizing risk, obtaining informed consent from both adults and minors and finally, employing research methods appropriately. These ethical principles were adopted from BERA (2018) and will be reflected on throughout this chapter, alongside the consideration of our collected data. In addition to reflectively considering these ethical codes, we were also cognizant of Harris's (2018) description of creativity, which is that it is not 'activated' in humans but emerges in the agency 'of the moment, an encounter, an exchange' (p.67), and it is these personalized agentive 'moments' that our research, using digital means, sought to capture. Consequently, eliciting the nature of interactions between peers, learner and teacher, the classroom context and the resources within the environment are *all* relevant in understanding and interpreting influences on the nature and emergence of creativity. To pay attention to each of these influencing factors (both human and material), that extend affordances to support and promote agency that results in the development of creativity, second generation activity theory (Roth and Lee 2007; Grimalt-Alvaro and Ametlier 2021) was applied.

Theorizing relevant aspects of cultural and historical activity theory

The theoretical framework of cultural and historical activity theory (CHAT) or second generation activity theory is drawn upon to highlight the ways that

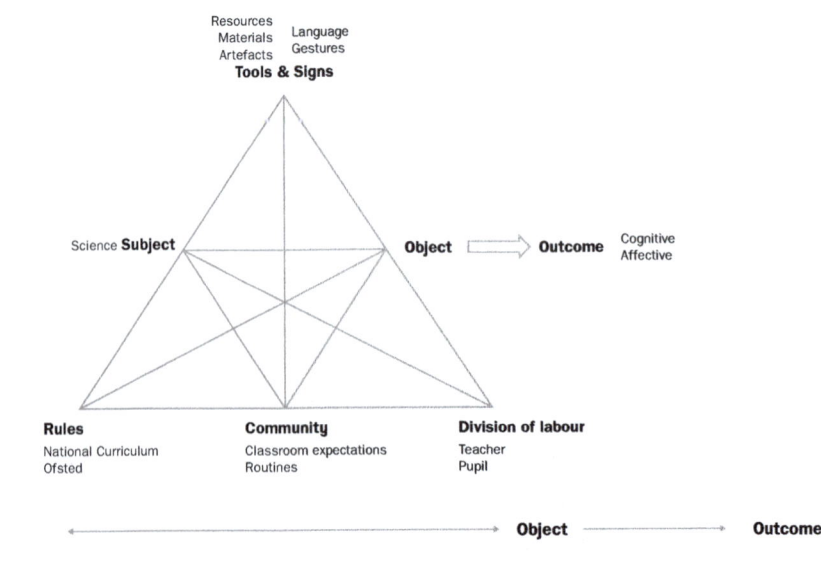

Figure 1 A diagrammatic representation of [second generation] CHAT (after Roth and Lee 2007 and Thompson 2015; Grimalt-Alvaro and Ametlier 2021) to provide context to the selected creative processes paid attention to for the purpose of this chapter

teachers engage in dialogue with learners and position them as agentive (or not) participants in learning (Roth and Lee 2007). In adopting the CHAT theoretical framework, we recognize that learning interactions are socially constructed phenomena (Kumplainen and Lipponen 2010), which is mediated by various pedagogical features which are highlighted in Figure 1.

In generating creative responses to the teacher's invitations, each student is offered a participatory position in the classroom community. Learning interactions [inter]actions are made visible through the ways that the students orient to the task and relate to the materials and objects made available, as well as how they engage with each other and interpret and construct meaning from ongoing exchanges. During the dialogic exchanges, the ways that resources (or objects), linguistic tools and signs adopted by the teacher offer affordances to promote original thought and action are deemed creative. To capture these features of CHAT, however, as previously noted, we needed to think ethically, with BERA's (2018:4) five key ethical principles in mind. These are described more fully below and reflected numerically through CHAT in Table 1 below.

1 Inclusivity of those with varying interests, values and perspectives.
2 Respecting participants' anonymity, confidentiality and dignity.
3 Ensuring the project employs appropriate research methods.
4 Maximizing research benefits whilst minimizing risks to participants.
5 Obtaining informed consent prior to data collection whilst ensuring the right to withdraw is explicit.

(adapted from McGregor et al. 2021: 19)

Table 1 indicates how four out of the five key ethical principles (1–4) were not only necessary to consider prior to data collection, but also during the process of evidencing the emergence of creativity. Obtaining informed consent and reminding the participants of the right to withdraw (the fifth principle), occurred on several occasions prior to the research activity and also immediately before any digital devices were employed to collect data. Principles 1–4 will be considered as we examine two selected creative moments. However, we shall discuss Principle 5 further first. This principle relates directly to protecting the best interests of the child as indicated in article 3 (UNICEF 2007) introduced in chapter I. The desire to elicit 'new' data that informs unique research about creativity from a fresh perspective had to be balanced with consideration about the rights and interests of the child, as they were the participant proffering their individual originality in the science lesson.

To collect and analyse (see table 1) the data, we needed to be able to apply our analytical framework, informed by CHAT, and we had to ensure that the concerns and individual values of the participants, including the headteacher, teacher, parent/guardian and the learners, were at the forefront of our minds (Van Mechelen et al. 2020) before pressing the record button. This was because the data we required involved evidencing the complexity of human behaviour and interactions to be subsequently examined. We needed to capture the physical, social, and ongoing development of the teachers and learners' thoughts and

Table 1 Features of CHAT to be captured with ethical values and principles in mind

Feature of CHAT to be evidenced		Ethical dilemmas (and suitable research methods)	Key BERA principles to be reflectively considered
Tools and signs	Language	Capturing student and teacher audible responses to dialogue (audio)	1,2,3,4
	Gestures	Capturing student and teacher actional responses to each other (video)	1,2,3,4
	Resources, materials and artefacts	Participatory [inter]actions being observed through the material affordances extended and provided by the teacher (audio and video)	1,2,3,4
Object		Meeting learning objective (video and/or audio) or generating a product (photograph)	1,2,3,4
Outcome	Cognitive	Mental action reflected through emergent dialogue (video)	1,2,3,4
	Affective	Emotional and social engagement of learners (audio and video)	1,2,3,4

ideas emerging withing the classroom. These recorded (and transcribed) observations needed to be detailed, reliable and verifiable (Cohen et al. 2018 p.561). This brought with it numerous ethical complexities that needed to be critically considered because, as Mercer and Hodgkinson (2008) stated, creative practices can not only be understood through exploring the nature of talk (as picked up through an audio recording), but can also be tied into: the physicality of the activities undertaken; the types of physical interactions between teacher and pupil; the social (non-verbal) actions between peers; and the learning outcomes produced during a science lesson. The data we needed had to be obtained through the use of wearable digital technology and non-intrusive videoing to be able to gain illustrative evidence of naturalistic creative learning processes, as they occurred during the course of a lesson. However, as Wilson (2015) reminds researchers, we were doing research *with* our participants and not *on* them; that is, data was being collected was just for our research purposes but would go beyond the perceived 'ivory towers' of academia and should benefit the public with minimal risk to the participants' health and wellbeing (reference BERA key principle 4). Thus, the participants needed to be fully informed of the purpose and intended audiences of the research prior to obtaining their signed consent and data collection.

To this end, to ensure participants were informed and we as researchers 'obtained informed consent prior to the data-gathering stage and ensured the right to withdraw was explicit' (informed by BERA 2018) we:

i. Invited headteachers (through our established professional networks) to consider whether they wished their schools (and their science teacher and his/her class) to be involved in the research project, which would involve the outcomes being shared via a publicly available website.
ii. Once headteachers agreed to be involved, other participants within their schools could be invited.
iii. Invitations including information sheets (and returnable consent forms) explaining the nature, focus and intent of the research were shared with the teacher. The nature of their involvement in the project was described and it was made clear they did not have to participate just because their headteacher had agreed.
iv. Invitations including information sheets (and returnable consent forms) explaining the nature, focus and intent of the research was shared with the parents and their children, who could volunteer to be involved. The nature of their involvement in the project was described and it was made clear they did not have to participate just because the teacher of their class had agreed.
v. Awaited the return of written assent from the teachers, children and their parents to be involved in the research project
vi. Established immediately prior to the digital recording whether any learners (or the teacher) had changed their minds about participation (even if their parents and their written assent had already been attained).

With all five principles in mind, we were aware that the lesson could only be videoed and audio recorded with the signed consent of the teacher, their learners and the learner's parents/guardians. The participants were invited to provide consent after they have read, and understood, their respective participant information sheets and privacy notices. These three documents, however, had to be tailored to the recipients; for example, the learners were given an age-appropriate participation sheet and the adults another. Parents/guardians and their children (who were under 16) were also afforded additional time (approximately one week) to mutually discuss and co-consider whether or not they wish to be involved. To ensure participants (teachers, learners and parents/guardians) did not feel 'railroaded' (Cohen et al 2011: 80) by the researchers, the headteacher of the school was initially contacted prior to any further communication. That is, the headteacher was invited to forward the appropriate ethical documentation to the class teacher for them to voluntarily contact the research team (via email). Only after the class teacher returned a consenting email, which indicated their interest in the project, were they and subsequently the pupils and their parents/guardians approached. It was with the asymmetrical interaction in mind, because relationships between researcher and the researched are rarely symmetrical (Cohen et al. 2011), that the opportunity for pupils to ask questions of familiar adults, such as their class teacher, prior to the observed lesson, provided them with their own agentive opportunities to decide whether or not they wished to participate in the research.

It was also recognized that the participants may have felt anxious and/or nervous when being videoed/audio recorded but they were reminded throughout that taking part in the research was entirely voluntary and if at any time they wanted to withdraw from the process they could do so without stating a reason (see also Brown, Chapter II). Whilst this did not occur, had it done so, any data relating to them would have been redacted (and audio destroyed). The researchers monitored any apparent discomfort, as part of the ongoing research (see also Capewell, Chapter VI). During the course of the observation no uneasiness was displayed by any of the participants, but had it done so we would have stopped the filming and, if requested, withdrawn the pupil from the research project. Having recognized a potential disadvantage of collecting data, we also wanted to highlight the benefits of their participation. We noted, on the information sheets, how the findings would inform other teachers (and fellow academics) about various ways that creative opportunities were augmented and developed in the science classroom. Additionally, the findings would subsequently illuminate the way creative teaching practices could influence learners to become impassioned and enthused with the subject, therefore, wanting to engage with it further (and animated enthusiasm and curiosity in science would only be discernible by triangulating what was said with bodily gestures).

The data was collected from the teacher's perspective via a wireless microphone attached to a dictaphone; there was also a camera video, situated at the back of the classroom, recording teaching as it naturally happened throughout the lesson. If the teacher interacted with any of his/her pupils who have not provided parental/guardian consent or completed their own consent forms, the data was not transcribed and was subsequently redacted from the raw data. Additionally, data was also collected from the student's perspective via wearable microphones. These recordings their voices throughout the science lesson was an attempt to capture any discussion between classroom peers. These protocols were clearly laid out in the individually tailored information sheets and consent forms to headteachers, teachers, pupils and their parents/guardians. We were also cognizant that we wanted to cause as little interruption to the scheduled school curriculum as possible, thus the science lesson took place, in collaboration with the class teacher, during the course of normal teaching school hours, and on school grounds using typical resources normally available.

As has been evidenced above, gaining the ethical approval and informed consent to video capture with additional audio a lesson was not straightforward (McGregor et al. 2021) but verbal exchanges, interactions, the use of artefacts, etc. were all necessary to evidence for CHAT analysis. This approach was justified, arguing that the use of video clips was not unprecedented – indeed there are even instances of these being uploaded to educational websites (Wilson and Mant 2010; McGregor et al. 2013; McGregor and Frodsham 2021) Through these existing, publicly available website materials, we acknowledged that participants may wish to seek recognition and waive their right to anonymity, especially when disseminated more widely. Whilst this did not occur in this particular research project, we could have applied for an ethical addendum, through university protocols, and sought further informed consent from all participants (headteacher, teacher, parents/carers and pupils) prior to data collection had they wished to be personally recognized. However, retrospective ethical approval may not have been granted post-data collection due to the anonymity guaranteed in the original ethical application.

We referred to BERA (2018) to consider all these forms of participatory ethical issues. They stated that 'researchers should recognize the entitlement of both institutions and individual participants to privacy, and should accord them their rights to confidentiality and anonymity' (BERA: 21). Contrastingly, schools can seemingly use personal data, such as pictures taken of their pupils for promotional reasons (e.g. a school prospectus and media interest), as long as the pupils and their guardians are made aware. This is not in breach of the child data protection act (CDPA) (ICO 2020). However, when collecting data for archival purposes in the public interest or for research, then the CDPA applies and safeguards have to be put into place. These safeguards included elements such as ensuring pseudonymization of schools, teachers and pupils. Thus, without consent being sought for personalized mentions, the names used in the excerpts (1 and 2) below are not the pupils' or the teacher's real names. These have been fictionalized, such as the girl called Olivia and Teacher being referred to as Ms McCabe. We also ensured that no photographs of the students or teacher faces were taken (Wilson 2015; Thomas 2017) and the video data collected was not shared beyond the immediate research team. Indeed, the raw data (audio and video) was destroyed once the research had concluded. This procedure meant that in our everyday dealings, as a researcher interacting with participants, we did our utmost to ensure participants' privacy (Thomas 2017). This practice was in line with BERA's second core principle.

It was by critically and constructively considering the ethical terrain of all five codes we were able to digitally capture excerpts from one teacher, four boys and four girls. This ensured equality, inclusivity and diversity, and demonstrated social responsibility by audio recording both the adult and eight children (four male, four female) perspectives (BERA's first key core principle). That is, all of these nine participants were individually miked up so that their verbal utterances were captured. There were also two cameras in the classroom – one photographic to take pictures of activities and original observable contributions and products. The other was placed at the back of the classroom to capture the ongoing actions of both the teacher and their 20 pupils to analyse through CHAT, as described in further detail below. Without the audio and video data we would not have been adhering to BERA's third key principle to provide the appropriate evidence to elucidate the elusive entity that is creativity.

Balancing the ethical selection of creative moments that demonstrate CHAT-in-action

The two moments described in this chapter, which occurred during a single science lesson, were selected to demonstrate how different influences inter-relate to generate opportunities or affordances that can promote creativity. The participatory interactions supported by the teacher in varied ways explicitly bring into play particular elements of the activity theory framework.

At the risk of ethically compromising the teacher and her practice, or the emergence of inspired thinking on a child's behalf, these two moments were chosen to demonstrate contrasting aspects of a lesson that illustrate creativity in quite distinct ways. The first, see Moment 1 below, demonstrates how the teacher imaginatively introduces the context, setting the scene for creativity to emerge. She adopts scientific tools and linguistic signs to introduce resources and artefacts that are materially relevant for the upcoming activities, all employed to mediate and engage the learners in thinking about how electricity works.

The second moment, offers an individual's original interpretation and consequent actions within the classroom community. This learner, faced with the challenge of a 'flat' or 'dead' battery, draws on her previous experiences to consider the problem and agentively respond by attempting to re-charge a failing source of chemical energy.

The details of the following two moments, collating the influence of the various factors identified through a CHAT analysis, would not be possible without a transcript of the classroom activities and associated dialogue. Research methods that adopted digital means to record the verbal and actional exchanges between teacher and learners made the following assertions possible. The implicit ethical issue in disseminating findings from this kind of illustrative research is balancing authenticity and the responsibility to ensure that participants would not feel at all uncomfortable reading about the study.

Moment 1: The Lighthouse Keeper's Son

In the first of the excerpts, seen below and as depicted through CHAT in Figure 2, the teacher is reading the class a story about Hamish and his father. The father is a lighthouse keeper and wants his son to take on his profession of maintaining three lighthouses, but Hamish is more interested in reading books from the comfort of his chair.

> Ms McCabe: Once there was an island far out to sea, where the wind blows hard and the wind blows fierce and the ships get blown right up on the rocky shore. On this island was a lighthouse keeper who had three sons. Every night two of his sons would follow him up the stairs. 'Let me light the lamp, Father!' they would cry, but not Hamish, who had his head in a book.
>
> Can you see the link in the story now? Their father showed his sons how to polish the lens and light the wick to burn the oil, to make the beacons shine out to the ships at sea. Hamish wasn't interested. Hamish just wanted to read (Excerpt 1).

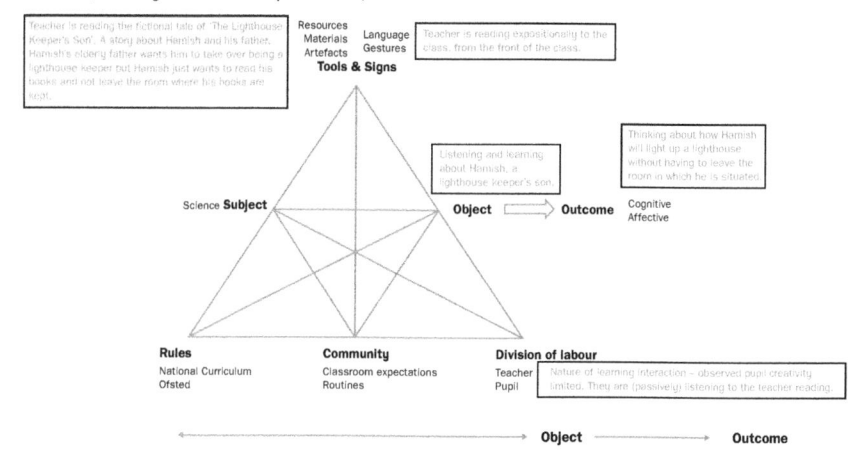

Figure 2 Diagrammatic representation of CHAT to illustrate foregrounded features of the first moment (The Lighthouse Keeper's Son)

Teacher is reading the fictional tale of 'The Lighthouse Keeper's Son'. A story about Hamish and his father. Hamish's elderly father wants him to take over being a lighthouse keeper but Hamish just wants to read his books and not leave the room where his books are kept.	Resources / Materials / Artefacts — **Tools & Signs** — Language / Gestures — Teacher is reading expositionally to the class, from the front of the class.

Science **Subject** — **Object** — **Outcome** — Cognitive / Affective

Listening and learning about Hamish, a lighthouse keeper's son.

Thinking about how Hamish will light up a lighthouse without having to leave the room in which he is situated.

Rules	**Community**	**Division of labour**	
National Curriculum / Ofsted	Classroom expectations / Routines	Teacher / Pupil	Nature of learning interaction – observed pupil creativity limited. They are (passively) listening to the teacher reading.

Object → **Outcome**

During this first moment, the teacher appears to have positioned the pupils as passive listeners. She sits at the front of the classroom, whilst they are situated at their desks, attentively listening to the story. Whilst this unidirectional exchange, Bredo (1999) claimed, would socially separate the pupils from the more experienced other (the teacher) and their surrounding physical environment, the story is being used to capture the pupil's imagination and interest (Turner and Bage 2006). The dialogic relationship, as indicated through the transcript (presented out of context here) could suggest she is leaving little room for the students' subjective creativity to be expressed (Rogoff 1995:156), consequently limiting learners' expressive opportunities conveying alternative viewpoints (core principle 1). However, as McCullagh et al. (2010) state, when a story is employed effectively, in conjunction with other creative teaching approaches, it could initiate child-led dialogue, the generation of ideas (McCullagh et al. 2010), questioning skills and problem solving (Turner and Bage 2006). Thus, whilst the division of labour is seemingly one-sided, Ms McCabe is setting up the opportunity for the pupils to become the active agents of their own learning (McGregor 2007). This example from the research evidence then, demonstrates how a teacher is attempting to provide the context for her learners to explore and investigate how to make series and parallel circuits within an imagined world. This provides the students with opportunities to discuss their own perspectives and to begin to conceive how Hamish could light the lighthouse without leaving the comfort of his reading chair.

Moment 1 therefore demonstrates elements of teacher's creativity within a CHAT framework. This also illuminates BERA's first and fourth core ethical principles in action, namely ensuring inclusivity whilst benefiting all the participants and researchers who are involved in the research study.

Moment 2: Keeping the lighthouse lamps alight

This moment occurs after the teacher describes how Hamish and his father had to look after three separate lighthouses, Hamish not wanting to leave his armchair because he sought to find out how to light all three lighthouses using one switch. Through this story, the teacher had sought to engage the children's imagination whilst also piquing their interest in proposing a solution to Hamish's predicament by making a parallel circuit out of the electrical components she has provided (bulbs, switch, wires, battery, etc.). The creative moment (see Excerpt 2 below), explored through CHAT analysis (Figure 3), illustrates how one out of a group of four pupils innovatively problem-solved when trying to make a parallel circuit.

> Katie: We need more batteries, I'll get more batteries.
> Harry: No we don't, no we don't. I can fix it.
> Olivia: Pass the battery to me cos I think I can recharge one.
> Mark: Why do that?
> Olivia: It might work.
> Mark: You're going to have to take out the battery first.
> Olivia: I'm going to charge it with static electricity [rubs the battery on the carpet]. It works. Oh gosh, it's working.
> [Ms McCabe walks over]
> Teacher: Why are you doing that?
> Olivia: I am recharging the battery through static electricity.
> Ms McCabe: Okay, let's see what happens.
> (Excerpt 2)

Olivia exemplifies an openness to other possibilities (or solutions) by manipulating the battery in a novel way, for whilst other batteries were available at the front of the class, she opted to recharge it with static electricity by rubbing it on another available resource – the carpet. By possibility thinking (Craft 2001) whilst tackling this problem, she was also drawing on her previous personalized experiences with a scientific phenomenon. This exemplifies an example of Olivia's right to freely articulate an ontological view of her own, no matter her age (resonating with BERA's first core principle of inclusivity). It also echoes with Runco's (2003: 318) everyday problem solving, which enables people to construct new meaning. Whilst Olivia's solution was not scientifically accurate (this battery could not be recharged this way) had she been provided with enough time, rather than an expedited answer by the authoritative other, she would have discovered this through further experimentation and critical reflection, thus mitigating any potential ridicule and distress. Akin to Moment 1, this episode, which could only be evidenced through the use of audio and video, highlights how Olivia was free to express her own perspective without fear of being rebuked.

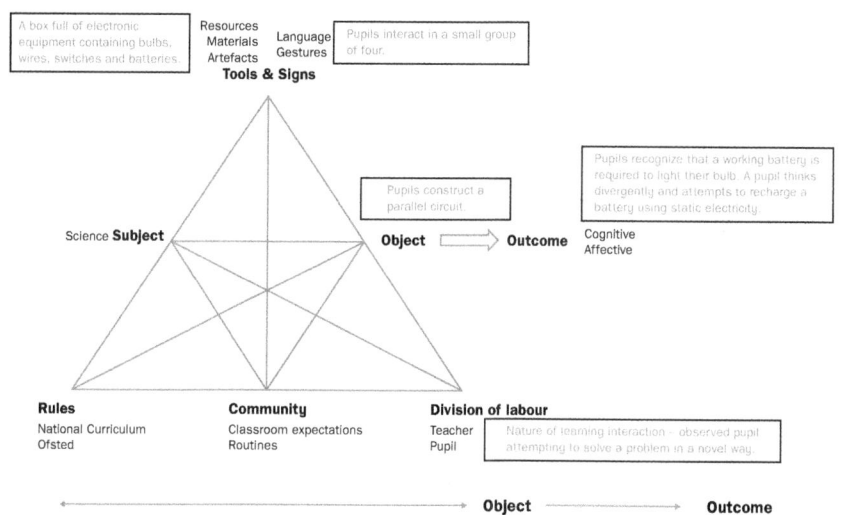

Figure 3 Diagrammatic representation of CHAT to illustrate the second moment (creating a parallel series circuit)

[Tools & Signs]
- A box full of electronic equipment containing bulbs, wires, switches and batteries.
- Resources, Materials, Artefacts
- Language, Gestures
- Pupils interact in a small group of four.

Science **Subject**

Pupils construct a parallel circuit.

Object ⟹ **Outcome** — Cognitive, Affective

Pupils recognize that a working battery is required to light their bulb. A pupil thinks divergently and attempts to recharge a battery using static electricity.

Rules — National Curriculum, Ofsted
Community — Classroom expectations, Routines
Division of labour — Teacher, Pupil — Nature of learning interaction – observed pupil attempting to solve a problem in a novel way.

⟵————— **Object** —————⟶ **Outcome**

Participants' emergent actions *and* talk: via merging digital video with individual audio recordings

As previously stated, eliciting how individuals participated in, and learned, about electricity through various classroom activities and social interactions was impossible without videoing the whole class *and* recording discussions through lapel-mounted microphones and audio-recorders, carried by the pupils and the teacher. As Mannay (2016: 28) suggests, this highlights how 'familiar territory' (in this case pupil talk and action in classrooms), are combined to look beyond what is oft-reported to elicit unique viewpoints that include being able to juxtapose learners' utterances with the ways they actually *engaged with* and *participated in* classroom activity (see core principles 1 and 3). As researchers we elicited fresh insights about the ways participants 'act' in learning, offering significant 'epistemic privilege' (Mannay 2016) concerned with understanding a challenging scientific concept – electricity (Principle 4).

Interestingly, the details required to apply (and check the usefulness and validity of) the CHAT framework requires empathetic understanding about the ways that teachers' and children's rights, voice, and privacy should all be paid attention to. In Table 2 below, the summary of different elements of the CHAT framework, which are required to illustrate how creativity can manifest differently between people or as a result of an individual's actions or dialogue, iterate the need for detailed digital recordings of happenings. Ethical consent and subsequent sensitivity in the ways that CHAT data is presented to share evident contrasts with classroom practitioners are one of the key reasons for examining the nature of teacher and/or learner creativity. This kind of detailed analysis is required because, as Davies (2016) and Johnston (2007) have shown, teachers

88 Ethical Dilemmas in Educational Research

Table 2 Relating ethical concerns: the nature of data required to evidence the nature of creativity in classrooms

Feature of CHAT to be evidenced		Ethical dilemma (Research method required)	Ethical guidance to be considered (BERA 2018)	Ethical Solutions related to core principles 1–4
Tools and signs	Language	Capturing student and teacher audible responses to dialogue (audio)	1,2,3,4	• Pseudonymization of schools, teachers and pupils • No photographs of faces only material processes and final products • Freedom to articulate ontological views without fear of detrimental result (ridicule) • Methods of data collection that ensures equality, inclusivity and diversity and demonstrates social responsibility by capturing both adult and 8 children (4 male, 4 female) perspectives • Data not used for other purposes, e.g. in other research projects • Dissemination of findings (e.g. this chapter and paper presentations) to benefit both the research and educational environment. Produce a summary of findings and publications to be sent to participants upon request
	Gestures	Capturing student and teacher actional responses to dialogue (video)	1,2,3,4	
	Resources, materials and artefacts	Participatory [interJactions being observed through the material affordances offered by the teacher (audio and video)	1,2,3,4	
Object		Objective to meet (video and/or audio) or a product is created (photograph)	1,2,3,4	
Outcome	Cognitive	Mental action to acquire knowledge or understanding (video)	1,2,3,4	
	Affective	Emotional and social engagement (audio and video)	1,2,3,4	

believe they are teaching for particular forms of learning, but objective observation indicates the reality is somewhat different. In the case of teaching for creativity (Frodsham 2018), there is a need for clarity about the nature of pedagogy and practice (McGregor and Frodsham 2019) that ensures it is pragmatically supported when there are international calls for it to be developed more widely in school science (OECD 2019). PISA, for example, defines creative thinking as, 'the competence to engage productively in the generation, evaluation and improvement of ideas that can result in original and effective solutions, advances in knowledge and impactful expressions of imagination' (OECD 2019: 8).

Reflecting back on the ethical dilemmas about the research data collected: Affordances and constraints

What becomes apparent from this chapter applying aspects of CHAT theorization, is that it enables elements of creative processes to be made more explicit so data can be analysed to inform findings about influences upon the nature of creativity as generated in a single science lesson. This was not possible without the ethical approval to video (capture individuals' utterances and actions as they interact and enact their thinking) and audio record the ongoing group discussions between young students.

This required securing ethical approval for the collection of such detailed information about classroom happenings as they unfolded. It also afforded microanalysis of collective and individual discussion and action, which provided unique insights into some of the pedagogic and epistemic processes that underpin creativity. What was also evidenced was the two ways (each moment described above) in which tools and signs (resources, materials, artefacts language, and gesture) influenced the object (creative outcomes) achieved within the episodes of the lesson.

In a longer-term study, further insight about the influence of cultural and historical experiences could be explored, but a significant constraint of engaging in research that draws on the use of video, audio and interview material requires much painstaking transcription prior to analysis. To probe further how family and other social, cultural and historical experiences influenced learner's unique contributions in classroom contexts that can contribute to collective creative outcomes also requires careful verbal and actional data collection, which is challenging for the researcher and can be perceived by participants as quite intrusive.

Conclusion

Some aspects of education cannot be researched without extensive investment in justifying why detailed information about practice (including eliciting emergent dialogue, mapping actions, documenting the use of tools, signs and artefacts) and various individuals' responses to teacher's instructions or guidance are collected (within the classroom community). The ethical dilemmas, when endeavouring to collect this kind of spontaneously emerging data, when using wearable technology (dictaphones) as well as collecting video material, means that the researcher needs to critically consider the research from their participants' perspective, not just their own, to engage in ensuring a consensual and voluntary acceptance (by teacher, pupils and parents/carers) as to why these data sets are necessary. The participants also need assurances of confidentiality (hence the fictionalization of names) and an open, honest, consistent experience practice of integrity. Thinking ethically, therefore, could be viewed as incurring an incredibly extensive workload for researchers as well as being interpreted by participants as quite intrusive in classroom settings. However, it was by capturing both the audio and video of both teacher and pupils that it became possible to illuminate varied ontological values and perspectives, meaning-making processes and learning outcomes through a CHAT theoretical framework. This illuminates important influences on learning processes, particularly with respect to creativity. This chapter has thus emphasized how examining influences on the emergence of originality in learning can inform the future development of teaching and that nurturing creativity and innovation is challenging. That is, eliciting (and following) the emergent narratives of individuals' learning journeys, eliciting their influence on others' thinking and actions throughout a lesson and consequently contrasting moments of creativity within the same classroom community presented a range of ethical dilemmas. However, these have been, and were, responded to effectively and reflectively through retaining BERA's five core principles at the forefront of our minds and applying them empathetically.

References

Bell, P. and McGregor, D. (2021) The nature of creativity in Arts and Science teaching: views from the primary classroom, *Journal of Emergent Science*, 21(June): 37–45.
BERA (British Educational Research Association) (2018) *Ethical Guidelines for Educational Research*. Available at: https:// www.bera.ac.uk/publication/ethical-guidelines-for-educational-research-2018 (accessed 16 February 2022).
Bredo, E. (1999) Reconstructing educational psychology, in P. Murphy (ed.) *Learners, Learning and Assessment*. London: Paul Chapman Publishing Ltd.
Cohen, L., Manion, L. and Morrison, K. (2011) *Research Methods in Education* (7th edn). London: Routledge.
Craft, A. (2008) Studying collaborative creativity: implication for education, *Thinking Skills and Creativity*, 3(3): 241–245.
Cremin, T and Chappell, K (2021) Creative pedagogies: a systematic review, *Research Papers in Education*, 36(3): 299–331.
Davies, D. (2016) *Creative Teaching in Primary Science*. London : Routledge
Davies, D. and McGregor, D. (2017) *Creative Teaching in Primary Science* (2nd edn) London: Routledge.

Durham Commissionris (2019) *Durham Commission on Creativity and Education*. Available at: https://www.dur.ac.uk/creativitycommission/report/ (accessed 27 January 2020).

Frodsham, S. (2018) *Developing creativity within primary science teaching. What does it look like and how can formative assessment augment the process?*. Unpublished PhD thesis. Oxford: Oxford Brookes University.

Glaveanu, V.P. (2018) Educating which creativity? *Thinking Skills and Creativity*, 27(2018), 25–32.

Grigorenko, E. L. (2019) Creativity : A challenge for contemporary education. *Comparative Education* 55(1): 116–132.

Grimalt-Alvaro, C. and Ametlier, J. (2021) A Cultural-Historical Activity Theory Approach for the Design of a Qualitative Methodology in Science Educational Research. *International Journal of Qualitative methods* (20) p.1–12.

Harris, A. (2018) Creative agency/creative ecologies, in K. Snepvangers, P. Thomson and A. Harris (eds). *Creativity Policy, Partnerships and Practice in Education*. Gewerbestrasse, Switzerland: Palgrave Macmillan.

Information Commissioner's Office (ICO) (2021) Taking Photos in Schools. Available at: https://ico.org.uk/your-data-matters/schools/photos/ (accessed 31 December 2021).

Johnston, J. (2007) What is creativity in science education?, in A. Wilson (ed), *Creativity in Primary Education* (2nd edn) Exeter: Learning Matters Ltd.

Kind, P.M. and Kind, V. (2007) Creativity in science education: perspectives and challenges for developing school science. *Studies in Science Education*, 43(1): 1–37, DOI: 10.1080/03057260708560225

Kumplainen, K. and Lipponen, L. (2010) Productive interaction as agentic participation in dialogic enquiry, in K. Littleton and C. Howe (eds) *Educational Dialogues. Understanding and Promoting Productive Interaction*. London: Routledge.

Mannay, D. (2016) *Visual, Narrative and Creative Research Methods*. London: Routledge.

McCullagh, J., Walsh, G. and Greenwood, J. (2010) Books and Stories in children's science, *Primary Science*, 111(Jan/Feb): 21–24.

McGregor, D. (2007) *Developing Thinking Developing Learning: A Guide to Thinking Skills in Education*. Maidenhead: Open University Press.

McGregor, D. and Frodsham, S. (2019) Epistemic insights: contemplating tensions between policy influences and creativity in school science, *British Educational Research Journal*, 45(4): 770–790.

McGregor, D. and Frodsham, S. (2021) Persistence and perseverance: working with University Research Ethics Committee (UREC) processes to elicit children's views, voices and volitions, in A. Fox, H. Busher and C. Capewell (eds) *Thinking Critically and Ethically about Research for Education: Engaging with Voice and Empowerment in International Contexts*. Abingdon: Routledge.

McGregor, D. Frodsham, S. & Deller, C. (2022) From slavery to scientist : Dramatising an historical story to creatively engage learners in resolving STEM problems. In K. Murcia, C. Campbell, M. Joubert & S. Wilson (Eds) *Children's Creative Inquiry in STEM*.

McGregor, D, Frodsham, S. & Deller, C. (2021) Persistence and perseverance : Overcoming University Research Ethics Committee (UREC) processes to elicit childrens' views, voices and volitions. In A Fox, H Busher and C Capewell (Eds.), Thinking critically and ethically about research in education, London: Routledge.

McGregor, D. and Gaciu, N. (2018) Creativity in Teaching Science, in J. Hillier and I. Banner (eds) *ASE Guide to Secondary Science Education*. Hatfield: ASE.

Mercer, N. and Hodgkinson, S. (2008) *Exploring Talk in School*. London: Sage.

OECD (2019) PISA 2021 *Creative Thinking Framework* (third draft). Available at: https://www.oecd.org/pisa/publications/PISA-2021-creative-thinking-framework.pdf (accessed 10 January 2022).

Rogoff, B. (1995) Observing sociocultural activity on three planes: participatory appropriation, guided participation and apprenticeship, in J.V. Wertsch, P. Del Rio and A. Alvarez (eds) *Sociocultural Studies of the Mind*. Cambridge: Cambridge University Press.

Roth, M-W. and Lee, Y. L. (2007) 'Vygotsky's Neglected Legacy': cultural historical activity theory, *Review of Educational Research*, 77(2): 186–232.

Runco, M.A. and Jaeger, G.J. (2012) The standard definition of creativity, *Creativity Research Journal*, 24(1): 92–96.

Thomas, G. (2017) *How to Do Your Research Project: A Guide for Students in Education and Applied Social Sciences* (3rd edn) London: Sage.

Turner, J. and Bage, G. (2006) Real stories, real science, *Primary Science*, 92(Mar/Apr): 4–6.

UNICEF (2007) *Implementation Handbook the Convention on the Rights of the Child*. United Nations Children's Fund.

Van Mechelen, M., Baykal, G.E., Dindler, C. et al. (2020) *18 Years of Ethics in Child-Computer Interaction Research: A Systematic Literature Review*. Presented at ACM Interaction Design and Children (IDC) conference 2020: London. England, 10 June 2020.

Wilson, H. and Mant, J. (2010) *Bright Ideas in Primary Science*. Available at: https://www.pstt-cpd.org.uk/ext/cpd/bright-ideas/introduction-to-the-bright-ideas-time.html (accessed 30 October 2017).

Wilson, M. (2015) Ethical considerations, in G. Butt (ed.) *MasterClass in Geography Education: Transforming Teaching and Learning*. London: Bloomsbury.

VIII Statistically Speaking: Ethical Dilemmas in Handling Numerical Data

Mary Wild and Sarah Frodsham

Numbers are often reified as 'facts' and therefore can be seen as likely to be less problematic for the researcher than some of the more obviously personal and highly contextualized forms of research that are highlighted elsewhere in this book. But in reality, numbers are not neutral nor incontrovertible. They are just as susceptible to producing ethical dilemmas for researchers as other forms of research. In this chapter, we will consider statistically based evidence, drawn from established national and internationally recognized comparative research, to illustrate the dilemmas in ethically producing and drawing conclusions based on highly aggregated data.

As has been noted in Chapter IV (Victoria Pratt), the ethical dilemmas of empirical work, whether quantitative or qualitative in nature, have led some institutions to guide students towards desk-based research, thereby avoiding the manifold dilemmas that the primary researcher can encounter. Whilst personalized, sensitive and confidential data is not collected directly, analysing comparative databases in extant data bases such as that provided by the OECD in longitudinal cohort studies (Cave and Von Stumm 2021) or publicly available national pupil databases (Gov.uk 2018) is not unproblematic.

Philosophically, there is the dilemma of the appropriateness of this type of collective data that can unduly obscure the significance of the individual and context. We will consider whether, and how, it may be ethical for policymakers and/or those who implement pedagogical practice to attempt to ground their teaching practices in this type of numerically driven and replicable evidence. The chapter will also flag ways in which demands upon the researcher to demonstrate impact of research can distort the significance of that research. This raises ethical issues around integrity of research and for the wellbeing of the researcher (Khazragui and Hudson 2014).

Looking for 'what works' in educational research

In considering the ethical ramifications of focusing on extant data sets, it is important to contextualize this form of research as part of a fiercely contested broader debate about the nature and purposes of education. The agenda for this kind of educational research can be characterized as pragmatically oriented, looking for effectiveness or 'what works', in a generalizable sense via statistically measurable data, rather than 'how it works'. This highlights a debate relating to whether researchers need to be cautious of what is seen by some as a truncated perspective (Oancea and Pring 2008).

The reference to 'what works' research is sometimes referred to as the 'datafication' of education (Bradbury and Roberts-Holmes 2017). It is seen by many educationalists as being part of a neoliberal and marketized view of education, which is inappropriate. Biesta (2015) refers to 'two cultures' in research and more broadly in education, one of which is a technological culture in which cause and effect are sought, variables are defined and outcomes measured. It is assumed here that extant truths can be determined and demonstrated and are essentially situated within a positivist paradigm. The alternative culture regards education as fundamentally a dynamic human process and therefore it cannot be objectified and measured in this manner, but it is an inherently fluid process involving communication and meaning-making as central – it is arguably seen through an interpretivist lens. This divide extrapolates to our wider vision of education beyond the research context meaning, as Biesta contends, that:

> We need to engage with the question of what good education is, rather than say, the question of what effective education is, which is only a question about the capacity of processes to bring about certain results, but does not say anything about why such results ..... are desirable. (Biesta 2015: 18)

Having given attention to the two paradigmatic stances of educational research (i.e. the 'what' and 'how') through Biesta we turn to Peter Moss, who, from the early years academic base has also drawn attention to this 'paradigmatic divide' (Moss 2007). He problematizes the growth of positivistic and modernist understandings as a dominant discourse in research and of childhood more generally, which he contends have a privileged 'assertion of the importance of early childhood education for economic and social goals' (p.229). This, he claims, is linked to neoliberalist economic and political agendas.

In a subsequent article, co-authored by Matthias Urban (Moss and Urban 2017) the authors challenge the UK government's decision to sign up the country to the Organization for Economic Co-operation and Development's International Early Learning Study (IELS). This move is characterized as an extension into the early years of the PISA-style reviews already adopted for older children, which foreground measurements and outcomes (OECD 2017), and they argue this is particularly inappropriate in regard to such young children.

It should, perhaps, be acknowledged that the purpose of the IELS study is noted on the OECD website (https; //www.oecd.org/unitedkingdom/) as being to provide countries with a common language and framework, encompassing a collection of robust empirical information and in-depth insights on children's learning development at a critical age. Indeed, Slavin (2004) helpfully highlights how professionals in education, at all levels, need to take manifold decisions that will impact on their students throughout their education, and having recourse to a body of evidence of 'what works' in education could provide beneficial insights. Similarly, the comparative use of quantitative findings or meta reviews of findings (Higgins and Katsipataki 2016) can help 'to identify which approaches have, on average, made the most difference to tested learning outcomes, in terms of effect size' (p.237). Similarly to Oancea and Pring (2008), these authors also urge caution in making comparative inferences and suggest that reflecting on 'what has worked' might be more judicious than claims about 'what works'. This more caveated advice would seem to offer an ethical way in which to present such findings and from which to make onward recommendations, but thinking about *what has worked* still does not delve deep enough to understand *how it worked*. The distinction between the utility of producing comparative datasets and how they are subsequently used, both positively and negatively, is highlighted by Hopfenbeck et al. (2018) in their systematic review of peer-reviewed articles derived from PISA iterations from 2000–2015. They argued that there are benefits from this measurable approach in terms of the research base in education, even if policymakers and other stakeholders may have interpreted and translated these findings into policy in ways that fit their own agenda. For example, they specifically mention the negative impact of crude league tables between countries and the consequential generalizations that are made about national education systems. This illuminates the ethical tension for the researcher in aligning themselves to a specific but contested philosophy of educational purpose in both the production and analysis of findings. However, it is likely that policymakers will inevitably seek to generate such conclusions and, arguably, it might be preferable for researchers to be involved in such research to bring rigour and integrity to the process. Whether or not we, as a community of researchers, are better off being involved in 'what works' research is not addressed in this chapter, as we do not seek to judge individual researchers or teams, national or international, on the specific forms of research that they espouse. However, we would argue that it is important that researchers have reflected upon their own beliefs and positionality such that that feel they have made an informed ethical decision about the ways in which they engage with measurable research.

Using secondary data

Researchers may choose to engage with secondary data sources because they are publicly available. This is understandable, and perhaps there are perceivably fewer ethical conundrums to consider by doing so, due to its accessibility. However, this does not mean researchers, who choose to use such data, are absolved from thinking carefully about their responsibilities. Cohen et al. (2018) describes this particular ethical dilemma aptly and it is discussed further with regards to the social sensitivity of data by Wild and Brown in Chapter X:

> ...regardless of whether the [secondary] data [is or is] not public, the researcher has to address responsibilities to the original participants, including the original researchers, and must avoid misinterpretation to the original findings and their contexts. (Cohen et al. 2018 p. 589)

Thus, as researchers we should still acknowledge that we are accountable even when critically interpreting data from publicly disseminated sources. After all

> As a [researcher we]... are part of this community of critical inquiry, and by being part of it have conferred upon us some important privileges. Those privileges, though, are balanced with responsibilities, and it is in the balancing of the one with the other that ethics come in. (Thomas, 2017:37)

To consider our duty of care towards those originally involved in the collection of secondary data we will, in this chapter, focus on examining it on three levels. These are: i) an international level; ii) at a localized level; and iii) via the original participants taking part in these globalized surveys. These levels will be contextualized through the disseminated results of a singular global scale survey, namely the 2018 Programme for International Student Assessment (PISA) – the original data from PISA being collected three years prior to it being made publicly available in 2021.

Evaluating education: The international level

The OECD has set out, since 1997, to understand how countries' children (aged 15 years) on average academically achieve on a triennial basis. This worldwide survey nominally focuses on the domains of reading, mathematics and science. These three core disciplinary areas were selected, Salganik et al. (1999) stated, because of the already pre-existing interest in these subjects from policymakers, measurement technology in place, and already established national conceptual and empirical frameworks. This has been criticized as being an overly narrow and reductionist approach with a focus on specified measurable outcomes. However, there may be some underlying justification in that these are the very skills that are seen as privileged across so many economic and social contexts, whereby the future life opportunities and trajectories of young people are seen to be boosted depending on their level of competencies in these core areas. This notion of facilitating future career choices is supported by the Educational Endowment Fund (2018), who suggest that very many rewarding and interesting careers require the attainment of 'good' grades, especially these three core disciplines. Recently, the OCED have also highlighted the importance of these disciplines, especially when navigating the '21st century' (OECD 2021b).

In 1997, over 40 countries took part in PISA and the statistically analysed results were disseminated in 2000. In the latest round, the number of countries participating have almost doubled (80 in total). That is, 600,000 students were involved in the survey. The subsequent report according to the OECD (2021a) indicates the countrywide ability and skills of the pupils to meet real-life challenges. However, this raises two questions. They are:

1. Who exactly benefits from these international pupil surveys?
2. What are the ethical conundrums researchers have to consider when choosing to use these publicly available secondary measurements as sources of information?'

These questions will be answered in the following subsection of this chapter.

Guror (2016) proposed the educative metaphor of mass deforestation to describe how students could be seen as commodities or 'natural resources' in the same way trees were '…viewed through a fiscal lens' in the nineteenth and twentieth centuries (p.600). Mass testing in the educational context and the impact of globalized data gathering through testing for attainment in education can arguably be seen as competitive in its nature, especially when examining where a country fails within PISA league tables. In the latest results, from PISA 2018 (Table 3) we can visually see a snapshot of a country's students, aged 15, mean performance in the three domains (OECD 2021a).

According to Bulle (2011), this international comparative format, such as that depicted in Table 3, which has been championed for over 20 years, not only leads to an environment of competition it also encourages countries at the top of the league table to promote their practices globally and acts as a foil to others (Buelle 2011). Thus, it can be used as a political tool and lead to a potential normative standardization of educative practices under the banner of 'best practice' without considering the individual pupil's wants or needs. This standardized end product, produced by running a complex statistical analysis, has also ignored the countries multifaceted, individualized educational system. For example, these statistics do not differentiate between the 80 countries' historical context and national values. It is with this in mind, alongside the competences that PISA reports to measure, that paying attention to specific geographical locations may help answer the first ethical question raised above. For example, we could compare performances between the United Kingdom and New Zealand. These two countries have some historical and cultural interconnections, but also very specific contrasts related to Indigenous community traditions and ways of thinking about education. This is discussed in more detail by Patrick Alexander in Chapter XI of this book.

What is not evident when comparing reading, mathematics and science PISA results from the United Kingdom (UK) and New Zealand (see Figure 4) is the emphasis that the countries place on their core competencies. As ethical beings we must ask ourselves the following question: how does Figure 4 help us to understand the participants? After all, as Wilson (2015) stated, we should be doing research with participants and not on them, and these decontextualized numbers place the researcher, and more importantly, the participant into a position of passive spectator of the results rather than an agentive individual.

Table 3 A global snapshot of students' performance in reading, mathematics and science (OECD 2021a)

Country	Reading (mean average)	Mathematics (mean average)	Science (mean average)
B-S-3-2* China	555	591	590
Singapore	549	569	551
Macao (China)	525	558	544
Hong Kong (China)	524	551	517
Estonia	523	523	530
Canada	520	512	518
Finland	520	507	522
Ireland	518	500	496
Korea	514	526	519
Poland	512	516	511
Sweden	506	502	499
New Zealand	506	494	508
United States	505	478	502
United Kingdom	504	502	505
Japan	504	527	529
Australia	503	491	503
Chinese Taipei	503	531	516
Denmark	501	509	493
Norway	499	501	490
Germany	498	500	503
Slovenia	495	509	507
Belgium	493	508	499
France	493	495	493
Portugal	492	492	492
Czech Republic	490	499	497
Netherlands	485	519	503
Austria	484	499	490
Switzerland	484	515	495
Croatia	479	464	472

Table 3 (continued)

Country	Reading (mean average)	Mathematics (mean average)	Science (mean average)
Latvia	479	496	487
Russia	479	488	476
Italy	476	487	468
Hungary	476	481	481
Lithuania	476	481	482
Iceland	474	495	475
Belarus	474	472	471
Israel	470	463	462
Luxembourg	470	483	477
Ukraine	466	453	469
Turkey	466	454	468
Slovak Republic	458	486	464
Greece	457	451	452
Chile	452	417	444
Malta	448	472	457
Serbia	439	448	440
United Arab Emirates	432	435	434
Romania	428	430	426
Uruguay	427	418	426
Costa Rica	426	402	416
Cyprus	424	451	439
Moldova	424	421	428
Montenegro	421	430	415
Mexico	420	409	419
Bulgaria	420	436	424
Jordan	419	400	429
Malaysia	415	440	438
Brazil	413	384	404
Colombia	412	391	413

(continued)

Table 3 *(continued)*

Country	Reading (mean average)	Mathematics (mean average)	Science (mean average)
Brunei Daraussalam	408	430	431
Qatar	407	414	419
Albania	405	437	417
Bosnia & Herzegovia	403	406	398
Argentina	402	379	404
Peru	401	400	404
Saudi Arabia	399	373	386
Thailand	393	419	426
North Macedonia	393	394	413
Baku (Azerbaijan)	389	420	398
Kazakhstan	387	423	397
Georgia	386	398	383
Panama	377	353	365
Indonesia	371	379	396
Morocco	359	368	377
Lebanon	353	393	384
Kosovo	353	366	365
Dominican Republic	342	325	336
Philippines	340	353	357
Spain	Not Available	481	483

We also need to consider how to read Figure 4. These are static, decontextualized and organized into a hierarchical order, with New Zealand seemingly doing better than the UK in reading, mathematics and science. Upon inspection, the PISA website tells us that the numbers represented are the mean score (OECD 2021a). Anyone with a mathematical background will know that this is a descriptive statistic that can present data as a frequency (Cohen et al. 2018). More simply, it is the sum of the total results being measured, divided by how many pupils took the survey. As Cohen et al. (2018: 727) state, the score only reflects 'enumeration and organization' and makes no attempt to bound the population parameters (i.e., hone in on the localized context). For the desk-based researcher this may be problematic as they may not have ready access to this geographic and demographical underlying information.

Figure 4 Averages for 15 years PISA a) Reading, b) Mathematics and c) Science scale by all student participants for New Zealand and the United Kingdom in 2018 (OECD 2021a)

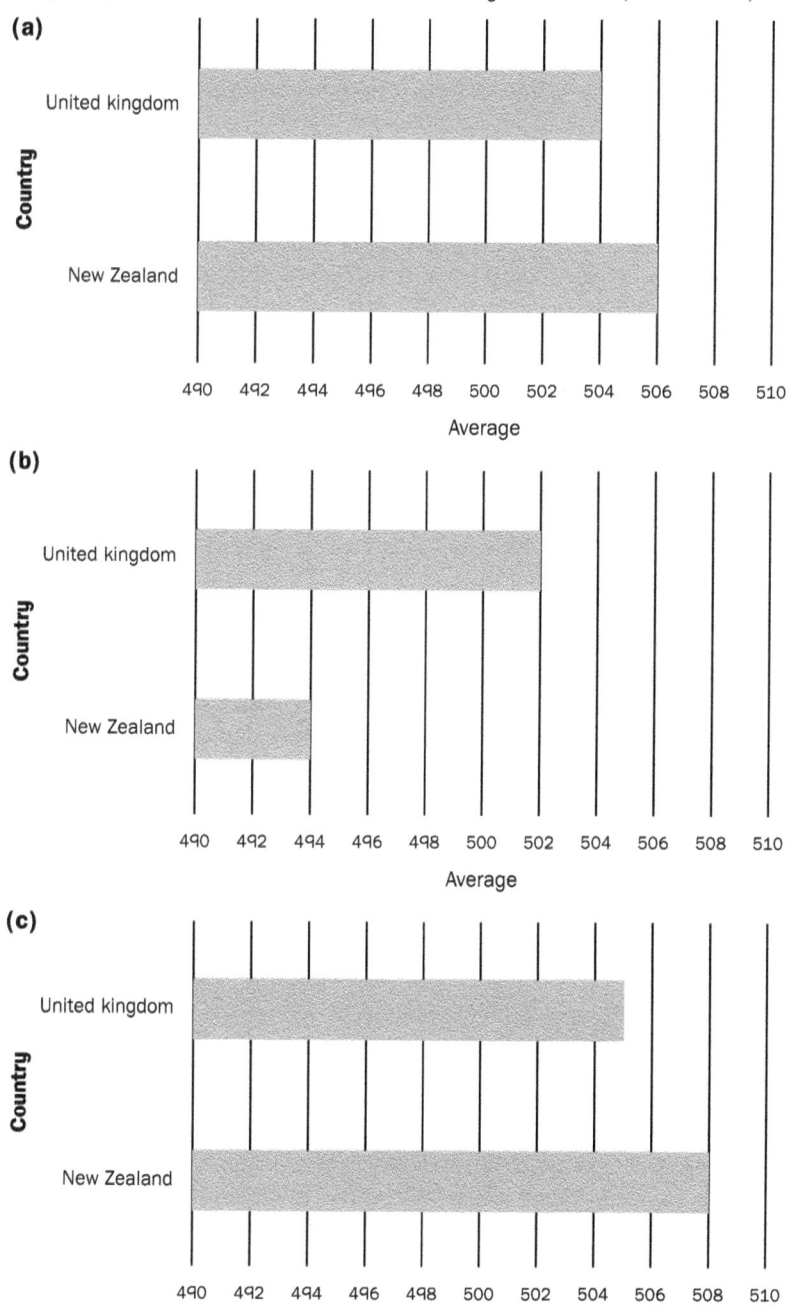

Evaluating the local from a global measurement

If we were to examine data by country, the UK for example, when we zoom into the detail of who takes the PISA survey we find out that only a small sample of UK schools have participated. That is, 170 secondary schools out of 4,190 volunteered (four per cent of all UK schools). Pupils from within these schools were subsequently randomly nominated to represent these individual schools' communities. Thus, in 2018 a total 5,174 of 15-year-old pupils took the survey out of a possible 3,258,451 pupils situated in state-funded secondary schools across the UK (Gov.uk 2021). This is 0.2 per cent of the overall population of 15-year-olds in state secondary education. These averages, taken from a small percentage of schools and even smaller percentage of overall pupils in the UK, becomes problematic when the disseminated results are making measurable generalizations that are reportedly representative of the entire country's student population (Mitchell 2006).

Not only does the researcher, who uses this type of data, have to consider if we are to generalize about an entire population in this manner through these disseminated mean averages, but we have an additional conundrum concerning participatory ethics that has thus far, in this chapter, not been considered. This 'concerns the value of participation and representation, and how we engage children [those under the age of 16] actively in the research' (Van Mechelen et al. 2020: 5). This underpins the key principles in research according to the British Educational Research Association (BERA 2018) and as discussed by Brown in Chapter I, who describes maximizing benefits but also protecting and minimizing risk or likelihood of harm for participants. To this end, obtaining informed consent from the participant is a necessary provision. Thomas (2017: 46) aptly described what voluntary informed consent is and why it must be sought:

> Because of the harm that might be caused during research involving people, an important concept when considering the ethics of research is that of consent..... This is more than a simple agreement to take part, however, it is voluntary [I]nformed consent (ibid).

BERA's (2018: 9) ethical guidelines state it is '...expected that participants [the pupils] provide voluntary informed consent to be involved in the study [and this must] be obtained at the start of the study'. However, because these students are under the age of 16, their parents'/carers' consent would also have to be obtained. This process is integral to research because, as Wilson (2015:137) stated, '...researchers have to be on their guard to ensure that coercion or undue influence... is not present' especially when minors are concerned. Details regarding informed participation are available through the technical reports (OECD 2017). At a school level, information packs are distributed to the school and thence to parents and pupils (PISA 2020; OECD 2020) but as a desk-based researcher it may be more difficult to fully source these chains of consent and to establish a connection to an individual participant's experience.

Evaluating the participants' experience

Building on this point about the individual experience underpinning the PISA datasets, an initiative entitled 'PISA for schools' (PISA 2020) was established. It was designed as a 'digital assessment to help school leaders understand their 15-year-old students' abilities to think critically and apply their knowledge creatively in novel contexts' (PISA:para.1) through a PISA-based Test for Schools (PBTS). In contrast to PISA the PBTS was designed to be seen at a national level, that is, to provide 'school-level results for benchmarking and school-improvement purposes' across the UK (PISA 2020). As of April 2020, there were 5500 schools in 10 countries that have reportedly taken part in this more localized enterprise. The notion of accountability at the national level is not new in the UK, although it might be noted that the UK as an educational entity ignores the distinctions that exist within the devolved nations (England, Wales, Northern Ireland and Scotland) and their individual curricula. For example, at the end of Key Stage 2 (ages 10–11) pupils are expected to sit exams known as summative assessment tests (SATs) for both mathematics and English. In contrast to PISA, SATs in primary school science, which were usually taken at the end of Key Stage 2, were abolished in 2009. This summative testing was reportedly halted due to the failure to produce complete and relevant information on the performance of individual children and having narrowing constraints on the teacher's ability to teach creatively (Harlen 2012) and develop the pupils' competencies. The ultimate purpose of SATs is to measure the pupil's attainment in mathematics, reading, grammar, punctuation and spelling, the results of which, described numerically through levels (1–6), are presented to those beyond the classroom, such as to parents/carers, to secondary schools to which the students are transitioning and for publicly published national performance tables (Headington 2003). Thus again, we are looking beyond the pupil (or the participant) into a public forum of accountability through descriptive frequency statistics.

It is with the individual storied narrative in mind that we will reflect on the effects of a high stakes testing regime through a personalized account of a secondary school student in the next subsection. The narrative we are about to recollect may sound like a work of fiction, but, in the words of BERA (2018: 21), we, like any good researchers, will be taking a 'fictionalized approach'. That is, the name of the town, school and the student we are about to meet have been pseudonymized to ensure confidentiality (Wilson 2015; Thomas 2017). This contrasts with the schools who take the triennial PISA survey whereby the schools' identity is not disclosed. If the school, however, chooses to take part in the PBTS then they will have the opportunity to access the PISA for Schools online network – this is a peer-learning platform that reportedly connects educators and teachers globally. Thus, these members, if they use this platform, will no longer be anonymous and neither will the teachers or teaching assistants who work within the school due to jigsaw identification. This type of identification occurs when someone can be identified by using two or more sources of information, in this case, the published PBST results and the publicly available staff list at the academic institution. The desk-based researcher needs to be aware of the potential form of inadvertent identification and adopt a further level of appropriate and respectful anonymization. They also need to be alert to the need to secure permissions and consents to use such online data.

Placing a spotlight on the unseen

Desk-based researchers, who choose to examine national and international secondary data sets, should keep in mind that they will only be viewing the decontextualized average mean of a small subsection of students. Yet it is arguably within the personalized account that the fundamental ethical dilemmas of this kind of testing regime can be illuminated. With this in mind, let us direct our attention to a 'fictionalized' narrative set in a school gymnasium.

This large, spacious room belongs to the state school called Avon Secondary and is located in the county of Middleshire. The gym contains 150 seated 15–16-year-olds. They are all busy, pens in hand, seemingly scribbling on A4 booklets. They are sitting at individual desks, in neatly ordered rows and in complete silence whilst five adults stand on the edges of the room monitoring the exam space. Two at the front, one at the side and two at the back, one of these latter two stands next to the double doors, to ensure noise levels from outside are restricted and to all intents and purposes blocking the exit. These five adults have the perceived authority over the students by ensuring the young adults adhere to the regulations and guidelines of the exams regulatory board. Forty-five minutes into the two-hour exam, one of the newly recruited invigilators, who is standing at the front of the hall, notices a student looking down at the exam paper, letting her hair cascade over her face. Nothing unusual in an exam hall but then the girls hand wipes her face and this is when droplets start to splash onto the exam paper.

The invigilator acts swiftly grabbing a handful of tissues, which are situated on a spare table to her left and walks towards the distressed pupil. As they kneel at the side of the small desk, they look under the young girl's cascading hair, directly into the student's watery eyes.

'Here, take these,' the invigilator says, as she holds up a handful of crumpled tissues.

The girl sniffs and takes the tissues. She continues to sob but this time a little more loudly and with more than the occasional sniff.

'Do you want a 10-minute break in the fresh air? I can add the time to the end of the exam if you like,' the new employee said.

The student nods.

'Okay, quietly stand up and we'll go outside just for a few minutes.'

As they get to the double doors, which are guarded by a more experienced invigilator, the newer, younger employee gets a disapproving look from their colleague.

'She's upset. She just needs a few minutes.'

The student and invigilator both exit the gym and find a space, away from the building, to sit. The young pupil continues to wipe her eyes and nose and then after what seems like a minute breaks the muffled silence.

'My mum and dad are divorcing and my nan went into hospital last week. I've not told anyone at school.' She pauses. 'And now I am going to fail my exam.'

Stunned by this outpouring of emotion, the invigilator replies, 'I am so sorry to hear that. Perhaps you should talk to someone you trust here at the school and see about getting some sort of mitigating circumstances.'

The student continues to cry for a few minutes.

'Can I finish this exam first?' the girl pupil asks. 'I just need to get in control.'

'Of course you can. When you are ready, we'll go back, but you must promise me you will talk to someone.'

After another minute or two of comforting the student, the disapproving colleague from the gym arrives.

'She needs to go back,' the more experienced colleague sternly states. 'She should not be out the hall. Five minutes is long enough.'

The girl begins crying again, this time a little more vigorously. The more experienced employee raises his eyebrows and looks directly, and somewhat uncomfortably, at the newly appointed invigilator.

'She needs a few minutes more.' A hand is placed against the young girl's back in a protective gesture.

'Time is ticking away. Do not be long,' the man answers.

'I promised her she could have an extra 10 minutes at the end.'

The elder invigilator's eyes widen, but he nods, turns around and walks back towards the gym.

The student wipes her eyes with her sleeves and continues to talk between sobs. 'I am usually an A-grade student, but everything is just getting to me. Mum, Dad and now my nan. I don't know what to do.'

'After the exam, talk to your teacher and then find someone you trust and tell them. Additionally, if you are up to it, tell the exams office too. Life is not being good to you at the moment. It's okay to be this upset,' the invigilator replies.

The girl nods and they sit there in silence for a couple more minutes, or maybe five, until the young student decides to stand up and go back to complete her exam. At the end of two hours, the rest of the students leave but the girl remains. She is given an extra 15 minutes. When she has finished, she look towards the newly recruited invigilator, as her paper is collected by the stern-looking male colleague and smile ever so slightly in the invigilator's direction. The student then turns around and walk away through the double doors. What happen next to this pupil, after she exite the room, the new invigilator never knows. But for her empathetic efforts, this fresh-faced recruit is reprimanded.

'Never to do that again without consulting me,' says the stern invigilator. 'What happens if someone else complains about her unfair treatment, her extra time?'

Reflecting on the unseen context

It is the recollection of these moments that can provide a spotlight on the individual and their lives beyond the exam hall. It can also highlight what our responsibilities are as researchers or gatekeepers of these testing regimes. So, just like a school volunteering to take part in either the PISA survey, the PBST, or a person who is perceived to be in a position of authority (akin to the invigilators), any researcher should carefully consider the power relations at play.

To begin to think about authoritative positionality, let us examine the seating arrangement in the gymnasium. In the case of the recounted story above, it was the stern invigilator, prior to the exam, who had precisely measured the gap between all the desks so that each was the same distance apart. Additionally, when the students entered the exam hall, strict guidelines were adhered to. For example, the length of the test, when it is sat and the noise levels (i.e. it must be completed in silence). This ensures that the administration of the test is appropriately handled, according to the regulations. These guidelines for the PISA and PBTS tests can be found in documents such as OECD (2021) and PISA for schools (2019). However, these protocols do not take account of the social and cultural diversity of the students and taken to the extreme, it minimizes considerations about conduct of the self and respect for individual participants.

The storied narrative above, however, only introduces us to one pupil out of 150. As she entered the gymnasium, none of us was aware that her parents were divorcing and her nan was in hospital. She had chosen not to disclose this information to anyone within the educational setting, as is her, and any participants', right not to do so. Arguably, the employee who was new to her post was vigilant to the students' needs and placed them above her more experienced colleague's pragmatic guidelines, but was she right to offer the student a break and counselling? As researchers, we are aware that we should offer participants breaks if they become visibly distressed. We are even told to offer to delete any data and stop the data collection process entirely. Obviously, the latter of these did not take place in the narrative above. Additionally, as researchers we should be aware of protocol regarding who the participant can talk to about any undisclosed issues, but simultaneously we must maintain an objective stance if they are discussed, something the invigilator did not do. Whether you think she, or the other pragmatic, more experienced colleague acted appropriately or not, there is more at play here than what is ethically right or wrong. It is at this point that we highlight how being empathic and taking an appropriate ethical pragmatic stance go hand in hand when researching. As Thomas (2017) implied at the beginning of this chapter, these authoritative privileges that are arguably perceived by those we are researching are our responsibilities, and it is in this mutual duality between balancing the pragmatic with the individual that ethical dilemma lies.

The tale recounted above was recollected in order to understand how aggregated results can mask the individual rights of the participants. When this fictionalized narrative is placed in a juxtaposition to the levelled account of the PISA studies, it illustrates how large and numerically oriented datasets have layers of social and cultural experiences hidden and unseen beneath. It is therefore incumbent on those drawing on such extant and publicly accessible datasets to present and reflect on findings in ways that can acknowledge and respect these multiple layers of experience.

Concluding thoughts

The availability of wide-ranging and large data sets offers much opportunity for desk-based research. Indeed, Cave and van Stumm (2021) reviewed the range of population cohort studies and list eight seminal studies over the past 40 years that collated and analysed data, including scholastic performance over time periods ranging between 7 and 29 years. Such a duration provides valuable opportunities for researchers to study patterns and trends across time in relation to societal and policy developments. But just because the opportunity exists, it does not mean it should be taken without due ethical consideration. Thus, such desk-bound research demands a valid and educationally legitimate rationale to avoid the pitfall of passive and objective data dredging (Plewis and Fielding 2003). This is a phenomenon that all researchers involved in the consideration of large data sets need to be actively cognizant of (Morrison 2019) and be mindful about. It is an understandable temptation to revisit such sets of data in the hope of detecting further statistically significant effects but without a theoretically sound rationale for further mining of data, academic integrity can be undermined. The pressures and demands on researchers is further explored by Wild and Brown in Chapter X. They are often measured by outputs in terms of papers and impact assessments for the purposes of the REF (Khazragui and Hudson 2014) and other accountability measures (Chubb and Watermeyer 2017).

Having focused earlier on publicly available statistics, it is worth noting the number of other datasets available for the desk-based researcher to access and draw upon. For example, the National Pupil Database (NPD) in England and Wales, which was established by the DfE in 2012 (https://find-npd-data.education.gov.uk). In recommending the greater use of these datasets, Cave and van Stumm (2021) are careful to highlight the ethical requirement for researchers to adhere to GDPR regulations in applying for access to data and in subsequent analyses. They also draw an important distinction for researchers between data that are designated as either 'safeguarded' or 'controlled'. Safeguarded data have been classified as potentially disclosive and mean that researchers are required to register with the UK data service and to accept the terms of the related end user licence. https://www.ukdataservice.ac.uk/get-data/how-to-access/conditions.aspx). Data designated as controlled, however, cannot be downloaded and accessed directly by researchers unless more stringent conditions apply and must include explicit permission form the original data owners (secure.applications@ukdataservice.ac.uk). The UK data service will also require researchers to complete mandatory training on the use of controlled data sets. There may also be other ethical preconditions that the desk-based researcher needs to have considered and in some instances actioned before they can begin to work on and with extant databases. For example, access to the NPD specifies a range of requirements including the requirement to hold a current Disclosure and Barring Service (DBS) clearance and to be accredited under the ONS-approved researcher scheme (https://www.gov.uk/guidance/how-to-access-department-for-education-dfe-data-extracts).

Extant databases offer the independent researcher tantalizing opportunities for desk-based and practicable research. However, returning to the two questions posed earlier, that is, who benefits from international surveys and what are the ethical conundrums faced by the desk-based researcher, we can see how the use of comparative quantitative findings (Higgins and Katsipataki 2016) from a publicly available dataset can help to identify 'what works', but only from a decontextualized standpoint. In relation to PISA, the casual observer of this data can know which country achieved greater, on average, attainment values through this international survey. This global testing system can, and seemingly does, benefit those countries at the top of the league table who can subsequently promote their teaching as 'best practice' under the banner of 'what works'. However, as McGregor, Frodsham and Wilson (2020) highlighted, without research evidence that is elicited through a range of forms of qualitative data it is not possible to substantiate *how* and *why* it works. Without this qualitative data, the desk-based researcher will not be able to appreciate how the disseminated best pedagogical approaches enhance the student's core competencies. Additionally, the social and cultural diversity and values of those who take part (from the school's community through to the individual participants) is missing. This globalized testing regime has also brought to bear an additional conundrum, which was summed up aptly by Cohen et al. (2018: 584), who stated that ethically 'tests should benefit the testee'. It is unclear how these comparative statistics will directly benefit those who took part, although the EEF states that good grades matter for future employment. However, we are also reminded of the girl in the examination hall, who was normally an A-grade student but was experiencing trauma due to external familial factors. Arguably, the strict regime of the exam hall was not suited to her emotional state at that time. This illuminates the potential multifaceted complexities of any individual social being, especially one who would not, and did not, benefit from being in this test environment at that point in time.

We write this chapter not to steer the researcher away from using publicly available statistics, but to leave you, the desktop researcher, with this final thought. Participants have to be considered in all elements of research from the beginning to the end (Thomas 2017: 44). Ethical considerations, therefore, begin from the moment you, the researcher, conceive of your potential research, be it empirical or library-based.

References

Bradbury, A. and Roberts-Holmes, G. (2017) *The Datafication of Primary and Early Years Education: Playing with Numbers*. Abingdon: Routledge.

BERA (British Educational Research Association) (2018) Ethical Guidelines for Educational Research. Available at: https:// www.bera.ac.uk/publication/ethical-guidelines-for-educational-research-2018 (accessed 16 February 2022).

Biesta, G. (2015) On the two cultures of educational research, and how we might move ahead: Reconsidering the ontology, axiology and praxeology of education, *European Educational Research Journal 2015*, 14(1): 11–22.

Bulle, N. (2011) Comparing OECD educational models through the prism of PISA, *Comparative Education*, 47(4): 503–521.

Cave, N. and van Stumm, S. (2021) Secondary data analysis of British population cohort studies: a practical guide for education researchers, *British Journal of Educational Psychology*, 91: 531–546.

Chubb, J. and Watermeyer, R. (2017) Artifice or integrity in the marketization of research impact? Investigating the moral economy of (pathways to) impact statements within research funding. *Studies in Higher Education*, 42(12): 2360–2372.

Cohen, L., Manion, L. and Morrison, K. (2018) *Research Methods in Education* (8th edn). London: Routledge.

Educational Endowment Fund (EEF) (2018) Improving Secondary Science: Guidance Report. Available at: https://educationendowmentfoundation.org.uk/tools/guidance-reports/improving-secondary-science/ (accessed 25 June 2019).

Gov.uk (2021) Schools, pupils and their characteristics: January 2018. Available at: https://www.gov.uk/government/statistics/schools-pupils-and-their-characteristics-january-2018. (accessed 14 November 2021).

Gov.uk (2018) National Pupil Database. Available at: https://www.gov.uk/government/collections/national-pupil-database (accessed 21 December 2021).

Guror, R. (2016) Seeing like PISA: a cautionary tale about the performativity of international assessments, *European Educational Research Journal*, 15(5): 598–616.

Harlen, W. (2009) Improving assessment of learning and for learning, *Education 3–13*, 37(3): 247–257.

Harlen, W. (2012) *Developing Policy, Principles and Practice in Primary School Science Assessment*. Available at: http://www.nuffieldfoundation.org/sites/default/files/files/Developing_policy_principles_and_practice_in_primary_school_science_assessment_Nuffield_Foundation_v_FINAL.pdf. (accessed 15 November 2021).

Headington, R. (2003) *Monitoring, Assessment, Recording, Reporting and Accountability*. London: David Fulton Publishers.

Higgins, S. and Katsipataki, M. (2016) Communicating comparative findings from meta-analysis in educational research: some examples and suggestions, *International Journal of Research and Method in Education*, 39(3): 237–254.

Hopfenbeck, T.N., Lenkeit, J., El Masri, Y. et al. (2018) Lessons learned from PISA: a systematic review of peer-reviewed articles on the Programme for International Student Assessment, *Scandinavian Journal of Educational Research*, 62(3): 333–353.

Khazragui, H. and Hudson, J. (2014) Measuring the benefits of university research: impact and the REF in the UK, *Research Evaluation*, 24(1): 51.

McGregor, D., Frodsham, S. and Wilson, H. (2020) 'The nature of epistemological opportunities for doing, thinking and talking about science: Reflections on an effective intervention that promotes creativity', *Research in Science & Technological Education*, DOI: 10.1080/02635143.2020.1799778.

Mitchell, C.J. (2006) Case and situational analysis, in T.M.S. Evens and D. Handelmann (eds) *The Manchester School. Practice and Ethnographic Praxis in Anthropology*. New York: Berghahn Books.

Moss P. (2007) Meetings Across the Paradigmatic Divide, *Educational Philosophy and Theory*, 39(3): 229–245.

Moss, P. and Urban, M. (2017) The Organisation for Economic Co-operation and Development's International Early Learning Study: What happened next? *Contemporary Issues in Early Childhood*, 18(2): 250–258.

Oancea, A. and Pring, R. (2008) The importance of being thorough: on systematic accumulations of 'what works' in education research, *Journal of Philosophy of Education,* (42) S1: 200.

Organisation for Economic Co-operation and Development (OECD) (2017) PISA for Development Strand C Technical Standards. Available at: https://www.oecd.org/pisa/pisaproducts/PISA-D%20Technical%20Standards%20OS.pdf (accessed 21 December 2021).

Organisation for Economic Co-operation and Development (OECD) (2019) PISA for Schools: A Readers Guide to the Schools Report. Available at: https://www.oecd.org/pisa/pisa-for-schools/ (accessed 13 November 2021).

Organisation for Economic Co-operation and Development (OECD) (2021a) OECD Data. Available at: https://data.oecd.org/pisa/reading-performance-pisa.htm (accessed 15 November 2021).

Organisation for Economic Co-operation and Development (OECD) (2021b) Policies for Better Lives. Available at: https://www.oecd.org/about/ (accessed 15 November 2021).

PISA (2020) General guidelines for use and availability. Available at: https://www.oecd.org/pisa/pisa-for-schools/PFS-Guidelines-for-Use-and-Availability-of-the-Assessment-August-2019.pdf (accessed 21 December 2021).

Plewis, I. and Fielding, A. (2003) What is multi-level modelling for? A critical response to Gorard, *British Journal of Educational Studies,* 51(4): 408–419.

Salganik, L.S., Rychen, D.S. and Konstant, J.W. (1999) *Projects on competencies in the OECD context, analysis of theoretical and conceptual foundations.* Neuchâtel: Education Statistics Services Institute.

Slavin, R.E. (2004) Education research can and must address 'what works' questions, *Educational Researcher,* 33(1): 27–28.

Thomas, G. (2017) *How to Do your Research Project: A Guide for Students in Education and Applied Social Sciences,* 3rd edition. London: Sage.

Van Mechelen, M., Baykal, G.E., Dindler, C., Eriksson, E. and Iversen, O.S. (2020) '18 years of ethics in child-computer interaction research: A systematic literature review'. Presented at ACM Interaction Design and Children (IDC) Conference 2020, London, 10 June.

Wilson, M. (2015) Ethical considerations, in G. Butt (ed.) *MasterClass in Geography Education: Transforming Teaching and Learning.* London: Bloomsbury.

IX Starting with Self: Researching as an Insider

Jane Spiro

Introduction

This chapter aims to interrogate the ethical issues connected with making oneself, one's practice or practice environment, the focus of research. Approaches in which the researcher is explicit within the research are numerous and include: auto-ethnography in which everything in one's natural setting has the potential to be research data (see Roth 2009; Reed-Dunahay 2021); action research as the study of one's own practice and its impact on the practice environment (Coghlan and Shani 2005; McNiff 2013); narrative research as the study of personal stories and the interrogation of these as sources of knowledge (Specter-Mersel 2010; Andrews et al. 2013); and living theories or the study of personal values and their embodiment in practice (see *Educational Journal of Living Theories* https//ejolts.org). These approaches share the position that the insider perspective is a contribution to, rather than a threat to, the validity of the research. Insiders offer insights that richly enhance research acquired through positivist and scientific approaches, for example, how teachers really experience the teaching of phonics (see Meyer 2001) or the real processes by which headteachers turn around challenging schools (Turner and Mavin 2008; Laar 2017). These forms of enquiry are positioned very differently from research that claims to be objective, distanced from the self and freed from individual bias. They, in fact, claim the opposite – that the very insider voice that makes it subjective also provides the contribution to knowledge. This contribution does not claim to be generalizable, but rather to have the potential for readers/researchers to find parallels in their own context and to be sufficiently evidenced to be trustworthy (Bassey 2000). Such approaches have been legitimated in the past two decades. Researcher-as-self paradigms have been published in recognized academic journals, (for example *Qualitative Research; Reflective Practice, Narrative Inquiry*), received high quality research ratings, been showcased by publishers such as Sage, Taylor Francis and Prentice Hall, embedded into research methods programmes and gathered a critical mass of doctoral dissertations. (See for example www.actionresearch.co.uk.)

This does not mean, however, that there are no longer questions to ask. On the contrary, asking questions about the rigour and validity of research, its contribution to knowledge and its ethical position are continuous and all researchers need to subject themselves to these questions. This is particularly so where core principles can be construed in several different ways that at face value appear contradictory. This chapter grapples with these apparent contradictions for researcher-focused researchers and explores the challenge of negotiating core principles so these are meaningful in different kinds of research. Section 1 looks at core ethical values and the potential conflicts for the insider-researcher. Section 2 involves the voices of researchers-of-the-self, discussing their responses to ethical questions about their research. Section 3 looks at examples of insider research projects as they arrive at solutions to the difficult fit between insider research and the varied received interpretations of ethical core values. Section 4 makes recommendations for building bridges between insider researchers and ethics committees, as they work towards a shared community of practice that allows researchers across paradigms to learn from one another.

Section 1 Researching the self and core ethical values

It has become a matter of urgency to consider the ethical positioning of researchers whose focus of enquiry is their own practice and themselves within it because the past two decades have changed expectations of the researcher–practitioner. Teacher education programmes build in reflective development as expectation; research methods programmes include action research, narrative and autoethnographies as routine options; and practitioners as part of their ongoing development are expected to track and evidence their own development. In parallel to this, positivist and scientific research communities have come to recognize that knowledge from insider experience and practice complements and expands the knowledge yielded by quantitative methods. For example, statistics about teacher attrition are enriched by narratives that explain teacher exits and returns to the profession (Harfitt 2015; Borman and Dowling 2017). The narratives of BME students in higher education provide the lived stories behind statistics revealing an attainment gap (see Cotton et al. 2016). Thus, a shared understanding of ethical principles is essential for diverse kinds of research to inform one another as equal partners and with a common ethical foundation.

International research such as AMA (2001) (American Medical Association) names three principles which are fundamental to research that includes human subjects: respect for persons, beneficence and justice. Though springing from the medical professions, these form a gold standard of ethical quality across all disciplines, for example: BERA (see updated framework 2018 and discussion by Brown in Chapter I) and AERA (2000); education and science councils such as ESRC (2019) (Education and Science Research Council). Yet, whilst these principles are widely endorsed, what remains contentious is how they are interpreted and realized within very different research paradigms, one newly emerging relative to the other.

Respect for participants is clearly the bedrock of ethical research. Whilst caring and nurturing professions such as medicine, nursing and education assume a principle of beneficence towards their participants, this cannot be left to chance. Seldon (2017) describes the 'whistleblower' Dr Maurice Pappworth who revealed the extent of unethical behaviour amongst medical practitioners supposedly honouring the Hippocratic oath. Nor can 'respect for participants' be defined in the abstract. It needs to be anatomized into acts which can be demonstrated and evidenced, namely informed consent, confidentiality and voluntary participation (see also Brown, Chapter I).

Informed consent

Respect for participants entails their right to be

> informed about the likely risks involved in the research and of potential consequences for participants, and to give their informed consent before participating in research. (AERA 2000 II.B.1)

To be fully informed places the burden on the researcher to explain, with transparency and honesty, what participation involves, its purpose and consequences. At face value this seems uncontentious. However, to inform transparently presupposes a number of conditions. Firstly, that the participants share the language of the researcher, and that the research complexity can be adequately and accurately conveyed to a non-specialist audience. Secondly, that the purpose and methods of the project are predetermined and unchangeable from the start. Thirdly, that the moment when a participant gives informed consent is the moment research can begin; any knowledge emerging before this moment of consent cannot contribute to the pool of ethically gathered data. This clean-cut separation between informal interactions and formally gathered data is not so self-evident where research knowledge emerges from the natural, organic and uninterrupted.

Each of these presuppositions could present problems for the researcher themselves or their own practice. In an action research paradigm, research outcomes change in the light of new data, so aims and strategies cannot be definitively explained in advance. In an auto-ethnography, everyone in the researcher's setting is a potential source of learning and it is difficult to separate organically occurring natural interactions from those designed into a research project. In some contexts, such as the sensitive data gathering of an anthropologist, or the building of rapport with children, information sheets and forms to fill in might crush, rather than build, trust and the richly informative moment might be lost.

Confidentiality: anonymity and naming

Respect for participants also includes the right to privacy. This means none of the data can be traced back to a specific institution or individual. This protects the participant when they may be sharing information that puts them at risk personally or professionally. It is also important where research might reflect negatively on specific institutions or individuals. The purpose of ethical research is to make a positive difference, not to expose or discredit participants or places.

Again, these principles seem uncontentious. Yet the researcher whose focus is her own practice clearly needs to identify as both researcher and researched. However far pseudonyms or numerical identities are used, or however the voices are camouflaged, the researcher's own context is thus suggested. It is insider researchers in conversation with ethics committees who have confronted this dilemma and sought to find compromises. One of these is to reveal identities essential to the research (for example, the name of the researchers themselves) whilst anonymizing those whose identities are not essential. In addition, since there is a risk of exposure, data entering the public domain needs to reflect positively and manifest beneficence in relation to all its participants. A duty of care falls on the researcher that any data that might be traceable to an individual or institution will not cause harm, offence or discredit; and in some cases where this is not possible, research might need to be withheld.

Voluntary involvement and beneficence

Respect for participants also means they have the freedom consciously and voluntarily to opt into research, knowing its purpose and benefits and understanding their own role in it.

Where a context is constructed for research purposes, the route to voluntarily opting in is more straightforward, for example, to choose to participate in an interview, complete a questionnaire or join a focus group. But a characteristic of researching the self is that daily practice is itself a source of knowledge. Researching the impact of new policy on a school may require an analysis of the organic life of the school as it responds to change, not the dynamics of a control group constructed for the purposes of enquiry. In other words, acting naturally within the daily context *becomes* participation in the research. To opt out of the research context would be to opt out of one's natural interactions and setting. However, this is problematic from an ethical perspective – privacy laws prescribe opting in as a voluntary proactive act and researchers are required to pre-empt the risk of any individual being a participant simply by accident, or by virtue of being in their usual place at the usual time. (See Hammersley and Traianou 2012.)

Many researchers of the self may take as self-evident that their work has a benign design. To work towards a benign betterment of others is the very foundation and essence of practice professions, such as teaching, nursing and law. Yet ethical principles have needed to deconstruct this trust, and for a good reason. Pappworth, the whistleblower noted earlier (Seldon 2017), observed multiple instances of practice dangerous to patients taken by doctors under the Hippocratic oath. This worst-case scenario may be many miles distant for the educational researcher, yet ethics for all human subjects has, of necessity, needed to abide by the same measures to stop such abuse ever happening again. This means beneficence cannot be assumed, and the qualities that make a research setting benign will always need to be evidenced.

Every researcher of self and practice needs to struggle with these dilemmas and identify where their own data gathering encroaches on the rights of someone else. It is important to learn how insiders and ethics committees have confronted these risks and continued to honour core principles whilst still giving the research design scope for insider data collection. (See Nolen and Vander Putten, 2007 for further analysis of these dilemmas.)

Justice: power, fairness and bias

The researcher of their own practice has much to contribute to knowledge on the one hand; they may understand the research setting deeply, be sensitive to knowledge not visible on the surface, be aware of pre-histories not known to outsiders and hidden cultures that might otherwise be missed (see Cochran and Lytle 2007; Mears 2017). Yet on the other hand, this sensitive relationship carries with it an inherent danger. By the nature of the researcher–researched relationship, the former has power; it is the researcher who formulates the hypotheses, designs the research instruments and chooses how to analyse and present the findings. This is the case, and needs to be carefully mitigated, in any research project (Jones et al. 2006; Brinkmann and Kvale 2018; Cohen et al. 2018), even more so when the researcher is an insider to the research setting. The first danger is that of over-personalization. The personal lens may skew or bias the emerging knowledge, assuming the researcher position is shared by others. The way data is analysed may silence those who do not fit the desired message (Jones et al. 2006; Flick 2018). In addition, there is likely to have been a connection between researcher and researched that significantly pre-dates the research design, whether teacher–student, leader–team member, peer to peer, and which may make the data unreliable (see Norton 2007; Brooks et al. 2014). These relationships belong to power systems; they are not free-standing and cannot claim to be impartial. Students may wish to please their teachers whilst peers or colleagues may connect their participation with promotion or acceptance in the team.

These kinds of questions have meant that insider research has taken its place alongside more scientific models only gradually, painstakingly and over decades. It has been able to do so because insider researchers have worked hard to mitigate the dangers described above, developing robust dialogue with ethics committees. To be ethical not only protects participants, it also ensures the rigour of the research design. Insider researchers have found solutions such as: working alongside an 'outsider' to verify their own position (Dhillon and Thomas 2019); inviting an outsider to analyse their data independently to compare interpretations; and gathering outsider data about themselves or their practice to shed light on their own insider experience (see Cypress 2017). In the next section, we hear the voices of educational researchers as they navigate ethical dilemmas in order to research themselves or their practice.

Section 2 Researching the self and researcher voices

This section considers what these ethical dilemmas really mean for education practitioner researchers. The participants in this section were part of a research ethics project conducted by Brown et al. (2020), asking how educational researchers related to their research ethics committees. Twenty-four people came forward in an open call for participants, which included two networks that represented researchers of self, their own practice or practice environment. An anonymized questionnaire included questions concerning the researcher–ethics committee relationship, but the following are of most relevance for the purposes of this chapter:

- In your opinion are there specific tensions between research ethics committees and education research?
- If you answered yes to the question above, please could you provide examples?
- Are there any other aspects of education research that increase ethical complexity?

Responses are classified here to map alongside the ethical principles discussed in Section 1.

Informed consent

One of the issues suggested above was the timing of informed consent, so that informally 'noticed' knowledge is separated from formally gathered data. Where there is specific intervention, as in medical research, this timing is clear but the educational researchers in this network note how much more difficult this is when researching one's own practice. For example, writes one educational researcher, when

> teaching innovation is a routine part of work, you get student evaluations/ evidence to show that it is successful and then want to present at conference/write up in journal as case study — at what point should ethical approval have been sought? My institution doesn't allow retrospective ethics applications, but there can be a very blurred line between teaching and research that makes it difficult.

The difficulty of articulating informed consent for a non-specialist audience was also suggested. One researcher describes the problem of consent and information forms couched in language that makes no sense to the participants:

> Ethics committee requirements, also, to present information for participants in a particular format and using particular wording can lead to modes of presentation which are difficult to understand and potentially off-putting for some.

This problem is even more evident where participant information needs to be communicated to children (see Capewell, Chapter XI in this volume). One informant complained that

> Sometimes the ethics committee has suggested a strategy that is simply impractical: e.g. participant information sheets for 5-year-olds.

This chapter mentioned earlier that action researcher's goals change in the light of new information, and the sources of this information cannot always be precisely predicted. As an example, one educational researcher describes gathering consent for children's sharing of written work. She had not predicted the value of children's drawings as a contribution to her research and had not built this into the consent forms. The ethics committee therefore 'disallow(ed) important visual data of how children work together'. This informant goes on to say:

> The more iterative nature of qualitative approaches can be difficult to articulate. Anything that involves children in the classroom increases ethical complexity, specifically due to the issues around informed consent and right to withdraw. If a researcher is conducting a class observation, can the children in the room give informed consent? What happens if they choose not to take part? These issues are central to the ethical dilemma in my opinion. For studies involving individual children (particularly those with SEND) how do we ensure that the research does not contribute to their 'otherisation'?

She mourned the difficulty, therefore, of focusing research attention on children with special needs, even though this was her intention, because the consent of children with cognitive or literacy challenges would always be contentious. 'It was easier in the end not to differentiate them, but the research ended up quite different to my intentions: useful, but not the same.'

Confidentiality and anonymized data

Several participants in the anonymized questionnaire raised issues related to confidentiality. They mentioned participants who wanted to be named, and were uneasy having ideas, information or narratives specific to them anonymized. Some felt they had lost agency in the anonymizing of their knowledge. Particularly so was this the case in the creative arts.

> In art and design, anonymity in talking about creative work is in tension with acknowledging artists.

One researcher describes the importance of contextual and insider knowledge when researching an institution. This places at risk the core principle of confidentiality.

> [S]ome 'gold-standards' such as anonymized data might not be possible in e.g. action research or small-scale case studies, or even when participants want to go 'on the record'.

> Insisting on anonymization of institutions as well as individuals (e.g. in school-based research) can also lead to the loss of important contextual information at the point of analysis, and make it difficult for participants to verify or check documents/outputs at a later stage.

Participants raised questions about ownership of data where rich narratives had been shared. Who has power over those narratives? If a participant who shared a narrative wishes to own it (for example, as a creative and named work) does he/she have power to do so if it has become part of research data for another person's project? At which point does the use of participant stories become appropriation of their stories? One participant felt that, even after ethical approval of a narrative research project, she began to feel uneasy about her control of important participant stories, and especially so where they wished to own them.

Voluntary involvement and beneficence

It is intrinsic to educational professionals that their goal is to enhance and benefit others. Yet, in the clarification of research ethics, nothing can be left to chance. Researchers-of-the-self and of personal practice may work for the best with passionate conviction, but this cannot be presumed where ethics are concerned.

> Action research entails research of one's own practice and learners, which raises issues of trust – not only between researcher-practitioner and their learners, but more problematically between action-researcher and the research committee. I say more problematic, because action researchers do work out careful and committed strategies to be fair, beneficial, and transparent to their participants; but these strategies are not always trusted by research panels.

Several participants struggled with the fact that the beneficence at the heart of their practice was misunderstood and mistrusted by non-educators.

> Beneficial learning between teacher-learner can be deemed by research panels to be 'coercion'. Organic and naturalistic research embedded into good practice can be seen by ethics panels to be interventionist.

The processes required to make their benign intent transparent meant some research had to be abandoned altogether. One participant describes her difficulty as director of studies wishing to research her own student community.

> Our ethical process makes it too difficult to collect data from our own students. Power relationships should definitely be considered carefully, but as programme director I then can't collect any data from students on my programme, but other staff members may not have the relevant experience to be able to conduct research that closely aligns to the programme.

Imposed standards suggest to principled practitioners a lack of trust. One participant felt that there was a 'lack of understanding, respect and acceptance of the ethical stance of educators'. She described ethical standards within her profession included 'values of care, respect, integrity and trust which far outstrip the usual institutional ethical committee guidelines'. In this climate of un-ease one educator describes an MA student asked by the ethics committee, 'Could you assure us that the students will be returned to the condition in which you found them?' She explained that 'transforming students for the better, expanding their lives, aspirations and minds' is what educators aim to do every day; yet 'intervention' or change is associated with negativity 'in the language of ethics'.

The participants suggest a gulf between the benign values of their profession and the need to evidence it – ethical conditions which they found to be restrictive, excessive, and indicative of lack of trust.

> There seems to be a lack of understanding about what happens in a primary classroom so restrictions are put in place not supportive of good research or compatible with classroom life.

The ethics committee's role as a gatekeeper of the law makes risk aversion inevitable. Changes in the law, such as GDPR (2018) have made voluntary opt-in essential and ethics committees more wary of the 'assumed beneficence' underlying researcher–researched relationships. Many of the participants reported an exaggerated sense of risk as a result, and restrictions which made them change research direction, or sometimes abandon research ideas altogether, as with the programme director above.

Ethics committees are becoming increasingly and inappropriately intrusive and frequently create unnecessary difficulties for researchers when there are no real ethical concerns.

> I think the current climate is making many people and establishments (in all sorts of areas) risk averse.
> in my view, the ethics committee has a tendency to see fairly straightforward matters through an exaggeratedly cautious lens that magnifies ethical sensitivities and vulnerabilities.

However, educational researchers describe mutual learning taking place as ethics boards and researchers-of-the-self resolve dilemmas and these resolutions begin to provide clear and helpful precedents. One participant describes an ideal world of collaboration with ethics committees, when they work with researchers-of-the self as 'on a safe, well-trodden path in good company with other universities worldwide'. This means educational researchers recognize the need for protocols and processes, whilst ethics committees appreciate the need to individualize their responses to proposals.

> I do appreciate the need for some common processes and protocols, but ethical working is premised on relationships of trust between academics and

research subjects, and often requires more individual and tailored overviewing of applications for research clearance.

Conversely, however, some of the participants spoke from the perspective of the ethics committee. They struggled with practitioner colleagues who felt their relationship with participants did not require further scrutiny and who had not sufficiently made transparent their ways of mitigating power imbalance. It emerges as urgent and essential that researchers-of-the-self and ethics committees start to use, or understand, the same language as they make their core claims to beneficence both transparent and tailored to suit their research endeavour.

Section 2 has provided a rare insider commentary that tracks a continuing unease between researchers of self and practice and the way core ethical principles are interpreted. There are mismatches regarding the transparency of values such as beneficence, methodological problems in the need for informed consent, areas which become out of bounds using ethical interpretations of power and justice and situations where anonymity is more problematic than naming. Whilst these are indeed areas of complexity, researchers-of-the-self have now worked with ethics panels worldwide over more than two decades to find new ways of meeting ethical issues midway. Section 3 considers some of these.

Section 3 Researching the self: process and principles

This section turns attention to research projects that have grappled with these core ethical principles and arrived at solutions and new theory that reaches a more nuanced understanding of core ethical principles.

Insider-outsider partnerships

One approach taken by researchers-of-the-self has been to work alongside a co-researcher to provide an outsider perspective that balances, repositions and triangulates insider knowledge.

Milligan's study (2016) with secondary school children in West Kenya created a partnership between herself as outsider and insider participants. She suggested the idea of 'inbetween' participation, where researchers work in partnerships with others who have different degrees of proximity to their subject. This mutual exchange is reflected too in the study of social communities. Dhillon and Thomas (2019) researched the experience of Sikh families in Britain. One of the researchers was an insider to this community (a Sikh), and brought to the research study cultural knowledge, sensitivity to the needs and expectations of the participant group and knowledge of the histories behind and beyond the data. The other researcher was a non-Sikh and an outsider to the specific community, although an insider to the experience of migration and otherness. Their study found that the insider–outsider distinction was not so easy a polarity and that the researchers did not form as clear-cut a divide between insider and outsider. They found that 'established binary polarities – such as insider/outsider' do not capture the complexity of co-researcher ethics. Instead, they suggest 'a more nuanced conceptualization' that takes account of multiple researcher positions and relationships between researcher and researched (Dhillon and Thomas 2019: 442).

Demirbag and Spiro (2018) is another example of insider–outsider co-researching. Here I, the co-author, researched the re-emergence of Hawaiian as an Indigenous language and culture alongside an insider-educator of the Hawaiian context. As with Dhillon and Thomas (2019), insider and outsider shared a common research enquiry. As insider, Romero Demirbag shared narratives of herself, relearning a recently silenced culture and then becoming an educator of that culture. As an outsider, I was able to ask about words that appeared to carry profound but tacit values, for example, *aina* and *aloha* – words that are windows into Hawaiian cosmology and philosophy. The different positioning meant that 'layers' of the story were unfolded to clarify meanings that were opaque to an outsider. As with Milligan's notion (2016) of the 'inbetween', the insider–outsider polarity was helpful, but far from clear-cut. Both researchers felt there were ways in which we were insiders (for example, having been brought up on the island, or having family growing up there), yet partly outsiders (in not being native speakers of Hawaiian).

However the insider–outsider spectrum may be conceptualized and nuanced, the combined positions of two researchers working side by side with a common research purpose but different relationships to the data provide a relatable methodology for the researcher-of-the-self. Issues of power relationships with participants might be more subtly and sensitively mediated by the insider researcher, whilst the outsider researcher might provide impartiality and distance between data and researcher.

Theorizing an ethics of care and reflection as method

Costley and Gibbs (2006) describe the dilemma of practitioner-researchers whose role by definition entails care for others. They review doctorate students in the UK and Cyprus as they undertake insider research into their own practice as community workers. They explain that, as insiders, they are different to other researchers who are able simply to 'leave the context of their research space'. Being compassionately and professionally connected to their research space, and to individuals within this, they argue for an enhanced 'ethics of care' (Costley and Gibbs 2006: 89).

Developing their theory over time, and with multiple projects amongst community and care doctorate-practitioners, they discuss how this ethic of care might be built into research methods, with reflective diary writing as a way for researchers to reflect and articulate the complexities of their approach to ethical considerations in their research (Gibbs and Costley 2006: 239).

In other words, their research design built in constant vigilance by researchers as to their relationship with participants, over and beyond the main methods and strategies set up within the research design. Briganti (2018) shares her ethical proposal to the University of Cumbria, explaining her theory of care based on respect for participants.

In her research, participants are seen, not as 'objects or sources of data' but rather as co-creators of 'knowledge on various issues such as poverty, human capabilities, sustainable (generative) development'. This co-creation and mutual influence also leads the researcher to 'improve [her] practice as a development worker through [her] own learning, the learning of others and the learning of social formations' (Briganti 2018 http://www.actionresearch.net/writings/ari/arianonethics14-02-17.pdf).

Briganti's ethics application explains that engagement as a development worker and researcher of her practice cannot be separated, but that both are founded on a fully transparent and consistently evidenced respect for her informants. This relationship is sensitive, complex and ever-changing. Her design entails extensive reflection about her role alongside her participants, through dialogue, diaries and self-checking.

Care and co-creation

A further example of care determining research direction and methods is a project engaged in by the current author and leading to the chapter 'The path less travelled' (Spiro and Crisfield 2018). The research project aimed to look at the impact of a training programme on a whole school approach to language policy. The training programme was co-facilitated by the researchers, but the aim was to discover if explicit development in language pedagogy made a difference to teacher attitudes to children with first languages other than English. A focus on the children themselves may have put undue pressure on both the children and teachers to demonstrate change during the period of the project. Children change at their own pace and rate, and the impact of a new pedagogy or policy may manifest results only gradually over time. The research, for this reason, refocused not on the children but on teacher perceptions and how far these were suggested by teacher use of classroom physical spaces, for example, the use of language labels, pictures, the whiteboard for summarizing and planning the day, and book corners for extensive reading at different levels. As we made observations of physical changes noted in the classrooms, these were shared and discussed with the teachers in focus groups and one-to-one interviews so the data could be co-created with the teachers. This meant the teachers had complete control over what was shared and what was made visible. It also meant they could focus on their teaching and the children themselves, without the research redirecting their focus. An 'ethic of care' and a co-creation of data were values that guided the research and the choice of data that was collected.

Insider researchers have been highly inventive in finding ways of demonstrating care and co-creating knowledge to rebalance participant-researcher power. Palaiologou (2017) describes research with young children using vignettes, or situations constructed from her insider knowledge as an action researcher. In constructing these vignettes, insider stories have been anonymized, distanced from specific individuals or places, and reframed as situations to explore *with* the children rather than about them. These are just some of the many examples in the public domain as researchers navigate the ethics of researching the self (See Gladwell 2001; Mercer 2007 for further examples).

Section 4 Building bridges: the insider researcher and a shared language of ethics

The survey conducted by Brown et al. (2020) invited educational researchers to share examples or ideas for best practice in working alongside their ethics committees. Four helpful strategies emerged that built bridges between researchers-of-the-self and ethics panels.

Firstly, informal dialogue between researcher and ethics committee was most frequently mentioned as a helpful way forward.

> an informal chat about my project before I completed the application paperwork. This meant that I was able to meet the people involved and that helped to demystify the process. I then felt able to ask questions whilst completing my application and the whole process felt more like a collaboration.

One-to-one conversation with the relevant research ethics officer.

> talking through potential responses and considerations to be negotiated

One participant noted how helpful it was to be contacted by 'a panel member initiating a conversation to clarify detail and help get the application to approval'. Another valued conversation concerning legal requirements – 'Most important thing is advising on appropriate data handling to ensure privacy and security'.

Secondly the opportunity to defend an ethics application more formally at the final stage was also suggested. One participant who had set this up for her students noted how much it had helped them appreciate the kind of questions ethics panels asked. The dialogue helped them articulate their theoretical positions and recognize gaps in their applications, but, conversely, it allowed ethics panels to appreciate more deeply the core values of practitioners and where these created conflict and ambiguity.

Thirdly, being connected with like-minded researchers further along the ethics application route was seen as very helpful and something that could be facilitated by ethics panels. It is useful to identify precedents and the ways they have navigated similar challenges, so researchers-of-the-self build a community of shared best practice.

Fourthly, teacher-researcher participation in research panels was seen as one of the most effective ways of building bridges. Inviting teacher researchers 'to serve as internal, external and community members of university research committees' (Nolen and Vander Putten 2007: 407) would serve several purposes. It would allow the teacher-researcher to be an insider to the research ethics process, rather than an outsider working with a different ethical language. It would entail development for the researcher, recognizing the gatekeeper role of the ethics committee, internalizing, and owning it within their own research paradigm. Importantly, it would also give ethics committees a perspective on the researcher-of-the-self paradigm, its dilemmas and its values, so the varied approaches to research come closer to one another in the spirit of mutual understanding (see Brown et al. 2020 for further development of these points).

At the start of this chapter, we noted the urgency for insider researchers to arrive at shared ethical values with researchers of other paradigms. We have seen that educators share similar ethical dilemmas as other care professions, such as community work and social care, and some solutions might usefully transfer from one setting to the other. What these professions have in common is the place of care and nurturing at the heart of practice and research. Educational researchers in this chapter described the fact that change and intervention emanate from this ethic of care, the wish to empower learners to find and fulfil their best selves. In addition, we have met researchers interrogating and improving their own practice through research, developing as professionals alongside developing as researchers, with the two closely bound together. Yet these two hallmarks of the researcher-of-self – the assumption of care and the valued role of self – require meticulous justification to be ethically compliant. What ethics committees require, and what researchers-of-the-self are energetically doing, is to interrogate each research question rigorously: how to gather informed consent in a language that makes sense to its participants; how to manage anonymity in a self-focused study; and how to mitigate bias or negotiate power when a researcher researches their own setting. These questions have led to nuanced, finely grained solutions, of which there are several in this chapter: new ideas of the researcher as 'inbetweener'; new methods such as partnered insider–outsider researchers; and new ways of co-creating data with participants. These are examples of the fact that ethical dilemmas, rather than closing down insider researchers, have made their endeavour ever more robust as they enter into rigorous and constructive dialogue with ethics committees about who they are, what they value and what the goals and purposes are of the educational research endeavour.

References

AERA (American Educational Research Association) (2000) *Ethical standards of the American Educational Research Association.* Available at: https://www.aera.net/About-AERA/AERA-Rules-Policies/Professional-Ethics (accessed 20 December 2021).

AMA (American Medical Association) (2001) *Council on Ethical and Judicial Affairs: Ethical considerations in international research.* Available at: https://www.ama-assn.org/delivering-care/ethics/code-medical-ethics-overview (accessed 20 December 2021).

Andrews, M., Squire, C. and Tamboukou, M. (eds) (2013) *Doing Narrative Research.* London: Sage.

Bassey, M. (2000) Fuzzy generalisations and best estimates of trustworthiness: a step towards transforming research knowledge about learning into effective teaching practice. Paper presented at the ESRC Teaching and Learning Research Programme First Annual Conference, University of Leicester.

BERA (British Educational Research Association) (2018) Ethical Guidelines for Educational Research. Available at: https://www.bera.ac.uk/publication/ethical-guidelines-for-educational-research-2018 (accessed 20 December 2021).

Borman, G.D. and Dowling, N.M. (2017) Teacher attrition and retention: a meta-analytic and narrative review of the research, *Review of Educational Research*, 78(3): 367–409.

Briganti, A. (2018) Ethics application: University of Cumbria. Available at: http://www.actionresearch.net/writings/ari/arianonethics14-02-17.pdf) (accessed 20 December 2021).

Brinkmann, S. and Kvale, S. (2018) *Doing Interviews*. London: Sage.

Brooks, R., Riele, K. and Maguire, M. (2014) *Ethics and Education Research*. London: Sage.

Brown, C., Spiro, J. and Quinton, S. (2020) The role of research ethics: friend or foe in educational research? An exploratory study, *British Educational Research Journal*, 46(4): 747–769.

Cochran-Smith, M. and Lytle, S. (2007) Everything's ethics: practitioner inquiry and university culture, in A. Campbell and S. Groundwater-Smith (eds) *An Ethical Approach to Practitioner Research*. Abingdon: Routledge.

Coghlan, D. and Shani, A.R. (2005) Roles, politics, and ethics in action research design, *Systemic Practice and Action Research*, 18(6): 533–546.

Cohen, L., Manion, L. and Morrison, K. (2018) *Research Methods in Education* (8th edn). Abingdon: Routledge.

Costley, C. and Gibbs, P. (2006) Researching others: care as an ethic for practitioner researchers, *Studies in Higher Education*, 31(1): 89–98.

Cotton, D.R.E., Joyner, M., George, R. et al. (2016) Understanding the gender and ethnicity attainment gap in UK higher education, *Innovations in Education and Teaching: International*, 53: 475–486.

Cypress, B.S. (2017) Rigor or reliability and validity in qualitative research: perspectives, strategies, reconceptualization, and recommendations, *Dimensions of Critical Care Nursing* 7/8, 36(4): 253–263.

Demirbag, J.R. and Spiro, J. (2018) Connecting students to a sense of place: reviving Hawaii, in J. Spiro, and E. Crisfield, 2018 *Linguistic and Cultural Innovation in Schools*. Palgrave Macmillan.

Dhillon, J.K. and Thomas, N. (2019) Ethics of engagement and insider-outsider perspectives: issues and dilemmas in cross-cultural interpretation, *International Journal of Research and Method in Education*, 42(4): 442–453.

ESRC (Economic and Social Research Council) (2019) Our Core Principles. Available at: https://esrc.ukri.org/funding/guidance-for-applicants/research-ethics/our-core-principles/ (accessed 2 August 2019).

Flick, U. (2018) *Designing Qualitative Research*. London: Sage.

GDPR (2018) General Data Protection Regulation, https://www.local.gov.uk/our-support/guidance-and-resources/general-data-protection-regulation, https://www.local.gov.uk/our-support/guidance-and-resources/general-data-protection-regulation, Accessed 13th December 2021.

Gibbs, P. and Costley, C. (2006) An ethics of community and care for practitioner researchers, *International Journal of Research and Method in Education*, 29(2): 239–249.

Gladwell, G. (2001) *The Ethics of Personal, Narrative, Subjective Research.* Brock University in October. Available at: http://www.living.actionresearch.net/writings/values/gsgma.PDF

Hammersley, M., and Traianou, A. (2012) *Ethics and Educational Research.* Available at: https://www.bera.ac.uk/publication/ethics-and-educational-research (accessed 2 August 2019).

Harfitt, J.G. (2015) From attrition to retention: a narrative inquiry of why beginning teachers leave and then rejoin the profession, *Asia-Pacific Journal of Teacher Education*, 43(1) 22–35.

Jones, S., Torres, V. and Arminio, J. (2006) *Negotiating the Complexities of Qualitative Research in Higher Education.* Abingdon: Routledge.

Laar, B. (2017) *Primary Heads: Exceptional Leadership in Primary Schools*, Carmarthen, Wales: Crown Publishing.

McNiff, J. (2013) *Action Research: Principles and Practice.* Abingdon: Routledge.

Mears, C. (2017) In-depth interviews, in R. Coe, M. Waring, L. Hedges and J. Arthur (eds) *Research Methods and Methodologies in Education.* London: Sage.

Mercer, J. (2007) The challenges of insider research in educational institutions: wielding a double-edged sword and resolving delicate dilemmas, *Oxford Review of Education*, 33(1): 1–17.

Meyer, R.J. (2001) *Phonics exposed: Understanding and resisting systematic direct intense phonics instruction.* Routledge.

Milligan, L. (2016) Insider-outsider-inbetweener? Researcher positioning, participative methods and cross-cultural educational research, *Compare: A Journal of Comparative and International Education*, 46(2): 235–250, DOI: 10.1080/03057925.2014.928510.

Nolen, A.L. and Vander Putten, J. (2007) Action research in education: addressing gaps in ethical principles and practice, *Educational Researcher*, 36(7): 401–407.

Norton, L. (2007) Pedagogical research in higher education: ethical issues facing the practitioner – researcher, in A. Campbell and S. Groundwater-Smith (eds) *An Ethical Approach to Practitioner Research.* Abingdon: Routledge.

Palaiologou, I. (2017) The use of vignettes in participatory research with young children, *International Journal of Early Years Education* 25(3): 308–322.

Reed-Danahay, D. (ed.) (2021) *Auto/ethnography: Rewriting the Self and the Social.* Abingdon: Routledge.

Roth, W.M. (2009) Auto/ethnography and the question of ethics, *Forum Qualitative Sozialforschung/Forum: Qualitative Social Research*, 10(1).

Seldon, J. (2017) *The Whistleblower: The Story of Maurice Pappworth.* Buckingham: University of Buckingham Press.

Spector-Mersel, G. (2010) Narrative research: time for a paradigm, *Narrative Inquiry*, 20(1): 204–224.

Spiro, J. and Crisfield, E. (2018) The road less travelled. In Spiro, J. and Crisfield, E. *Linguistic and Cultural Innovation in Schools.* London: Palgrave Macmillan.

Turner, J. and Mavin, S. (2008) What can we learn from senior leader narratives? The strutting and fretting of becoming a leader, *Leadership & Organization Development Journal*, ISSN: 0143-7739. https://www.emerald.com/insight/publication/issn/0143-7739.

X   Ethical Issues for the Researcher

Mary Wild and Carol Brown

Researchers in education are interested in exploring both process and outcomes for others within the educational system and for themselves as practitioners. Researchers may have differing focus on either process or outcomes, as has been noted elsewhere in this book. But in general, they are intent on unveiling and highlighting issues and practices within education so that a better experience, better learning or a better set of outcomes may be realized for those within the education system – children, students and the professionals who guide and work to support their learning. This intent to work for a greater purpose and to promote practice that is based on a deeper understanding of educative practice and environments extends into the application of ethics in research. As noted in several chapters of this book (e.g. Chapters III, V, IX), the researcher can sometimes feel overly constrained by specific requirements of ethical panels (see Chapter III) but the imperatives to be ethical in their approach towards participants is regarded as integral to their purpose and is embraced as a central part of the planning and conduct of the research. However, one aspect of ethical planning that can get overlooked by researchers is the impact that the intended research may have upon themselves –in specific terms, relating to the demands and challenges of particular projects. These in turn can be more readily identified than some of the broader challenges that also face the educational researcher in relation to the institutional and policy contexts in which they carry out their work. This chapter will discuss both of these sets of ethical dilemmas.

Ethical guidelines on researcher wellbeing

These twin dilemmas are accorded due recognition and weight in the BERA ethical guidelines (BERA 2018) in which articles 84 and 85 specify that:

> *84. Safeguarding the physical and psychological wellbeing of researchers is part of the ethical responsibility of employing institutions and sponsors, as well as of researchers themselves.*
>
> *85. Employers and sponsors need to avoid exploiting differences in the conditions of work and roles of other researchers, including student researchers and those on time-limited contracts. Employers are also responsible for supporting researchers' personal and professional career development.*

In more illustrative guidance, BERA has begun to collate a series of case studies in relation to research dilemmas, which include case studies with a focus on researcher wellbeing in different contexts, such as researchers working in an international context (Pennacchia 2019a) and for those focused on practitioner research (Pennachia 2019b). A striking feature of these guides is the space they provide for reflection on the part of the researcher who consults them, with specific prompts and questions for consideration by the reader. The importance of pre-emptive reflection on ethical issues on the part of the researcher is something that has been highlighted in preceding chapters in this book (see Chapters II, V and IX).

Identifying risks for researcher wellbeing

In 2006 an extensive enquiry was commissioned by the National Centre for Research Methods under the auspices of the ESRC to investigate risk to wellbeing that qualitative researchers in particular can face (Bloor et al. 2007). In addition to a comprehensive literature review, their study included interviews with 86 participants charged with managing research at institutions. Whilst the focus of the report was on qualitative research and was not confined to educational research contexts, their findings have been extrapolated to the educational context and are cited in the recent BERA case study guidance already referred to above.

Bloor at al. (2007) identified some overarching categories of risk: practical risks, emotional risks and institutional risk management. The interface they identify between individual risk and the institutional contexts in which they work is an important source of ethical dilemmas for the research community. In addition, they noted that the gender of researchers could also magnify degrees of risk and challenging experiences and, whilst not explicitly addressed in their study, it seems plausible that some degree of intersectionality for other researcher demographics would be pertinent too (Tefera et al. 2018).

Dilemmas and risks in the field

One of the perhaps more obviously envisioned practical risks is the issue of the safety of lone researchers in the field. Most universities will have specific policies drawn up in relation to risk assessment for researchers undertaking research in domestic and international contexts that are seen to be higher risk environments for projects (see also Chapters III and XI). The particular exigencies of working in an international context are covered in Chapter XI and in some cases, research will be precluded by advice from national government such as the Foreign and Commonwealth Office (FCO 2022) (https://www.gov.uk/foreign-travel-advice). However, even in seemingly more domestic and local circumstances, the researcher may face an ethical dilemma. The onus is placed on researchers to travel to places familiar to their participants but unfamiliar to them, or even potentially uncomfortable to them. This may be considered ethically supportive from the participant perspective, but it simultaneously raises ethical issues for the wellbeing and security of the researcher (Kenyon and Hawker 1999; Paterson et al. 1999). In these expositions of the risk to researchers of fieldwork conducted in participant homes, various precautions were proposed, for example ensuring a check-in and check-out procedure with other members of the research team or other colleagues. More recently, that might mean ensuring mobile phones are accessible and charged as a means of maintaining contact to others. Other strategies to safeguard the researcher may be less tangible but equally important such as undertaking training in how to handle situations that might become fraught or take an unexpected turn (examples given, for example, by Gilson in Chapter V). Where the lone worker in the field is a female on her own, for example, there may be additional gender-related concerns if confronted by a threatening or challenging participant. Reflective work by Kloß (2017) has highlighted the issue of sexual harassment and ethnographic fieldwork. Kloß powerfully foregrounds the emotional impact of such disturbing experiences and suggests that this is an aspect of social research that is under-acknowledged and that needs addressing within the broader research community.

As Parker and O'Reilly (2013) have pointed out, recent decades have seen an increasing awareness of potential risks and more overt focus on planning for these, for example, by recourse to risk assessment protocols at the ethical approval stage of a project. Notwithstanding this, Parker and O'Reilly highlight that the need for training in risk management is as important, and perhaps more so, than the advance completion of risk assessment protocols.

> Risk cannot be fully ameliorated and therefore it is equally important that the research community have strategies and systems in place to manage risk when it arises, not only working to prevent risk from occurring. (Parker and O'Reilly 2013: 350)

An added dimension to current ethical dilemmas is the rise in the use of online technologies for accessing and interacting with participants that has increased rapidly in more recent years and will have received a catalytic impetus following the Covid-19 pandemic with its consequent constraints on face-to-face research. Superficially, the rise in use of such technologies for data gathering could promise to mitigate some of the ethical conundrums of lone working experienced by preceding generations of researchers. However, the digital opportunities afforded to researchers carries its own intrinsic ethical dilemmas for both participants and researchers alike. For researcher wellbeing this includes issues of personal privacy and the separation of the personal and work context when both may be mediated through the same digital platforms.

The BERA ethical guidance (BERA 2018) refers in Article 84 to the requirement for researchers to 'be aware of the legal responsibilities as well as the moral duty of institutions towards the safety of staff and students' (p. 35). This reminds us of the need for researchers to be aware of issues around safeguarding for those they are working with in schools and other settings as well as for themselves. There is an ethical imperative to be aware of localized procedures, e.g. the referral to a designated safeguarding lead (DSL) or multi-agency safeguarding hubs (MASH) regarding any concerns they have.

Dilemmas in the research workplace/outfield

Moving away from a focus on the direct impact and the physical and emotional risks of working in the field, there is another significant space for researcher wellbeing. As signified in the BERA guidelines on researcher wellbeing (article 35, BERA 2018), the conditions of work, workplace relationship/hierarchies and career prospects bear many ethical implications and consequences for researchers.

Vostal (2015) has written about the experience of 'academic life in the fast lane', noting the negative impact that increasing workload and competing workload demands can place on the academic. He writes about the guilt that can be experienced by the academic at not accomplishing enough and of the additional emotional burden of the 'doctrine of excellence'. Similarly, Kinman and Jones (2008) point to research across many countries that charts the stressful nature of academic work and reports specifically on a UK-based study that demonstrates the extent to which academics are increasingly working well beyond their designated work hours. In subsequent work, Kinman (2014) draws on longitudinal research from the UK and Australia, which highlights how competing demands on academics have increased over recent times and to the deleterious effect of this on work-life balance with the attendant stress that accompanies this. There is also an argument that such pressure may disproportionally affect certain groups, such as women in the academic workplace (Caretta et al. 2018) or early career researchers (Sutherland 2017; Djerasimovic and Vilani 2020). Writing specifically about fieldwork in an international context, Jenkins (2020) notes that women may find it particularly difficult to schedule time away from family to conduct such work. Individual characteristics may also render the researcher more vulnerable in terms that are more general. In a very recent study, reported on as this chapter was being written, researchers at the University of Glasgow highlight some very concerning details of the stress and pressures that postgraduate researchers can experience (The National 2022). One of the study's authors, Jelena Milicev, is cited and notes links between 'maladaptive perfectionism and workaholism' and increased risks of a variety of mental health issues at levels above the national average. It is also noted that particular groups including postgraduate researchers who are female, transgender, non-binary, homosexual, bisexual and queer more commonly report this. However, the study also refers to the beneficial impact of strong social support networks, supportive supervisors and a 'positive departmental atmosphere'.

The pressure to take on new projects, write bids and to publish consistently, often whilst juggling teaching responsibilities and coping with high and increasing administrative work, all too frequently result in ethical tensions at the pragmatic level. This may occur on a day-to-day basis – whether to put in additional time into a work project or to spend time with family or friends – or it may be more strategic, such as deciding whether to say yes or no to a project that the researcher feels to be important and worthwhile, but for which there is no additional resource. This can be a difficult decision to take for the individual concerned, but it is also a significant and growing ethical responsibility that the Academy itself needs to step up to address.

The Neoliberal University

Much of the intensification of workload and an increasing culture of performativity has been attributed to the wider neoliberal and marketized conception of the role of academics in public life (Caretta et al. 2018). There is resonance here to the wider educational agenda noted by Wild and Frodsham in Chapter VIII that has driven a focus on measurement and quantifiable outcomes. Driven by policy imperatives such as the Research Excellence Framework (REF) in the UK (UKRI 2022) and similar accountability exercises elsewhere in the world, academic endeavour is increasingly scrutinized with metrics, impact and public engagement to the fore. As well as contributing to workload pressures, this can lead to more precise ethical dilemmas for researchers who may feel compelled to artificially distort the form of research undertaken or dissemination practices. Such pressures are likely to be especially acute when career progression is driven by performance against such externally imposed metrics (Watermeyer 2015; Chubb and Watermeyer 2017).

Reflective issues for the researchers

As well as these aforementioned practical issues for the researcher to consider, there are also several factors that are important specifically for their own emotional and psychological wellbeing. Whilst it may be standard practice in similar professions or areas of research (such as counselling or psychology for example) to prioritize these routinely, and even incorporate them as part of one's own reflective practice, this is not necessarily so in the educational field. In this section, a number of these issues are considered, including reflection on the social sensitivity of research, dealing with secondary trauma and preparation for researcher wellbeing. The common theme in this section is the need for ethical research in education to critically involve self-reflection and self-care on the part of the investigator and is an that is area often overlooked.

Socially sensitive research

In their seminal paper on the ethical and professional dimensions of socially sensitive research, Sieber and Stanley (1988) define socially sensitive research as 'studies in which there are potential social consequences or implications, either directly for the participants in the research or for the class of individuals represented by the research' (p. 49). Babacan and Babacan (2013) suggest that what is considered sensitive is however defined by cultural, social, historical, economic and political factors and that these, in turn, determine what is acceptable to be discussed in public, the emotional responses by members of society and the perception of risk involved. Babacan and Babacan (2013) acknowledge that sensitive research often focuses on people or communities who are marginalized, discriminated against and vulnerable.

Thus, the consideration of ethical dilemmas in socially sensitive research extends beyond simply ensuring that any research meets the basic ethical requirements stipulated by guidelines and due regulatory processes. Sieber and Stanley (1988) highlight that such research possesses special ethical problems for the investigator. These include ethical analysis of the research question itself, the research process and the potential application of the findings (p. 49). Examples they give are research examining the relative merit of daycare for infants versus full-time care of the mother or investigating the relationship between gender and mathematical ability. In such cases, the design and procedures used to conduct the research may meet regulatory guidelines but pose wider dilemmas around the societal implications in the very asking of the questions themselves or in the application of the findings. Such complex dilemmas are not uncommon in educational research and therefore require careful consideration. There have been other examples given throughout this book that align with this issue, for example in Chapter VIII where Wild and Frodsham discuss the dilemmas in handling numerical data and implications of generalizing findings to provide international comparisons of attainment and wellbeing using large-scale datasets.

One of the most important considerations for the researcher must therefore be the ways in which their findings might be applied, other than for those originally proposed. Further examples, cited by Sieber and Stanley (1988), include significant discussion on particularly sensitive areas such as the application of research findings where racial differences have been investigated, as may often be the case in educational research. They additionally refer to the example of how the knowledge of genetic inheritance and the use of psychological testing of IQ were, when taken together, used to promote a policy of sterilization for those suffering with what was then described as mental retardation. The original researchers had never intended their work to be applied in such a way and these illustrations can be used as helpful examples for the educational researcher to ponder when thinking about the ethical applications of their work.

One resolution for the researcher concerned with the dilemmas of socially sensitive research is to avoid conducting it and there was even early evidence (Ceci et al. 1985) that such work was much more likely to be rejected by ethics committees. However, one could argue that this is not a satisfactory, or ethical, resolution for either the researcher nor community, since new knowledge cannot be gained on populations who may benefit if it is deemed too sensitive to facilitate their inclusion or focus. As Sieber and Stanley (1988) conclude, the likelihood that research will raise socially sensitive issues is great and unavoidable if useful theory, knowledge and applications are to be achieved; restricting investigation of such areas would limit researchers to examining unimportant problems (p. 54). Therefore, the recommendation is that the researcher ensures they are aware of their relationship with society, since sensitive research addresses some of society's most pressing issues and policy questions and shying away from controversial topics is an avoidance of responsibility (p. 55). Babacan and Babacan (2013) argue that 'equipping people with relevant information or knowledge, opening up a debate itself and providing evidence with the voices of the marginalized and disadvantaged is a vital contribution to democratic reform and the struggle for a socially just society' (p. 60). Their work focused on case study, racism-related research and drew on their experiences, insights and challenges faced when balancing researcher responsibilities and communicating results. This sentiment is also reiterated by Isham et al. (2019 p. 69) who state that 'much sensitive research is underpinned by an ethical and intellectual commitment to develop new forms of knowledge that challenge traditional ways of knowing and exercising power, thereby giving credence to marginalized experiences and enabling hidden issues to be better heard and seen (Mantoura and Potvin 2013; Bradbury-Jones et al. 2014).

Babacan and Babacan (2013) suggest that undertaking socially sensitive research carries physical and/or psychological risks for several stakeholders, the focus on this chapter being on those for the researcher themselves. They refer to the work of Lee (1993) who highlighted how such research might effect both the personal life and security of the researcher. Babacan and Babacan (2013 p. 55) proclaim that 'in order to protect all participants' physical and psychological safety, protocols or guidelines need to be developed at the beginning of the research process to identify and minimize risk or respond to risks as they arise during the research process' (McCosker et al. 2001). The next section of this chapter will thus focus on these emotional risks in more detail, dealing with secondary trauma when conducting (sensitive) research and preparation for researcher wellbeing.

Secondary trauma for the educational researcher

As discussed earlier in this chapter, Bloor et al. (2007) produced a report on the risks to researcher wellbeing. One aspect focused on the emotional risks, which are now explored in more detail in this section. Bloor et al. (2007) suggest that several emotional risks may occur including the effort of the 'emotional labour' required to establish and maintain good relationships with participants, emotional distress, role conflict and anxiety and isolation in fieldwork settings. Some of these issues have been illustrated with practical exemplars by Gilson in Chapter V. Emerald and Carpenter (2015) used their own auto-ethnographies to create a co-constructed narrative to identify some of the emotional risks, concluding that these encompass vulnerability, emotional labour, emotions as data or evidence and emotionally sensed knowledges. Bloor et al. (2007) claim there may be a particular gender bias in emotional risks. They found evidence to indicate that research on emotive topics was disproportionally conducted by female researchers, which they believed is accounted for by feminist models stressing traditional gender roles in which such researchers are seen as confidantes sympathetic and trusting. However, the impact on wellbeing may be influenced by various factors including the age, background and life experiences of the researcher (Kennedy et al. 2013). These risks pose an ethical dilemma in educational research as the costs and benefits must be carefully balanced for the researcher themselves.

There has been interest in the traumatizing effects of the research process where, compared to clinical professions, less attention has been given to managing the emotional impacts (Dickson-Swift et al. 2006). Research is not, however, a neutral or impassive process (Hallowell et al. 2005). There are many formal psychological definitions of secondary trauma, which can be nicely encapsulated for educational professionals more succinctly as follows: secondary trauma is when one encounters someone else experiencing trauma and feels deeply the impact of their distress (Educationsupport.org 2022). Symptoms include: insomnia, nightmares, exhaustion, depression, headaches and gastro-intestinal issues (Dickson-Swift et al. 2006); flashbacks or repeating the traumatic experience over and over again; avoiding certain scenarios or situations that are reminders of what has been shared; negative changes in beliefs and feelings which can lead to anxiety and depression; and hyper arousal – a feeling of always being alert and that the littlest thing can set you on edge (Educationsupport.org 2022). Other factors associated with secondary trauma include compassion fatigue, burnout and vicarious trauma. The symptoms of trauma may affect various aspects of the researcher's life including their family and personal relationships and their professional ones (Sikic Micanovic et al. 2020).

For the educational researcher, trauma may arise from various circumstances, such as: exposure to challenging situations, narratives or emotive material, especially in the absence of clinical supervision (Craig et al. 2000; Raheim et al. 2016; Williamson et al. 2020); working with marginalized groups (von Benzon and van Blerk 2017); dealing with issues of social injustice, which may exacerbate feeling of hopelessness (Coles et al. 2014; Williamson et al. 2020); triggers directly from interviews as well as secondary data collection (Williamson et al. 2020); and assimilating the 'feeling states' induced by the research process (Lee-Treweek and Linkogle 2000). Notably, such effects can occur not just as part of the active data collection, but also as part of the transcription process (Kiyimba and O'Reilly 2016).

Many of the specific issues around insider research have been discussed in Chapter IX by Spiro. Here, only a very general reference is therefore made to some of the important ethical considerations in terms of emotional risks with regards to positionality. Fenge et al. (2019) define this as 'acknowledgement of the multiple roles and positions that researchers and research participants bring to the research process' (p. 3). They believe critical reflection on 'the self' can develop insight into the ways identity influences the research undertaken and that this is particularly pertinent when looking at sensitive topics. This, in turn, links to the notions of 'insider–outsider' perspectives and duality of roles and Fenge et al. (2019) highlight how this is particularly true for researchers who have previous professional backgrounds or dual roles, for example, whilst undertaking a PhD. These are not uncommon scenarios for the educational researcher, for example, the researcher who wants to investigate support for children with additional learning needs in mainstream schools because they have such a child themselves, or the mature PhD student who is a teacher in the local authority and wishes to use participants from schools she works in. Many similar examples are discussed in Chapters IV and XIII and arise in an educational context where researchers may have come to the field in mature years, with lived experience, personal interests or with a prior associated professional career in another sphere of the field. Fenge et al. (2019) argue that positionality concerns the ways researchers then make sense of their roles, their place in the community and the boundaries involved in the researcher-participant relationship – some seeing the roles as very separate, others more blurred and forming a 'counselling' relationship. Ethical dilemmas may then present in terms of power and inequality between the individuals and communities. Isham et al. (2019) state that there is a close association between sensitive research and more 'radical' forms of involvement and collaboration such as participatory approaches. They believe this is because such topics benefit from the insights of those with experience and insight and the breaking down of the power asymmetry between researchers and researched in order to facilitate empowerment, although ethical and methodological issues then become closely entwined. Isham et al. (2019) found that working with advisors using a network approach offered some helpful ways of addressing these ethical issues.

Although sensitive research may therefore carry a risk of trauma, the ethical dilemma for the researcher is whether those risks outweigh the wider benefits of the questions being explored. Perhaps a way to review such ethical dilemmas is to consider the notion that the researchers' emotional responses and reflexivity can actually be a necessary and helpful part of the process; providing insights, understandings and analyses (Hubbard et al. 2001; Sikic Micanovic et al. 2020).

Preparedness for researcher wellbeing

One of the key themes emerging from the literature is that whilst such emotional (and other) risks may not be possible to avoid in entirety, researchers can be vigilant in attempting to mitigate the risks of emotional harm. This can include counselling, peer support, reflexivity and, most critically, advance preparedness (Bloor et al. 2007).

It seems, however, that these considerations are often overlooked by regulatory processes (Fenge et al. 2019; McCosker et al. 2001). At the institutional level, research indicates that research ethics committees (REC) could helpfully ensure a focus on this as part of the review process or that the application processes at the very least could serve as a useful prompt for researchers to reflect on the issues (Emerald and Carpenter 2015; Kiyimba and O'Reilly 2016; Fenge et al. 2019).

Williamson et al. (2020), for example, included a researcher safety protocol in their submission to the REC. It included protocols such as peer check-ins post interviews, an open-door policy with team members agreeing to be visible and available to discuss arising issues and emotional wellbeing featuring as an overt agenda item on each team meeting.

Fenge et al. (2019) explored ten social science researchers' experiences of undertaking research on sensitive topics or with marginalized groups. Lack of preparedness – for both early career and experienced researchers – emerged as a key issue in dealing with emotional impact and was linked to a perceived lack of training or support. Recommendations include supportive supervision, which encourages a reflexive stance and safe reflection on experiences that may be useful and foster resilience, and peer-to-peer supervision. Prioritizing self-care needs were also identified as useful preparedness. This may include supervision outside of the immediate university setting (Hubbard et al. 2001).

McCosker et al. (2001) report strategies that they have helpfully used within their work, and although the work focused on women and abuse, the strategies may be equally applicable for the interviewer exploring sensitive topics in the educational context. Strategies for preparing for emotional distress included conducting interviews in the morning, limited to only one per week, using a transcriber to then transcribe the data, maximizing listening to data in no more than one-hour chunks, ensuring there was not simultaneous data collection and literature review of the topic and ensuring debriefing with a colleague and transcriber.

Sikic Micanovic et al. (2020), also conducting work outside the educational field, provides further interesting and applicable strategies for ensuring preparedness for emotional impacts. These incorporated the use of reflexive research diaries to provide a safe outlet for discharge and reflection on feelings and anxieties, agreed team debriefs that allow true emotional expression without fear that this will be perceived as researcher incompetence, embracing and acknowledging emotions, being honest about limits and capabilities, seeking external help from professionals if needed, working in pairs and again limiting the number of weekly interviews here to just two a week.

At an institutional level, Dickson-Swift et al. (2008, 2009) emphasize similar recommendations to these aforementioned studies including profession supervision, policy development and minimum training standards for researchers. However, on a personal level, there are also several useful self-care strategies that the researcher can implement to ensure emotional wellbeing. These can fall into restorative, recuperative and recreational self-care (Educationsupport. org 2022). For example, exercise, diet, relaxation therapies, socializing and ensuring a work-life balance, mindfulness, peer support, opportunities for respite, spirituality, hobbies, music and other recreational behaviours (Hunter and Schofield 2006; Kavanaugh and Campbell 2014; Decker et al. 2015; Berger 2021; Educationsupport.org 2022).

This section has attempted to provide some suggestions for the educational researcher in preparing themselves for the emotional impacts of their work. These include both organizational and personal strategies, which are often commonplace practices in professions where the emotional stakes of the work are high such as psychology, counselling and social care, but yet to be routinely considered within the field of research. Notably however much of the emerging work in the field concentrates on qualitative research rather than quantitative and still involves small-scale studies; there is more work to be done here in the educational arena. Emotional impact can be found in those conducting secondary analysis, as well as primary data collection. It is also important to acknowledge, as Hubbard et al. (2001) point out, that researchers should not seek to avoid emotional experiences but simply learn how to acknowledge, utilize and manage them at every stage of a project. This is similarly highlighted by Sikic Micanovic et al. (2020), who suggest that emotional challenges are difficult to predict or eliminate and hinge on a researcher's positionality and field context and therefore need to be risk-managed from the design stage to dissemination and beyond.

Conclusion

This chapter has focused on several ethical issues and dilemmas that arise for the researcher; these have been largely under-acknowledged in educational research but a more recent focus on ensuring the physical and psychological safety of the researcher is a welcome one. Some of the issues can be addressed by localized or international regulatory requirements associated with gaining institutional ethics or risk assessment approvals, but others are more nuanced and the dilemmas rest with the researcher themselves. Thus there are organizational, institutional and personal strategies for managing researcher wellbeing.

Bloor et al. (2007) make a number of helpful recommendations, for example:

- including content on researcher safety as part of in-service training courses for PhD supervisors and principal investigators
- university departments undergoing periodic health and safety audits, including examination of provision for researcher safety
- compliance with safety guidelines by principal investigators a requirement for funding
- funders formally asking referees to comment on researcher safety issues as part of their review of applications
- ethics committees accepting formal responsibility for safety issues and in the context of specific research questions.

Similarly some of BERA's recommendations (2018), in articles 84 and 85, are that:

- researchers should be aware of the legal responsibilities as well as the moral duty of institutions towards the safety of staff and students
- institutions, sponsors and independent researchers should consider whether an in-depth risk assessment form and ongoing monitoring of researcher safety is appropriate, especially for those undertaking fieldwork, working abroad and/or investigating sensitive issues
- researchers, principal investigators, students and their supervisors should ideally be offered training on researcher safety
- specialist training should be made available to researchers entering conflict or post-conflict settings internationally or areas with high risk of disease
- employers and sponsors need to avoid exploiting differences in the conditions of work and roles of other researchers, including student researchers and those on time-limited contracts.

References

Babacan, H. and Babacan, A. (2013) Difficult research conversations: sharing socially sensitive research in the public domain, *Etropic*, 21(1): 52–63.

Berger, R. (2021) Studying trauma: indirect effects on researchers and self – and strategies for addressing them, *European Journal of Trauma and Dissociation*, 5(1): 1–8.

Bloor, M., Fincham, B. and Sampson, H. (2007) *Qualiti (NCRM) Commissioned Inquiry into the Risk to Well-being of Researchers in Qualitative Research*. Cardiff.

Bradbury-Jones, C., Taylor, J. and Herber, O.R. (2014) Vignette development and administration: a framework for protecting research participants, *International Journal of Social Research Methodology*, 17(4): 427–440.

British Educational Research Association BERA. (2018) *Ethical Guidelines for Educational Research*. British Educational Research Association (BERA). Available at: https://www.bera.ac.uk/publication/ethical-guidelines-for-educational-research-2018 (accessed 10 July 2019).

Caretta, M.A., Drozdzewski, D., Jokinen, J.C. et al. (2018) 'Who can play this game?' The lived experiences of doctoral candidates and early career women in the neoliberal university, *Journal of Geography in Higher Education*, 42(2): 261–275.

Ceci, S.J., Peters, D. and Plotkin, J. (1985) Human subjects review, personal values and the regulation of social science research, *American Psychologist*, 40: 994–1002.

Chubb, J. and Watermeyer, R. (2017) Artifice or integrity in the marketization of research impact? Investigating the moral economy of (pathways to) impact statements within research funding proposals in the UK and Australia, *Studies in Higher Education*, 42(12): 2360–2372.

Coles, J., Astbury, J., Dartnall, E. and Limjerwala, S. (2014) A qualitative exploration of researcher trauma and researchers' responses to investigating sexual violence, *Violence Against Women*, 20: 95–117.

Craig, G., Corden, A. and Thornton, P. (2000) Safety in social research, *Social Research Update*, 29: 68–72.

Decker, J.T., Constantine Brown, J.L., Ong, J. and Stiney-Ziskind, C.A. (2015) Mindfulness, compassion fatigue, and compassion satisfaction among social work interns, *Social Work and Christianity*, 42: 28–42.

Dickson-Swift, V., James, E.L., Kippen, S. et al. (2006) Blurring boundaries in qualitative health research on sensitive topics. *Qualitative Health Research*, 16(6): 853–871.

Dickson-Swift, V., James, E.L., Kippen, S. et al. (2008) Risk to researchers in qualitative research on sensitive topics: issues and strategies, *Qualitative Health Research*, 18: 133–144.

Dickson-Swift, V., James, E.L., Kippen, S. et al. (2009) Researching sensitive topics: qualitative research as emotional work, *Qualitative Research*, 9: 61–79.

Djerasimovic, S. and Vilani, M. (2020) Constructing academic identity in the European higher education space: experiences of early career educational researchers, *European Educational Research Journal*, 119(2): 247–262.

Educationsupport.org (2022) *Secondary Trauma*. Available at: https://www.educationsupport.org.uk/resources/for-individuals/videos/secondary-trauma/Education support (accessed 7 January 2022).

Emerald, E. and Carpenter, L. (2015) Vulnerability and emotions in research: risks, dilemmas, and doubts, *Qualitative Inquiry*, 21(8):741–750.

FCO 2022 Foreign Travel Advice (2022) Available at: https://www.gov.uk/foreign-travel-advice

Fenge, L., Oakley, L., Taylor, B. and Beer, S. (2019) The impact of sensitive research on the researcher: preparedness and positionality, *International Journal of Qualitative Methods*, 18: 1–8.

Hallowell, N., Lawton, J. and Gregory, S. (2005) *Reflections on Research: The Realities of Doing Research in the Social Sciences*. Maidenhead: Open University Press.

Hubbard, G., Backett-Milburn, K. and Kemmer, D. (2001) Working with emotions: issues for the researcher in fieldwork and teamwork, *International Journal of Social Research Methodology*, 4: 119–137.

Hunter, S.V. and Schofield, M.J. (2006) How counsellors cope with traumatized clients: personal, professional and organizational strategies, *International Journal for the Advancement of Counselling*, 28: 121–138.

Isham, L., Bradbury-Jones, C. and Hewison, A. (2019) Reflections on engaging with an advisory network in the context of a 'sensitive' research study, *International Journal of Social Research Methodology*, 22(1): 67–79.

Jenkins, K. (2020) Academic motherhood and fieldwork: juggling time, emotions, and competing demands, *Transactions of the Institute of British Geographers* 45(3): 693–704. https://doi.org/10.1111/tran.12376 (accessed 29 June 2022).

Kavanaugh, K.L. and Campbell, M.L. (2014) Conducting end-of-life research: strategies for success, *Nursing Science Quarterly*, 27(1): 4–19.

Kennedy, F., Hicks, B. and Yarker, J. (2013). Work stress and cancer researchers: An exploration of the challenges, experiences and training needs of UK cancer researchers', *European Journal of Cancer Care*, 23: 462–471. doi:10.1111/ec.12135.

Kenyon, E. and Hawker, S. (1999) 'Once would be enough': some reflections on the issue of safety for lone researchers, *International Journal of Social Research Methodology*, 2(4): 313–327.

Kinman, G. (2014) Doing more with less? Work and wellbeing in academics, *Somatechnics*, 4(2): 219–235.

Kinman, G. and Jones, F. (2008) A life beyond work? Job demands, work-life balance, and wellbeing in UK academics, *Journal of Human Behavior in the Social Environment*, 17(1–2): 41–60.

Kiyimba, N. and O'Reilly, M. (2016) The risk of secondary traumatic stress in the qualitative transcription process: a research note *Qualitative Research*, 16(4): 468–476.

Kloß, S.T. (2017) Sexual(ized) harassment and ethnographic fieldwork: a silenced aspect of social research, *Ethnography*, 18(3): 396–414.

Lee-Treweek, G. and Linkogle, S. (2000 *Danger in the Field: Risk and Ethics in Social Research*. Abingdon: Routledge.

Lee, R.M. (1993) *Doing Research on Sensitive Topics*. Sage Publications.

Mantoura, P. and Potvin, L. (2013 A realist–constructionist perspective on participatory research in health promotion, *Health Promotion International*, 28(1): 61–72.

McCosker, H., Barnard, A. and Gerber, R. (2001) Undertaking sensitive research: issues and strategies for meeting the safety needs of all participants, *Forum Qualitative Research*, 2(1, Article 22).

Parker, N. and O'Reilly, M. (2013) "We are alone in the house": a case study addressing researcher safety and risk, *Qualitative Research in Psychology*, 10(4): 341–354.

Paterson, B., Gregory, D. and Thorne, S. (1999) A protocol for researcher safet, *Qualitative Health Research*, 9(2): 259–69.

Pennacchia, J. (ed.) (2019, a) *BERA Research Ethics Case Studies: 2. Researcher Wellbeing and International Fieldwork*. London: British Educational Research Association. Available at: https://www.bera.ac.uk/publication/researcher-wellbeing-international-fieldwork

Pennacchia, J. (ed.) (2019b) *BERA Research Ethics Case Studies: 3. Anticipating the Application and Unintended Consequences of Practitioner Research*. London: British Educational Research Association. Available at: https://www.bera.ac.uk/publication/anticipating-the-application-unintended-consequences-of-practitioner-research. (accessed 29 June 2022)

Raheim, M., Magnussen, L.H., Sekse, R.J.T. et al. (2016) Researcher-researched relationship in qualitative research: shifts in positions and researcher vulnerability, *International Journal of Qualitative Studies on Health and Well-Being*, 11: 1–12.

Rose, G. (2007) *Visual Methodologies* (2nd edn). London: Sage.

Rose, J. (1983) *Sexuality in the Field of Vision*. Verso.

Sieber, J.E. and Stanley, B. (1988) Ethical and professional dimensions of socially sensitive research, *American Psychologist*, 43(1): 49–55.

Sikes, P. and Piper, H. (2010) Ethical research, academic freedom and the role of ethics committees and review procedures in educational research, *International Journal of Research and Method in Education*, 33(3): 205–213.

Sikic Micanovic, L., Stelko, S. and Sakic, S. (2020) Who else needs protection? Reflecting on researcher vulnerability in sensitive research, *Societies*, 10(3): 1–12.

Sutherland, K.A. (2017) Constructions of success in academia: an early career perspective, *Studies in Higher Education*, 42(4): 743–759.

Tefera, A.A., Powers, J.M. and Fischman, G.E. (2018) Intersectionality in education: a conceptual aspiration and research imperative, *Review of Research in Education* (42): vii–xvii.

The National (2022) *Glasgow University research reveals stark wellbong findings*. Reported in The National newspaper Scotland 10 .01. 2022.

UKRI (2022) *Research Excellence Framework*. Available at: https://re.ukri.org/research/research-excellence-framework-ref/ (accessed 29 June 2022).

UNICEF (2007) *Implementation Handbook the Convention on the Rights of the Child*. United Nations Children's Fund.

United Nations Convention on the Rights of the Child (UNCRC) (1989) *United Nations Convention on the Rights of the Child*. Available at: https://www.unicef.org.uk/what-we-do/un-convention-child-rights/ (accessed 20 July 2021).

von Benzon, N. and van Blerk, L. (2017) Research relationships and responsibilities: 'doing' research with 'vulnerable' participants: introduction to the special edition, *Social and Cultural Geography*, 18(7): 895–905.

Vostal, F. (2015) Academic life in the fast lane: the experience of time and speed in British academia, *Time and Society*, 24(1): 71–95.

Watermeyer, R. (2015) Lost in the 'third space': the impact of public engagement in higher education on academic identity, research practice and career progression, *European Journal of Higher Education*, 5(3): 331–347.

Williamson, E., Gregory, A., Abrahams, H. et al. (2020) Secondary trauma: emotional safety in sensitive research, *Journal of Academic Ethics*, 18(1): 55–70.

Zimbardo, P.G. (1973) On the ethics of intervention in human psychological research with special reference to the Stanford Prison Experiment, *Cognition*, 2: 243–256.

XI Ethics in Educational Research with Indigenous Communities

Patrick Alexander

Introduction

In this chapter, I will propose a series of points of contention that derive from an engagement with the ethics of educational research conducted with Indigenous communities (below I provide a rationale for the use of this term). I argue that whilst there are specific issues and concerns that must be addressed in educational research with Indigenous communities, broadly defined, the concerted involvement of Indigenous actors in the process of research also raises some foundational concerns about the ethics of educational research in general (Smith 2005). Firstly, I will ground this argument by considering the history of educational research and its relationship to Indigenous communities, particularly in the context of mass education and education policy that has focused largely on the assimilation of Indigenous communities into the wider architecture of colonization and the modern nation-state. This process has often involved symbolic, structural and actual violence against Indigenous persons. In considering this history, I draw links between educational research and the broader range of technologies of discipline (Foucault 1975) of incursions made on Indigenous worlds through different means of taxonomy, whether orchestrated by the state or reified in the practice of social scientists (or both). That is, the broader epistemic violence (Hunt 2014) of the taxonomy of modernity can also be seen in the disciplining of educational research and its ethical framing. Secondly, I will explore the ways in which educational research privileges the school as a taken-for-granted and natural site of learning that is unproblematic in its benefits for Indigenous communities. Following Ball and Collet-Sabe (2021), I will suggest that the inverse is often true in Indigenous experiences of school and that 'ethical' educational research aimed at redeeming school practice may instead serve to reproduce inequities of power that marginalize Indigenous populations. In doing this, I critique the extent to which the forms of knowledge represented in mainstream educational research and in schooling are commensurate with championing Indigenous forms of knowledge (Harrington and CHiXapkaid 2013). Finally, I will contend that in order to conduct ethical research with Indigenous communities, it is important to reconsider what is the purpose and outcome of educational research in general. Where research continues to adopt an extractive approach to 'data collection', and where the ultimate outcome of educational research is to reproduce an essentially colonialist framing of what 'research' is for, I contend that the ethics of educational research remains contested and is in need of continued decolonization, not least when applied to marginal populations, including many Indigenous communities (Bunda 2017). Doing so presents a profound opportunity to expand the horizons of what educational research might constitute in the future.

Defining Indigenous communities

Before developing the above argument, I would like to recognize that the very term 'Indigenous communities' is problematic when deployed to essentialize consistency in the experience or characteristics of individuals who identify or are identified as 'Indigenous'. To do so is a crude oversimplification of the rich diversity of cultures and modes of social organization and meaning-making that can be seen across the world in communities of Indigenous persons. The term 'Indigenous communities' is used here as a shorthand in so much as it is useful to define the experiences or means of organization practiced by Indigenous actors vis-a-vis the state and in the context of modernity and in so much as those who identify as Native, First Nation or Indigenous (Bron and Sant 1999) are also defined as such by the state. There is a long and sinister history of academic categorization of those considered other to the Western Euro-American experience (Said 1978; Kuper 1988), and it would be remiss to assume that the current nomenclature of indigeneity is beyond the problems and shortcomings of previous labels that would have included 'primitive' and 'savage' – especially when deployed by individuals, like the author, who do not identify as Indigenous. I therefore invoke this term in the spirit advocated by Linda Tuhiwai Smith (2021), recognizing that the experiences of English-speaking Indigenous persons in Canada or the United States will be vastly different to those of Indigenous communities in the Ecuadorian Amazon, in Indonesia or in the Arctic Circle. What brings these disparate communities together is their experience of violence, difference, marginalization and othering through discourses of racism and colonialism and in relation to institutions of the nation-state that serve to establish an assumed cultural 'mainstream' that is, by definition, not 'Indigenous'. Below I present examples of Indigenous experiences of educational research in an attempt to avoid the misconception that these communities share an uncomplicated history or unifying set of cultural beliefs or values. I also defer to Indigenous scholars as the voices most important in defining what it means to be Indigenous and in illuminating what are the implications of Indigenous forms of knowledge for ethical practice in educational research. The arguments summarized here are therefore not new, but rather celebrate the scholarship first and foremost of Indigenous persons.

Do more harm: Historical context and educational research as disciplinary technology

The historical shifts outlined in Chapters I and II provide a clear indication of how debates about research ethics emerged in the twentieth century. The postwar era ushered in a new period of deep reflection about research ethics and, following the Nuremburg trials, of a call for universal standards that would protect participants from the kinds of organized terror perpetrated in the name of scientific research during the Second World War. Beginning in the fields of clinical and behavioural research, the discourse of universal ethical standards slowly reached the social sciences during the second half of the twentieth century, although the histories of disciplines including sociology, psychology, anthropology and education are of course darkened by numerous examples where research has not been ethical in word or in deed. In fact, one of the most arresting aspects of the history of ethical codes of practice in the social sciences is that it is so short and recent. However, professional bodies across the social sciences now aim to ensure ethical research is conducted in keeping with codes of practice. To take one example from a discipline with a long history of working with (and sometimes against) Indigenous communities, the American Anthropological Association's ethical code (2012) suggests that researchers should: do no harm; be open and honest regarding their work; obtain informed consent and necessary permissions; weigh competing ethical obligations due collaborators and affected parties; make results accessible; protect and preserve their records; maintain respectful and ethical professional relationships. The American Educational Research Association's (AERA 2011) code of ethics demonstrates a similar sentiment (although, notably, makes no explicit mention of Indigenous communities), focusing on the principles of: professional competence; integrity; professional, scientific and scholarly responsibility; respect for people's rights, dignity and diversity; and social responsibility. The British Educational Research Association (BERA) established a similar set of ethical guidelines beginning in the late 1980s and revised in 2018 (see chapter II) which, similarly, do not explicitly mention Indigenous communities, but which raise important questions of diversity and inclusion in ethical practice (we will return to this specific example towards the end of the chapter). Given the focus of much educational research in contexts involving children and young people, many such sets of ethical guidelines also refer to the broader rights discourse articulated in the UN Convention on the Rights of the Child (UNCRC 1989). The UNCRC does explicitly recognize the rights of Indigenous children, and like the AAA, AERA, and particularly the BERA ethical guidelines, is clearly framed with laudable intentions and with the best interests of participants in mind.

The move towards these kinds of universal standards of ethics across different fields of educational research is in many ways a positive one that helps to begin the conversation about what ethical educational research with Indigenous communities (and in general) might look like. However, this is not to say that the discursive shift towards the architecture of standardized ethical practice – university ethics boards, institutionally approved methods, ethics bureaucracy, and so on – is not unproblematic as a means of safeguarding the interests of participants in research. On the contrary, there are several foundational problems with framing ethical practice in this way, not least when involving Indigenous communities. As Linda Tuhiwai Smith clearly articulates (2021), ethical procedures can form part of a much longer narrative of research with Indigenous communities that is framed by colonial discourse. The history speaks for itself. Some of the earliest forays into researching Indigenous communities can be considered to be 'educational', in so much as they were oriented towards understanding 'primitive' or 'savage' ways of thinking, often characterized in evolutionist terms as inferior to Western scientific rationality (Finnegan and Horton 1973; Kuper 1988). The crude anthropometrics of race science, propagated by anthropologists and other social scientists, was (and remains) essentially a means to justify White supremacy by confirming the myth of the intellectual inferiority of non-White persons. After genocide, education has been a most effective means of subjugating Indigenous communities. For example, as Michael Tlanusta Garrett and Eugene F. Pichette argue of the Native American experience.

As it became increasingly apparent that Native Americans had no interest in adopting White cultural standards and practices, Whites turned to the power of education to civilize Indian children early in life. Most treaty agreements included provisions for the education of Native American youth by establishing church-affiliated schools. Native American children were deliberately taken from their homes at a young age and forced to attend boarding schools as far away from home as possible (Tlanusta Garrett and Pichette 2000: 4).

The devastating legacy of residential schools in Canada and the wholesale removal and 're-education' of Aboriginal 'Stolen Children' in Australia are two among many other examples of how state-sponsored education initiatives, informed by academic thinking, have led to structural and symbolic violence against Indigenous communities. These are not only injustices of the past. The KISS Academy in India, for example, is a 'factory school' explicitly dedicated to the re-education of Indigenous communities, turning them, in the words of KISS, from 'tax consumers into tax payers [sic], liabilities into assets' (KISS 2019). In 2020, the KISS Academy courted the international education research community as a means of legitimating its treatment of over 30,000 Indigenous children, offering to host the annual conference of the International Union of Anthropological and Ethnological Sciences. Fortunately, this offer was rejected after intervention from Survival International, but this demonstrates the continued relationship between academic scholarship and educational institutions and/or policymakers that reproduce relations of marginalization for Indigenous communities.

When ethical procedures do not directly challenge the colonial legacy of educational research, it is possible that instead they become an extension of this legacy. Or to put it another way, if historically social science research has been done *on* or *to* Indigenous communities, often to the effect of justifying colonial practices and racist discourses, then the introduction of ethical guidelines for this framing of research does not necessarily resolve the underlying issues of research conducted in a colonial frame. This includes, as I develop below, the reproduction of forms of knowledge – namely, Western legal-rational, scientific discourse, the search for evidence, truth or evidence-based claims of 'what works' (Davis 2017; Menter 2021) – that may run counter both to the interests and modes of knowledge of Indigenous communities. Rather, ethical guidelines may instead become part of a wider set of disciplinary technologies (means of disciplining people, bodies, bodies of knowledge) (Foucault 1975) and at worst may represent a form of litigious absolution from the underpinning ethical concerns of how research involving Indigenous communities is conducted. In short, research that receives institutional ethical approval is not necessarily ethical, because it may still represent a form of research that in the essence of its practices – in its approach to methodology, to data collection, to representation, ontology – remains Eurocentric and bound tightly to modernity and to the colonial past. Returning to the post-war moment of reflection that engendered the ethical guidelines referenced above, the sociologist Zigmund Bauman (1989) argued that the cultural and legal response to the Holocaust was limited by its focus on seeking to blame individual perpetrators, rather than interrogating the conditions of modernity that would allow such an atrocity to occur. Zoe Todd (2016) points to Bauman in her own illumination of the continued ways in which the conditions of modernity – a privileging of Euro-American modes of knowledge production, the rapacious neoliberal capitalism, neo-colonialism and persistent asymmetries of power that subordinate Indigenous communities to Whiteness – also shape academic scholarship in general. From an Indigenous perspective, research may also be synonymous with the wider extractive and disciplinary practices of the modern nation-state. With this in mind, Linda Tuhiwai Smith provides a valuable and challenging framing of the historical relationship between Indigenous communities and researchers when she suggests the following:

> The word itself, 'research', is probably one of the dirtiest words in the Indigenous world's vocabulary. When mentioned in many Indigenous contexts, it stirs up silence, it conjures up bad memories, it raises a smile that is knowing and distrustful.... The ways in which scientific research is implicated in the worst excesses of colonialism remains a powerful remembered history for many of the world's colonized peoples. It is a history that still offends the deepest sense of our humanity. Just knowing that someone measured our 'faculties' by filling the skulls of our ancestors with millet seeds and compared the amount of millet seed to the capacity for mental thought offends our sense of who and what we are...It galls us that Western researchers and intellectuals can assume to know all that it is possible to know of us, on the basis of their brief encounters with some of us. It appals us that the West can desire, extract and claim ownership of our ways of knowing, our imagery, the things we create and produce, and then simultaneously reject the people who created and developed those ideas and seek to deny them further opportunities to be creators of their own culture and own nations. It angers

us when practices linked to the last century, and the centuries before that, are still employed to deny the validity of Indigenous peoples' claim to existence, to land and territories, to the right of self-determination, to the survival of our languages and forms of cultural knowledge, to our natural resources and systems for living within our environments. (2021:1)

The sentiment articulated here suggests the need for a more profound decolonization of educational research beyond what gains have been made in recent years to highlight the need for ethical practice. Part of this process also involves critiquing the unit of analysis, or of concern, in standard approaches to ethics in educational research – that is, the individual. It is important to note that the individual human being is not a universal category of personhood across all cultural contexts. Rather, thinking about rights and agency as purely human qualities is culturally specific to the cartesian traditions of modernity. In other cultural contexts, the locus of personhood may be much more expansive, meaning that concepts such as 'human rights' or the application of the UNCRC (1989) are not unproblematic in how they position the individual human being at the heart of ethical practice. This is a fundamental challenge to the universalizing essentialism (Ortner 1995) that underpins centrality of the educated subject as the focus of ethical procedure in much educational research. Vivieros de Castro (2015) points to the importance, for example, of recognizing Indigenous ontologies if one is to appropriately recognize an Indigenous reckoning of reality in research, including in the ethics of research. In his perspectivist approach, Vivieros de Castro points to the fact that Amerindian Indigenous communities may hold reality to consist of multiple natural worlds in which personhood is not only the domain of humans, but that many or all things in nature may embody personhood. If a human participant in educational research does not consider there to be a discreet distinction between their role as an actor in a social context and the role of other non-human animals or objects, then this significantly complicates the ways in which ethical procedures are positioned. Beyond questions of literacy or informed assent to written ethical protocols, how does one factor into ethical procedures the assent of non-human actors, if such actors are recognized as such in Indigenous modes of knowledge and meaning-making? This question has been raised by the so-called 'ontological turn' in the social sciences (particularly in anthropology) and in a growing interest in posthuman framings of the research process (Braidotti 2019), although Indigenous scholars like Todd (2016) and Hunt (2014) have also noted how even these shifts towards a more expansive understanding of ontological complexity have also commandeered Indigenous knowledge without giving due recognition to the long history of these ideas in Indigenous communities. As both Todd and Hunt suggest, there is epistemic violence in the imposition of a Western framing of the educated subject – so often the subject of educational research and research ethics procedures – and also in the co-opting of Indigenous modes of knowledge to promote 'new' means of thinking about ontology in scholarship that remains overwhelmingly White, Western and English-speaking in its make-up. Countering this epistemic violence demands, as Tuhiwai Smith (2021) suggests, a more thoughtful engagement with Indigenous modes of knowledge and a concomitant rethinking of the means by which research and its ethics are carried out.

Against school

One starting point for rethinking the methodologies and ethics of educational research is to revisit and problematize one of the principal sites of educational research – the school. As Ball and Collet-Sabé (2021) argue, educational research has long focused on investigating how schooling may be improved, or how it may offer better opportunities to children, young people, teachers and society. The ethical propriety of research in schools might be partly measured against its engagement in this redemptive discourse – that is, not only doing no harm, but also advocating doing good through improving schooling. Menter (2021) provides a clear historical picture of how educational research in the British context has focused predominantly on improvements to school practice, but that the increasing commercialization and politicization of educational research has led to a preoccupation with research that seeks to find straightforward and replicable 'evidence-based' solutions to educational or social problems. Whilst the search for better practice begins from an ethically sound basis, clearly there are ethical questions about research in search of 'easy answers', as Menter puts it (2021). Ball and Collet-Sabé (2021) go further still to argue that a redemptive framing of the relationship between educational research and school may itself be unethical, because the modern school is, as they put it, an 'intolerable institution'. Whilst the UNCRC would propose that school is a universal right of all children, the historical and contemporary examples of Indigenous experiences of modern schooling above point to the potentially devastating impacts of school on the lives of its subjects. Ball and Collet-Sabé point to six aspects of the school episteme that render the modern school 'intolerable', namely:

1 School is imagined as a self-evident and unproblematically positive and progressive mode of education.
2 School is the means by which binary discourses of the enlightenment and of modernity are reproduced (including the seemingly self-evident benefits of school vs not-school).
3 School reproduces discourse of universality (per the argument about personhood above.
4 Schooling regularly reproduces the inequalities of contemporary society, in spite of laudable progressive discourse to the contrary.
5 Schools reproduce a universal discourse of individualization (currently, in the mode of neoliberal capitalism).
6 School serves to reify particular forms of professional and technical knowledge (of teachers, psychologists, educational researchers) as superior to other forms of knowledge (including Indigenous forms of knowledge).

I synthesize this argument because it is important to consider how educational research, emanating as it has done in the wake of the emergence of the modern school and mass systems of education, may be implicated in reproducing the episteme of the modern school but is also characterized by these epistemic conditions. The implication of these two claims – that educational research both reproduces and is defined by the above six aspects of the school espiteme – are considerable. In relation to school-oriented research, the ethics of educational research with Indigenous communities must account for a radically different experience of schooling in the history and present of Indigenous communities, where the modern school more regularly reveals itself as a violent imposition on these communities and their modes of knowledge and meaning-making (Rival 2000). Of course, not all educational research focuses on school (as highlighted already in Chapters II and III), but thinking critically about the epistemic qualities of the modern school, and about the role of educational research in reproducing these qualities, might also require a concomitant radical rethinking of what ethical educational research might look like generally in the future. We might consider, for instance, how the shadows of schooling (summarized in the characteristics of its episteme) linger in attempts of educational researchers to assess the effectiveness of learning in non-school contexts and learning of diverse kinds in informal contexts. Considering these questions in the context of educational research with Indigenous communities presents various avenues for thinking, to paraphrase Ball and Collet-Sabé (2021), of educational research beyond its current ethical and methodological horizons.

Decolonizing educational research

So how then, might we resolve the enduring ethical tension at the heart of traditional educational research and its ethics, especially when working with Indigenous communities? One approach would be to champion the value of methodologies traditionally invoked with Indigenous communities, namely ethnography, as does Ortner (1995). More specifically, Ortner argues for the power of the 'ethnographic stance' – 'the ethnographic stance (as we may call it) is as much an intellectual (and moral) positionality, a constructive and interpretive mode, as it is a bodily process in space and time' (1995: 173). Others would rightly point out that traditional ethnography as a methodology is particularly problematic given the history of anthropological misrepresentations of Indigenous communities. Perhaps it is in the application of the 'ethnographic stance' to a wider range of methodological possibilities that we consider productive ways of carrying out educational research with Indigenous communities in an ethical and thoughtful way. Central to such a proposition is the visibility of Indigenous persons and the audibility of Indigenous voices. Linda Tuhiwai Smith (2021) recounts a wide range of innovative approaches to research led by Indigenous actors, including community research and insider research (see Spiro, Chapter IX for further discussions on such research). Tuhiwai Smith is quick to point out, however, that it would be equally reductive to presume that insider research is more ethically sound if the individual Indigenous researcher is given 'official' status to speak in general for a community by virtue of their membership in it. Rather, such research demands a sensitive approach to mediating one's findings, often in dialogue with existing systems of community governance or mediation. As Tuhiwai Smith suggests,

> The complexities of an insider research approach can be mediated by building support structures...[for example,] *whanau* structures used by Māori researchers to ensure that relationships and issues, problems and strategies can be discussed and resolved. (2021: 160)

Tuhiwai Smith goes on to recount more than 40 diverse Indigenous research projects that encounter other methodologies aimed at ethical engagement. At the heart of many of these projects is the act of storytelling – an act that resonates with the spirit of the 'ethnographic stance' articulated above:

> Story telling [sic], oral histories, the perspectives of elders and of women have become an integral part of all Indigenous research. Each individual story is powerful. But the point about the stories is not that they simply tell a story, or tell a story simply. These new stories contribute to a collective story in which every Indigenous person has a place. For many Indigenous writers stories are ways of passing down the beliefs and values of a culture in the hope that the new generations will treasure them and pass the story down further. The story and the story teller both serve to connect the past with the future, one generation with the other, the land with the people and the people with the story. As a research tool, Russell Bishop suggests, story telling is a useful and culturally appropriate way of representing the 'diversities of truth' within which the story teller rather than the researcher retains control. (2021: 166)

Of course, storytelling can take many forms and represent diverse voices and may involve conversation, collaboration, dialogue or silence, resistance and refusal (Simpson, 2007; McGranahan, 2016), which can also be generative in its engagement with the complex history of educational research. In her recounting of Indigenous education in a Métis community, Yvonne Poitras Pratt (2021) also points to the many modalities that stories may take, invoking the power of digital storytelling as a tool for decolonizing educational research. Storytelling is of course not a new way of producing and sharing knowledge and that is partly the point. What is novel, however, is the potential of storytelling as a means of privileging Indigenous voices and expanding the horizon of how the practice, purpose and power of educational research is framed.

Conclusions

By considering the ethics of educational research with Indigenous communities, this chapter has raised some fundamental questions about the ethics of educational research in general. I began by considering the intellectual history of ethics in educational research and the sinister legacy of social science research in the histories of Indigenous communities. This raised several questions about the Eurocentric, modernist forms of knowledge regularly reproduced through educational research, including the nature of the subject at the heart of ethics procedures. One might assume, given the parameters for human and humane existence outlined in Chapters I and II, that the establishment of a universal declaration of human rights was also an assertion for a universal understanding of personhood. However, I have argued that this is not the case even in Western liberal democracies where individual citizenship and neoliberal individualism are fetishized as the essential locus of social existence. For many other communities, personhood is equally complex and rarely only tied to one's existence as a human individual. I would like to conclude this chapter with a number of questions: what would the ethics of educational research look like if we were to instead start by drawing on the ethics of practice from Indigenous communities? What are the radical challenges for educational researchers who start their approach to ethical engagement not with a plan for the extraction of data but with the will to listen and to spend time understanding local context in order to begin to understand what questions they might be asking, if they ask any at all? What are the challenges for ethics committees in recognizing that this kind of unpredictable, unplanned approach to research may in many cases be the more humane, the more ethical approach to adopt? How are the parameters of consent complicated, for example, when one is attempting to document an educative process that is transspecies, or that involves 'nature' as much as it does the world of human persons? Fortunately, the process of addressing these questions is already underway, as we can see by returning to the ethical guidance provided by BERA. Perhaps more than any other professional body in the realm of educational research, BERA's guidelines recognize the importance of maintaining a broad horizon of possibility for what the ethics of educational research may look like, in a way that is directly relevant to research with Indigenous communities. This is summarized in the following statement from the introduction to the guidelines:

> In sum, and for each research project, researchers will need to devise specific ethical courses of action...they may draw on ethical approaches that reflect a range of philosophical orientations (virtue ethics, or deontological ethics, for example). It is adherence to the *spirit* of the guidelines that we consider most vital to protect all who are involved in or affected by a piece of research. (BERA 2018)

With this spirit in mind, the radical challenge of conducting ethical educational research with Indigenous communities is in thinking differently and more expansively about many educative processes, including about the nature of educational research and its methodologies.

References

Ahmed, S. (2012) *On Being Included*. Durham: Duke University Press.
American Anthropological Association (2012) Principles of Professional Responsibility, available at https://ethics.americananthro.org/category/statement/ [accessed 1 July 2022].
American Educational Research Association, Code of Ethics, Approved by the AERA Council February 2011, available at https://www.aera.net/About-AERA/AERA-Rules-Policies/Professional-Ethics [accessed 1 July 2022].
Ball, S. and Collet-Sabe, J. (2021) Against school: an epistemological critique, *Discourse: Studies in the Cultural Politics of Education*, pp.1–15.
Bauman, Z. (1989) *Modernity and the Holocaust*. Ithaca, NY: Cornell University Press.
Braidotti, R. (2019) A theoretical framework for the critical posthumanities, *Theory, Culture and Society*, 36(6): 31–61.
British Educational Research Association. (2018) *Ethical Guidelines for Educational Research*. British Educational Research Association (BERA). Available at: https://www.bera.ac.uk/publication/ethical-guidelines-for-educational-research-2018 (accessed 16th February 2022).
Brown, J.N. and Sant, P.M. (eds) (1999) *Indigeneity: Construction and Re/presentation*. Hauppauge, NY: Nova Science.
Bunda, T. (2017) Special issue: indigenous educational research, *Australian Educational Research*, 44: 1–4.
Davis, A. (2017) It worked there. Will it work here? Researching teaching methods, *Ethics and Education*, 12(3): 289–303.
Finnegan, R. and Horton, R. (1973) Introduction, in R. Horton and R. Finnegan (eds) *Modes of Thought: Essays on Thinking in Western and Non-Western Societies*. London: Faber.
Foucault, M. (1975) *Discipline and Punish: The Birth of the Prison*. New York: Vintage.
Haraway, D. (2015) Anthroposcene, Capitaloscene, Plantationoscene, Cthuluscene: making kin, *Environmental Humanities*, 6: 159–165.
Harrington, B.G. and CHiXapkaid, P. (2013) Using Indigenous educational research to transform mainstream education: a guide for P-12 school leaders, *American Journal of Education*, 119: 487–511.
Hunt, S. (2014) Ontologies of Indigeneity: the politics of embodying a concept, *Cultural Geographies*, 21(1): 27–32.
Kuper, A. (1988) *The Invention of Primitive Society: Transformations of an Illusion*. London: Routledge.
McGranahan, C. (2016) Theorizing refusal: an introduction, *Cultural Anthropology*, 31(3): 319–325.
Menter, I. (2021) Snake oil or hard struggle? Research to address the reality of social injustice in education, in A. Ross (ed.) *Educational Research for Social Justice: Education Science, Evidence, and the Public Good, vol 1*. Cham: Springer.
Ortner, S.B. (1995). Resistance and the problem of ethnographic refusal. *Comparative Studies in Society and History*, 37(1): 173–193.

Poitras Pratt, Y. (2021) *Digital Storytelling in Indigenous Education: A Decolonizing Journey for a Métis Community*. New York: Routledge.

Rival, L. (2000) Formal schooling and the production of modern citizens in the Ecuadorian Amazon, in L. Bradley (ed.) *Schooling the Symbolic Animal: Social and Cultural Dimensions of Education*. London: Rowman and Littlefield.

Said, E. (1978) *Orientalism*. London: Vintage Books.

Simpson, A. (2007) Ethnographic refusal: Indigeneity, 'voice' and colonial citizenship. junctures, *The Journal for Thematic Dialogue*, 9: 67–80.

Smith, L.T. (2005) Building a research agenda for Indigenous epistemologies and education, *Anthropology and Education Quarterly*, 36: 93–95.

Tuhiwai Smith, L. (2021) *Decolonizing Methodologies: Research and Indigenous Peoples*. London: Zed Books.

Todd, Z. (2016) An Indigenous feminist's take on the ontological turn. Ontology is just another word for colonialism. *Journal of Historical Sociology*, 29(1): 4–22.

UN Commission on Human Rights, *Convention on the Rights of the Child*, 7 March 1990, E/CN.4/RES/1990/74, available at: https://www.refworld.org/docid/3b00f03d30.html [accessed 1 July 2022].

Vivieros de Castro, E. (2015) *The Relative Native: Essays on Indigenous Conceptual Worlds*. Chicago: Hau Books – Special Collections in Ethnographic Theory.

XII Jolts in the Margins: Probing the Ethical Dimensions of Post-Paradigms in Educational Research

Linda J Shaw

Introduction

In any piece of research before it is placed in front of the ethics committee, there are ethical considerations beyond the correct and efficient completion of ethics documentation. There are the ethical dilemmas around participants and their recruitment and around the research design, and there is the problem of finding an ethical research question.

The methodologies touched upon in this chapter trouble the very premises on which 'scientific' research has been applied to social science-based fields such as education (Humes and Bryce 2003). A single chapter cannot hope to do justice to the complexity of paradigms such as post-structuralism and allied theoretical positioning found in, for instance, post-humanism and post-colonialism. I will, however, try to draw out common features which relate these post-modernist approaches to educational research and the ethical tribulations which underpins them (DiQuinzio and Young 1997; Ball 2021).

In an effort to (re)present some of the ideas provoked by paradigms which set out to trouble modernist (and therefore humanist) assumptions about ontology and epistemology (Ball 1990) this chapter is split into three parts. In using the term (re)present, rather than simply represent, my desire is not merely to describe but also to deconstruct (Silverman 1989) the underpinnings of my own research into childhood and education. My hope is that this makes space for an engagement with the complexity of ethical research into the lived experiences of children, young people and educators. A starting point and a thread running through each of the sections is that complexity is an important ethical concept in its own right and 'perhaps the most important theoretical statement of our time' (Gordon 2008:3).

My own work draws primarily on post-structuralism as a way of engaging critically with educational policy at a national, local and school setting level.

As Humes and Bryce (2003) point out, the relationship between education research and post-structuralism is problematic since education as a structure tends to draw on Enlightenment assumptions about progress and rationality. Post-structuralism sets out to disrupt these Enlightenment suppositions in a number of different ways that defy a 'fixed characterization of it [post-structuralism] (or anything else)' (Humes and Bryce 2003:175). However, I also take a post-feminist positioning which turns to French philosophy and the work of writers such as Luce Iregary and Lois McNay. Post-feminism actively searches out tensions and juxtaposition of academic theories which hide (and sometimes generate) inequality relating to gender and other characteristics of social identity (McNay 1992). Many feminist theorizations have more recently acknowledged the importance of intersectionality (Davis et al. 2015), the idea that our identity is made up of a combination of characteristics, including physical or mental ability, class, race and gender (Rivers and Zotzmann 2017). In the context of intersectionality, it would be implausible to ignore post-colonialism, which tackles issues of imperialism, anti-imperialism and colonization (Coloma 2009).

The first section in the chapter considers post-modernism as an umbrella term under which are nestled several theories, which have in common a concern with highlighting issues relating to human rights and social justice. The middle part of the text thinks about the foundations of ethnography as a methodology which continues to be turned to in the study of pedagogy and sociologies of education. Finally, I will address the role of imagination, particularly the sociological imagination (Mills 2000), in my continuing explorations of what makes for ethical research into early childhood, education and play.

What is argued throughout is that ethical processes as they pertain to educational research, whether from within academia or externally funded, are a necessary quality system. They are a safeguard and the minimum standards to be adhered to in the planning and execution of research. However, ethical paperwork, even when very well designed, is never sufficient. The onus to trouble existing and unfolding power relations remains with the researcher and research term throughout and following the collection of data and the writing and other types of dissemination. This means working with other human agents in ways that recognize the complexities of personhood (Gordon 2008) and social structures that imply the complicity of all of us in inequality and social injustices (de Lauretis 1989).

The ethics of a post-modern classroom

There is no such thing as post-modern education or a post-modern classroom. Contemporary education is an institution. Like all social institutions, it is built on ideologies (Meyer 2009), which are constructed from historical concepts, politics, culture and regimes of power (Foucault and Gordon 1980). Philosophy, sociology, psychology and science weave together to produce an entanglement of discourses and counter-discourses, which intertwine in educational research to produce both discernible patterns and oppositions. It is these tensions within and between educational concepts that have been the focus of my research and writing (Shaw and Manchester Metropolitan University 2017; Shaw 2020). Previously, my attention has centred on tensions between teaching and learning, early childhood and pupilhood, care and education, and education and play. In this chapter, the focus shifts towards rigidities that might be noted between ethics and aesthetics and how these might relate to the enactments of ethical teaching and ethical research.

For Edwards and Ribbens (1998) one ethical failure of qualitative research lies in the unequal valuing of public knowledge (or research into public institutions) over the significance of investigations that seek to better understand private lives or topics pertaining to the domestic. This is a significant ethical dilemma within the study of all phases of education. In early childhood and primary education, the importance of knowledge acquisition expressed through acts of teaching continues to compete with values associated with caring (particularly mothering); in middle and late childhood this translates into undervaluing of learning that takes place outside of formal education settings and inequalities of status between science, technology, engineering and maths (STEM) subjects and the arts and humanities within school curricula (Al Salami et al. 2017).

The consequences of ignoring the private and the domestic in social research is that certain groups of people are silenced, or at the very least their voices are never heard (Mauthner and Doucet 1998). In the case of education, this is primarily female (as measured against the norm of male) and other non-normative gendered teachers (Preston 2018) and children and young people who become the objects of research rather than subjects (in the sense of active agents) in their own learning and parents/carers (Kellet 2010).

In post-colonial terminology, these social consortiums or sociocultural natives of education spaces, teachers who do not aspire to managerial or other positions of power, young children, adolescents and parents are cast into the role of the subaltern. The subaltern, according to Spivak (1993), are those occupying the lowest status, displaced to the margins of a society and unable to assert human agency. In this reading of educational research, the ethical imperative is to find a way in which the subaltern can speak in their own language and on their own terms. This has forged a pathway towards research *with*, not *on*, *about* or *for*, children and young people (Tisdall et al. 2009) and growing interest in methodologies that draw on critical race theory (Zamudio et al. 2010), queer theory (Pinar 1998) and other post(modern) paradigms. However, there is no doubt that these positionings fall outside of the mainstream of educational research and may clash with ethical processes that seek to protect groups constructed as vulnerable, including children and young people (Tisdall et al. 2009).

Writing from a post-feminist perspective, DiQuinzio and Young (1997) critique ultra-normative interpretations of ethics as unbiased analysis of what is right or wrong in the treatment of human and non-human subjects. A normative ethical position is one that privileges universality and impartiality over diversity (Silvers 1997), pulling the gaze toward male values of public performativity in male-dominated sectors such as finance, the judiciary or business. Much ethical theory, DiQuinzio and Young (1997) claim, is blind to gender and therefore biased in its production of oppositions between reason and emotion, the public and the private, and intellectualism versus caring.

One thing that post-paradigms have in common is that they attempt to decentre universality and heteronormativity in all its different forms in order to open the way to other possibilities for ethical questions, discourses and enactments. The feminist philosopher Irigaray (1985) reassess moral assumptions about female sexuality and economic exploitation of women and women's bodies as objects of economic exchange. All of this may seem a long way from the concerns of educators and educational researchers, but that is the point. The language and culture of schools is as white, middle class and patriarchal as any other social institution (Adkins and Skeggs 2004) but primary schools in particular are encased within discourses of childhood innocence that banishes these more difficult questions about power and performativity. As Raey (2006: 117) has argued, gendered power relations in primary classrooms are 'more complicated and contradictory than any simplistic binary discourse of boys versus girls'.

One way in which these complexities around binary discourses of gender has been approached in the field of education is through the concept of intersectionality. Even so, Bhopal and Preston (2011) characterize the study of difference in education as possible only through multi-disciplinary research that draws on a variety of theoretical perspectives. Education studies in the UK in the twenty-first century have been particularly resistant to these more radical ways of thinking about gender, banishing them to the margins of educational research or ignoring them all together. Weaver-Hightower and Skelton (2013) give interesting perspectives on what they call 'pro-feminist' education writers in their editing of a selection of feminist academics' self-portraits of their work.

The ethical dilemmas for researchers hoping to engage with questions of fairness and 'good practices' in education begins with how we might remain open to methodologies that peel back layers of social injustice. The intention of such an uncovering is not to reach a single correct solution, which is an impossibility, but to reveal prospects for pedagogical enactments that resist symbolic violence (McRobbie 2004). Even after these operational quandaries of finding an ethical project and carrying it out have been addressed, there remains the predicament of how to ethically speak and write up the findings (Derrida 1978).

I have found the idea of decentring or destabilizing orthodox views (including my own) particularly useful in a field such as education, which incorporates tensions between social welfare ideals and neoliberal functionalism. Ball (2021) points to changes in education systems and policies in the United Kingdom and elsewhere since 1976, which have seen profound shifts in teaching as a profession. The impact has been generated by a movement away from a public service ethos and towards a market economy of welfare. For a definition of neoliberalism in an educational context, Ball (2021) settles on Jones' (2016) description of ideologies based on a rolling back of the state in order to further the interests of free market economies and individual freedom and a competitive marketplace.

Contesting post-modernism in education, Rikowski and McLaren (1999) maintain that 'education has a crucial role to play in the struggle for a future where social, economic and political options are not *closed* by the domination of capital...' (Rikowski and McLaren 1999: 1). Rikowski and McLaren (1999) argue that post-modernism stands in the way of equality and social progress by turning away from progressive ideologies such as Marxism, to a fragmentary world view that addresses only local concerns. This misses the point that post-modernism is not a single ethical viewpoint and therefore has the potential to go beyond theoretical foundations such as educational reproduction (Adkins and Skeggs 2004), Marxism (Derrida 1994) and feminism (Irigaray 1977). The ethical standpoint of post-theories is often that knowledge is a shared enterprise that should resist top-down claims to legitimacy. This would suggest the need for a far more equal partnership between academics and others (Gordon 2018) that acknowledges the challenging and contested landscape between educational theory, educational research and pedagogical practices both within and beyond formal schooling.

Ethnography and ethno-methodology in education research

Whilst ethnography is an established method in British educational research, it has emerged primarily as a branch of sociology. I am most interested in post-structuralist ethnographies but for a more comprehensive overview of ethnography in education, see Gordon et al. (2001). The technique of a researcher immersing herself into a cultural context in order to observe and theorize the sociocultural landscape (or field) is taken from North American cultural anthropology and British social anthropology (Atkins et al. 2001). The ethical impasses of traditional and historical approaches to anthropology are well documented (Caplan 2003). They include the colonial power discrepancies between the researcher who enters an Indigenous community in order to 'make the strange familiar' and report back on native values and rituals (see also Alexander's discussions in Chapter XI).

Traditional anthropology is written in a very particular academic style. First, a context is given, often an account of the arrival of the researcher into 'the field' to be studied. In this introductory section, the strange habits of the Indigenous population (in our case children, teachers and other education professionals) are (re)counted. This is usually the only place within the text where the subjects appear as human agents (MacLure 2003). In this reading of the stories that are told by research, it is not that output is seen as more important than process but that both empirical action and the writing up are production. The completed report is not an end point since it lives on in the interpretations of its readers. Both starting points and endings, according to Derrida (1978), are arbitrary beyond the circumstance that the authors have had to decide where to begin and when to withdraw. What is (re)told after this is given the legitimacy of analytical text through the style of the writing. Academic writing of research is skilled in hiding the author within the text, but the world view is very much that of the researcher, not the researched (MacLure 2003). Issues around insider research have been considered more fully by Spiro in Chapter IX.

The manifestation of this unease over the unpredictability of impacts in conducting and then presenting (as in gifting through my writing) research was expressed in the introduction to my PhD thesis (written sometime after the fieldwork was complete). The aims of the research expressed a desire to create 'different spaces', in which the exchanges between adults and young children can be (re)cognized (MacRae 2011) as a process of meaning-making that values equality, diversity and social justice and co-constructs knowledge. This position is/was continually disrupted (or haunted) by archetypes of the adult as teacher, professional or technocrat, within a system that frames knowledge exchange as a financial transaction and early years education and care (EYEC) as no more and no less than a tool of a market economy (Shaw and Manchester Metropolitan University 2017).

Post-structural ethnographic techniques attempt to challenge the unequal power balance between the gaze of the researcher and the shared lived experience of all those involved in the undertaking of the research project. In other words, the investigator situates herself inside of the research (or acknowledges that she cannot be anywhere else except inside her own life and identity as a researcher). Attention is paid to all of the complex minutiae of everyday life in the research setting, for example sounds and smells (Cooper 2014); what is said and written (so that nothing is outside the text) (Derrida 1978); and/or what objects are permitted or excluded from the classroom (Jones et al. 2012). The starting point is not to 'make the strange familiar' but 'to make the familiar strange' (Gordon et al. 2001). This makes sense in a field such as education, since everyone has some sort of personal experience of being educated and projects are routinely initiated and carried out by education professionals of some sort or another. The 'some sort or another' may be teachers or educational psychologists, sociologists of education, advisors, or consultants and so forth. In my own research, I have struggled with the improbability of finding methodologies that are 'empowering and responsive' (Pascal 1993: 73) with the capacity to provide reliability and rigour, in the sense of attention to detail, beyond that claimed by traditional positive methods (Shaw 2017).

The impossibility of disentangling myself and my research from the modes of production of contemporary society, education policy and academic research conventions (De Lauritis 1987) has been one of the central ethical concerns of my enactments of educational investigation. My PhD journey began when working for a local authority practitioner-led project on young children's transitions ended. Within the methodological positioning that emerged, this might be classified as a rupture in the sense of an event experienced as a sort of violence that signalled the ending of something valued and the beginning of new possibilities for conceptualizing (Foucault 1980; Foucault 2000) work undertaken in the field of EYEC. The violence was a sudden withdrawal of funding, following a change of government, meaning that there was no longer time, physical space or salary for a facilitator to continue a project that had enabled schools and settings to come together to engage with academics and practice discourses on children's transitions (Shaw 2017).

When the study was proposed, my thinking and experience framed it within a sociocultural perspective (Tharp and Gallimore 1991). Here, knowledge is understood to be co-produced through the planned/unplanned interactions between adults, children and the environment (Stephen 2010). The intention was to employ an interpretive discourse (O'Hanlon 2003) and by pursuing participant action research (PAR) (Carr 2002; McNiff 2010) to create opportunities to interrogate existing practices as well as consider alternatives. This would have meant an undetermined number of research cycles in which I effectively mentored practitioner-researchers in posing and investigating research questions of interest to them. On reflection, this approach had several ethical as well as practical challenges. It appears as over-reliant on the work of others with unclear benefits for them in terms of actual return such as achieving higher qualifications, funding or even recognition. There were also unresolved dilemmas around my role within the participating settings. Teachers and practitioners were often grateful for the extra pair of hands, but it is unclear whether it could be said to be working for and with participants, including children (Clark and Moss 2001) within an 'ontology of emergence' (Lee, 2001; Horton 2001; Gallacher and Gallagher 2008). I could participate in, even enjoy, interactions with children whilst bearing none of the responsibilities of working for the organizations, planning, learning, interacting with parents or any of a plethora of other daily duties that fall to practitioners (Shaw 2017). This was the catalyst for a reconstituting of the methods/methodology into ethnomethodology through ethnographic observation and documentary analysis, which is explored below.

Further along in the research story, after a substantial amount of ethnography had been completed, came another rupture requiring a further reflexive turn (Seidman 1994; Best and Kellner 1997). My post as a Workforce Development Officer changed to that of Early Years Teacher Consultant (EYTC). This brought my working life much closer to practice and made the power relationship between schools where I was advising and nursery/reception classes participating in the ethnography, ethically untenable. The response (agreed with the supervision team) was to (re)turn my attention to the reports that I was writing as part of the quality process of EYT consultancy. The reports could not be analysed as individual but apparently 'complete' texts because this would have risked identifying individual schools and staff members. Therefore, in line with the methodological underpinnings of the study, the reports were deconstructed into their constituent headings of leadership and management; outcomes for children; safeguarding and welfare; learning and development; and, finally, observation of practice.

Short sections from individual reports were selected for scrutiny. Words or phrases that seemed to merit attention in relation to hauntings of pedagogical discourses and enactments were highlighted in the extracts and then discussed in more depth. Of interest were the tensions or juxtapositions which speak of or to power. There are connections to be made with Foucault's technologies of power and of the self, drawing on Foucault (Rabinow 1997) and Gordon (2008) as well as other post-structural influences. The section addressing leadership and management highlighted Foucault's notion of normalizing judgements: 'Outcomes for Children' scrutinized the disciplinary powers of marking schemes and next steps; the sections on 'Safeguarding and Welfare' considered the absence of the word 'care' within the report extracts; and 'Learning and Development' played with the words that convey pedagogical (and social) tensions, including 'challenge', 'model' and 'free flow'. The final section on observation touched on issues around fiction, culture and gender in research involving early years pedagogy. Here is an example from the analysis of 'learning and development':

> The juxtaposition of learning with development (Dahlberg et al. 2007; Dahlberg et al. 1999; Burman 2008a) has been one of the starting points from which the thesis began and to which it has returned in the literature review and the analyses of heterotopic spaces, objects, materials, and artefacts. The following extract from the part of the reports presented as Learning and Development picks up on the complexity and instability of the language(s) which haunt early years' pedagogical articulations. Ways in which terms of control collide with others which hint of freedom so that if something is modelled it must also be valued. The way in which writing; the wider curriculum (The World and Creative Development) (DfE 2014); the inside and the outside; free-flow; sharing; judging; demonstrating; interests; challenges and independence become entangled, juxtaposed and configured (Foucault 1994a) into a story of children and practitioners told by the report (Derrida and Wolfreys 1998; Payne 1993a). The key terms pulled out from this longer extract are 'model, value, focus, free flow, share, routines, judge, group, interests, challenges and independence'.
>
> Discussed opportunities to model and value writing within the wider curriculum. This might include children writing and displaying labels, opportunities for writing in wet sand and encouragement to use a variety of media for writing inside and outside, for example writing with chalk on walls and pavements. School have requested this as a focused support visit after half term. Talked about the extension of free flow to maximize the learning environment now that a new road track has been painted on the shared nursery/YR outside area Agreed that it would be beneficial to staff and children to share the indoor and outdoor spaces as appropriate.
>
> Suggested that it would be beneficial to spend the early weeks establishing routines in consultation with the Y1/2 teachers. This will also provide opportunities to judge children's starting points and group them accordingly.
>
> Agreed that planning in Y1/YR is strong and should continue to reflect children's interests and to demonstrate challenges during continuous provision and/or independent learning activities. (EYQL report, Ashton First School 8.10.13)

The report extract was then discussed/written about under the headings: terminologies of control; challenge system; modelling and free flow. The ethical shift that I was able to make was a transferal of focus from the practices of others to the system and my own complicity within it through my authorship of the reports.

Ethnomethodology is one possible response to some of the ethical dilemmas above. By focusing on methodology as the basis of ethical research design in sociology, ethnomethodology troubles traditional theories of social action that dominated the field in North America from the 1950s (Pollner and Emerson 2001). The premise of such work is that sociology that relies on techniques, procedures and writing conventions taken directly from the physical sciences constructs a false representation of people's social worlds as universal and reproducible, in discursive texts, by an objective outsider in the guise of the researcher/author. As Pollner and Emmerson (2001: 119) express it, ethnomethodology concerns itself with 'the orderliness of social life as experienced, constructed and used from within the concrete and particular contexts and activities of which the society is composed'. In education, the society is composed of teachers, students, parents and others in schools, classrooms and any other institution in which pedagogical interaction might occur. Epistemological concerns of who holds legitimate social knowledge and how it should be (re)presented is problematized. This produces a tension between ethics procedures that resist or may be vigilant/apprehensive about insider research with ethical dilemmas around truth and power embodied in research with human participants.

Writing specifically about social research in education MacLure (2003) demonstrates the links between ethnomethodology and conversation analysis. Ethnomethodology pays attention to language as an unavoidable mediator between human experience and reality (Derrida 1978). Ethnomethodology rejects sociology's treatment of language as transparent and straightforward. The critique is that language used as a medium through which to express sociological categorization, for example class, ethnicity, normativity and deviance, overlooks language's 'role in creating social realities, including the reality of sociologists' *own* categories' (MacLure 2003: 188). Such deliberations take ethical research far beyond the necessity for informed consent and meeting the basic requirements of ethical permission to proceed with a research project.

As an example of how ethnomethodology can operate in an educational context, I offer an extract and analysis of some of my fieldwork, which took place in nurseries and Key Stage 1 primary classrooms in England (Shaw 2017):

> Andrew is interested in the mark making. His speech is difficult to understand but he gives me directions which I attempt (badly) to follow. I draw a spiral. Later Andrew traces around this with a pencil. His fine motor skills appear well practised'. (Field notes, St Egberts, 24.11.11)

> Andrew is a magnet for the panics around children's language; he is described as 'one of several children in Nursery who have very poor speech'. He is likely to be labelled as 'emerging' in this prime area of EYFS learning and development (DfE 2014) and will carry this construction of his identity with him into Reception. It is not so much that he does not engage with the learning on offer, mark making is perceived as an important pre-curser to writing,

but that he has not engaged in them in the 'correct order'. He needs to demonstrate his competence in 'speaking and listening' before his election of mark making can be endorsed. Perhaps he is also less skilled in interpreting the implied meanings of the emplacement of objects in an education setting than some of the other children [who featured in the writing up of the study].

Of course, the names of the school and the child conjured up in the field notes have been fictionalized to adhere to important rules about anonymity and the event was witnessed and date stamped. All ethical requirements in terms of carrying out the ethnography were met. However, ethical dilemmas reassert themselves in the writing up of the analysis. Andrew is given a pretend name so as not to dehumanize him with a number or a letter. He is an active agent, not just Child or Pupil 1/A.

Ethics and aesthetics

Aesthetics, the philosophical study of beauty and cultural taste (Lyas 1997), has tended to be ignored by educational research outside that specifically concerned with arts education. A dichotomy is thereby generated between aesthetics and ethics. It is within the remit of post-structuralism to dismantle all such false oppositions in order to examine their workings and reconstruct them in the image of the other. Post-structuralism (and other post-paradigms) challenge false dichotomies such as black and white, where whiteness has been historically valued above brown or blackness, masculinity above femininity, Christianity above other religions and so forth. All of these social constructions – ethnicity, gender, religion – could be said to contain both aesthetic judgements and moral ones.

There is a conscious effort in the choice of extract to make the role of the researcher in the encounter visible. The communication difficulties are not considered as being located in Andrew but also in the adult researcher, who finds it difficult to follow the instructions. The usual power relations are messed about with, although not entirely reversed. Critique is of the system and of ways in which we are all drawn into specific ways of viewing and interpreting our shared social worlds, particularly within culturally specific institutions such as schools. In other words, there is an ongoing desire to make the familiar strange in order to articulate differently the possibilities for speaking about and enacting practice. There is an intentional blurring or juxtaposition of ethics with aesthetics, that is an association is made between cultural good/diversity and social and moral justice.

Emerging from post-structural philosophers such as Foucault (2000) is an invitation to address cultural ideologies from the margins, so that their idiosyncrasies but also their ethics (by which I mean just and unjust practices) can be brought to the surface. In the collection of Foucault's essays 'Aesthetics essential works of Foucault 1954–1984' the threads which bind the essays together are concepts through which societies have operated regimes of power over citizens, such as ideas on madness, normality, social spaces and social roles. Much of Foucault's work is interested in the operation of power, which he presents as functioning not only from the top down but also through resistance and counter cultures. Post-structuralism is not what comes after structuralism, but a confronting of the continuing operation of constructions of power and hauntings from historical ideologies (Gordon 2008) such as those spawned from Marxism (Derrida 1978) and Freud (Buhle 1998). In educational theory, that has translated as going beyond entrenched and/or contested theoretical frames so that Ball (1990) has applied Foucault's theories to regimes of power and discipline in schools and feminist writers have taken a critical stance on concepts such as symbolic violence and social class as iterated by Bourdieu (Adkins and Skeggs 2004).

The recognition of aesthetics and ethics as two sides of a coin rather than separate conceptual entities has been most widely acknowledged within literary criticism (Palladino 2018; Ellison 2001). In the field of sociology, Gordon (2008) has extracted the metaphor of social haunting and technologies of the self from Foucault (Foucault 1988), but combined this with a consideration of what the fictive contributes to our understanding of human rights, social justice, racism and sexism. Gordon is making a powerful point about the multidisciplinary nature of these ethical concepts, which weave themselves through all social institutions (Gordon 2017). It is not a great leap to play with these ethical ideas in the context of children/childhood and education (Shaw 2020). I think that the artificial boundaries between art and science/aesthetics and ethics are also being tested (or pushed against) in renewed interest in creativity in schools and the translation of science, technology, engineering and maths (STEM) to STEAM, which incorporates the importance of art education (McGregor 2021). Links here can be made with Chapter VII, where Frodsham and McGregor look at issues of agency and privacy when exploring creative processes in the classroom. This takes us quite neatly onto a discussion of the imagination in educational research.

The imagination and the sociological imagination in research in education

Education is a field in which traditionalism (and traditional values) continually rub up against progressivism (and progressive values). More than traditional methods of either quantitative or qualitative research are needed in order to answer pedagogical questions such as: whether the onus should be on teachers to teach or learners to learn; whether schools should be ready for children or children ready for schools; whether curricula should meet the needs of the economy or a wider interpretation of society and social good; and whether research should be carried out by an academic elite or a broader range of social actors. In the fourth edition of *The Education Debate,* Ball (2021) considers the social/ethical implications of education reform in England, including the impact of globalization and internationalism, the marketization of education, social mobility and impacts of Covid-19. All are topics with moral dimensions both within and beyond the formal/public education system. Possibly what we might draw from this is that politics, an inherently ethical enterprise, has become a haunting of educational discourses which tends to banish it from enactments of teaching and educational research. What I mean is that politics in school hides itself in plain sight – we all know that it is unavoidably present but, possibly due to the way in which we construct childhood in the West (James and Prout 1997), it has become a taboo in education and other pedagogical spaces where children and young people are present.

With reference to Dahlberg et al. (2013), I am entering from a location where early years (and maybe every stage of education) has no pre-determined purposes, composition or meaning but is what we as human agents choose to construct. Much discourse around education, both domestically and internationally, has taken on languages of quality, standards and outcomes. 'Much of this work on quality has been undertaken in the United States' and 'can, in part be understood as a consequence of the particular conditions of that country. A dominant ideology of private responsibility for children, reliance on free market solutions, high levels of demand and large economic equalities between families' (Dahlberg et al. 2013: 30). In the UK, practitioners often look to the Scandinavian countries for better articulation of ethical practices (Centre for Educational Research and Innovation 2005) whilst policy seems to track North American discourses (Dahlberg et al. 2013). Other examples of international comparisons have been provided by Capewell in Chapter VI and Alexander in Chapter XI.

Kettley (2010) critiques education studies for its lack of engagement with debates about methodology and theory building. Kettley (2010: 3) argues that education research 'is remarkably silent with respect to the meaning, purposes and procedures of theory building'. This, in my view, is an ethical issue. If educational researchers weld themselves to a narrow range of theoretical paradigms, then the door to discussion, diversity and knowledge exchange about socially just methodologies is firmly closed. Ethics in research (and in life, for that matter) is not a fixed set of principles but a necessary debate about how human beings should respond to ever-changing social and physical aspects of people's lives (our lives and the lives of those others who do not share our privileges or resources).

This ethical emplacement of theory and methodology is particularly important in a field such as education studies where the hinterland between philosophy and practice is narrow and frequently traversed by academics, practitioners and others such as parents and politicians. The purpose of social science is to explain and potentially transform social processes (Kettley 2010). Disciplinary claims on particular types of knowledge have meant that philosophy (rather than social science or education) has been seen as the only domain from which questions about 'what an explanation *is*' (Kettley 2010: 113) can be decided. This is an argument for more methodological and ethical focused investigations within education research, as well as more openness to interdisciplinarity.

In his interpretation of how education studies might innovate its assemblage of new theory, Kettley (2010) stresses the role of imagination. This is a necessary part of scientific research but also denotes an ability to seek out and articulate questions of importance to social practices in education in the vein of Mills (1959/2000) 'sociological imagination'. 'This abstraction denotes the ability to explore biographical, interpersonal and historical data in pursuit of accurate and original explanations of schooling' (Kettley 2010: 139). Taking this notion of the sociological/educational imagination from an ethical perspective, I would say that it is particularly important in educational research which seeks to recognize 'the other' in relation to white male hegemony within education systems (Spivak 1993). Central to the achievement of social justice in education is recognition of the importance of practitioners, children and young people taking a more active role in research that involves their lives and experiences of pedagogy.

The term 'the sociological imagination' has crept into common usage, at least in the field of sociology. Gordon (2008) uses it in her title *Ghostly Matters: Haunting and the Sociological Imagination*, although she never directly references Mills (1959/2000), the North American sociologist who is generally credited with coining the phrase. Mills' ideas on the need for a different type of social science research have influenced my own approach to researching and writing about childhood and education (Shaw 2021).

It is Mills (1959/2000) who highlights 'the sociological imagination' as a response to a shift from a modernist age to a 'post-modern period', although his own work was founded on more traditional sociological paradigms. The trend that Mills identifies in the middle of the twentieth century carries through into the twenty-first as transition in public and academic consciousness of philosophy, economics, values (or ethics) and the instability of lived experiences (Hall 2012).

Post-modern thought troubles concepts such as truth, freedom and rationality as they have been constructed since the Enlightenment (Dahlberg et al. 2013). In education this means facing up to the concept of childhood as a social construct which has changed (and continues to change) through history and location (Hendrick 1997). In England, childhood (and its counterpoint, pupilhood) has lengthened, with younger children occupying nursery provision on school sites and adolescence extended as far as 24 or 25 years (Deming and Dynarski 2008).

On the face of it, the ethical implications for research involving very young children are very different from those faced by researchers interested in adolescence or young adulthood. The dilemma is that approaches that construct children (of any age) as vulnerable, in need or fully reliant on adults casts them as something other than fully human (Woodhead 1997). It takes no account of situations where the intention of the adult differs significantly from that of the child and neither is either right or wrong. Although issues such as child protection remain important, they are not 'non-negotiables' in relation to conceptualization because this would (and arguably has) generated unforeseen social injustices as in the over-representations of Indigenous Australian children in the social care system (Tsantefski and Connolly 2013). What Woodhead (1997) argues is that by viewing children's needs as an enlightened and progressive way of working with children in comparison to practices of the past, which cast children as economic units, we fail to see injustices and inequalities within safeguarding and welfare systems. Systematic analysis of taken-for-granted concepts, such as that of 'need', has the potential to reveal 'a complex of latent assumptions and judgements about children' (Woodhead 1997: 61) by adults in education settings.

This ethical conundrum was also visible in my analysis of the safeguarding and welfare sections of the EYTC reports previously described. What emerged were themes around the disciplining of care and the absence of care. For a partial demonstration an extract of the analysis follows:

> Revisited key requirements including paediatric first aid; safeguarding; storage of medication; mobile phone, camera and e-safety; risk assessment (which should be carried out daily and visible within the classroom) and food hygiene. Referred to document Keeping Children Safe in Education, which can be downloaded from https://www.gov.uk/government/publications/keeping-children-safe-in-education. The SCB website is also an important source of up-to-date information, advice and guidance' (EYQL report, Heath Primary School, October 2015).
>
> As structuralist texts, the safeguarding and welfare sections of the reports are prominent in their success in redirecting matters of the body towards professional domains outside of the early years' heterotopic space of the Reception class unit. Apart from the juxtaposition of safeguarding and welfare in the title all possibility of alternative pedagogical positions is eradicated. This section is haunted (and a haunting) in the ways discussed by Gordon (2008) as a haunting by absence. The discourse is about requirements. The word 'requirements' is a symbol of non-negotiability and unquestionability, which is reinforced by the statement that they are key requirements. Turning the key would open the door to a forbidden and, therefore, a frightening room of unspeakable violations of the innocence of childhood (Shaw (2017) - PhD thesis).

Children's agency and power/permission to express their personal and cultural experiences is not only an ethical prosperity of protecting children. Adult perspectives also dominate the constructive processes of curricular. In her account of early years artmaking MacRae (2011: 103) discovered that her 'teacherly assumptions about representational intent are unsettled'. This type of reflexive turn (Seidman 1994) is more possible in post-paradigms, which allow for the concept of the researcher as insider because they actively urge a critical approach to the self (see also Spiro, Chapter IX). Such paradigms set out to dig deep and trouble the assumptions associated with our different, and sometimes conflicting, identities as teacher, researcher, parent, carer, advisor, mentor, consultant and citizen (Sarup and Raja 1996).

Before moving to the conclusion, here is a final example from my own ethnomethodological field work and its analysis, which exposes the application of the imagination over more 'fact bound' methodologies. The point being made is that allowing the child into the research, not by following them around or questioning their competency, reveals new truths and different perspectives on what might constitute socially just education:

> One Reception-aged child, Joseph, haunts the first participant observation in the newly created early years' cloakroom/corridor/learning space. He features as children drift in and out at break time, in the observation of the children sent out to use the area and at times in between this when he should officially have been in the classroom but has entered the space on the way to the toilets or the coat pegs (or for reasons of his own making).
>
> Joseph spends 5–10 minutes telling me and himself about the contents of the trays; 'The frogs are similar. Some have red eyes.' He shows me that the caterpillar is stretchy. I say, 'I hope it doesn't pull apart.' Joseph says, 'No it is stretchy.' (Fieldnotes, St Egbert's RC Primary School 26.5.2011)
>
> Joseph is a magnet for adult concern. He is particularly good at using language to express non-conformity, which leads to professional questioning of his behaviour since he is not always interested in completing tasks set at the times designated. While he has an abundance of curiosity and his own explanations for the contents of the environmental trays, efforts to get him to read and write in a more formal teaching scenario are exhausting and usually short lived, even tokenistic. He also fails the school readiness test. At five years old, Joseph has already read and decoded the notes which tell him that learning in school is about passivity and obedience, about completing tasks to satisfy adults or avoiding them if possible. That independent learning, exploration and intellectual stimulation are located behind him in the haunted space of a different pedagogy, gradually receding out of reach (Shaw (2017) - PhD thesis).

The ethics is not only contained within how the investigations are carried out but also how Joseph and other young people as the subjects/participants are (re)presented in the analysis, writing and dissemination of the research. It is this dilemma that has instigated my search for methodologies that bring into play post-structural and post-feminist work. Such paradigms tend to exist on the margins of sociology and education studies. This is a situation that leaves open the possibility of being and becoming a different type of researcher and educator (Masney 2013) for every occasion on which I engage with academia, education practises and that contested space between.

Conclusion

The chapter set out to trouble the ethics involved in research, which hopes to fairly (re)cognize the complexity of social worlds. It has suggested that there are times when the ethical certainties of research committee permissions need to dialogue with other ethical paradigms emerging from education studies and social research. This authorizes more experimental methods and theory building

(Kettley 2010) to occur safely rather than being stifled by limiting standpoints taken directly from the physical sciences.

Ethical concepts disturbed have included the impossibilities of positioning the researcher as outside this type of research and the undesirability of doing so. I have argued for a greater acceptance of education professionals as partners in academic investigation (or exploitation) in their field. I also suggest that there is an ethical imperative in education research to (re)consider constructions of childhood and the contribution that children and young people make to the study of their lives within and beyond the school gates.

Finally, I have questioned whether ethics should be seen as located primarily in the time and space in which ethics approval is being sought and the fieldwork carried out. Ethical choices haunt the selection of the question, the recruitment and continuing relationship with participants and all other stages of the research process. They are particularly present in those enactments and discourses that are never written up and remain within the realms of the 'messiness of research' (Gibbes and Skop 2020). Drawing on post-structural philosophy to be found in the work of Foucault and Derrida, I have suggested that the writing of research is just as important in acknowledging ethical issues of power between researcher and researched as well as author and reader.

References

Adkins, L. and Skeggs, B. (2004) *Feminism after Bourdieu*. Oxford: Blackwell (Sociological review monographs).
Al Salami, M.K., Makela, C.J. and de Miranda, M.A. (2017) Assessing changes in teachers' attitudes toward interdisciplinary stem teaching, *International Journal of Technology and Design Education*, 27(1): 63–88.
Atkins, P., Coffey, A., Delamont, S. et al.(2001) *Handbook of Ethnography*. London: Sage.
Ball, S. J. (1990) *Foucault and Education: Disciplines and Knowledge*. London: Routledge.
Ball, S.J. (2021) *The Education Debate* (4th edn). Bristol: Policy (Policy and politics in the twenty-first century).
Best, S. and Kellner, D. (1997) *The Postmodern Turn*. New York: Guilford Press (Critical perspectives).
Bhopal, K. and Preston, J. (2011) *Intersectionality and Race in Education*. Hoboken: Taylor & Francis (Routledge Research in Education).
Buhle, M.J. (1998) *Feminism and Its Discontents: A Century of Struggle with Psychoanalysis*. Cambridge, MA: Harvard University Press.
Caplan, P. (2003) *The Ethics of Anthropology: Debates and Dilemmas*. London: Routledge.
Carr, W. (2002) *Becoming critical education, knowledge and action research*. London: Routledge Falmer Press.
Centre for Educational Research and Innovation (2005) *Formative Assessment: Improving Learning in Secondary Classrooms*. Paris: OECD.
Clark, A and Moss P. (2001) *Listening to children: the mosaic approach*. London: National Children's Bureau.
Coloma, R.S. (2009) *Postcolonial challenges in education*. New York: Peter Lang (Counterpoints, v. 369).

Cooper, D. (2014) *Everyday Utopias the Conceptual Life of Promising Spaces*. London and Durham: Duke University Press.

Dahlberg, G., Moss, P. and Pence, A.R. (2013) *Beyond Quality in Early Childhood Education and Care: Languages of Evaluation*. Classic edn. London: Routledge (Routledge education classic edition series).

Davis, J.D., Olive, J.L. and Brynn-Bevel, R.J. (2015) *Intersectionality in Educational Research*. Dulles: Stylus Publishing (Engaged research and practice for social justice in education series).

De Lauretis, T. (1987) *Technologies of Gender: Essays on Theory, Film, and Fiction*. Basingstoke: Macmillan (Language, discourse, society series).

Deming, D. and Dynarski, S. (2008) The lengthening of childhood, *Journal of Economic Perspectives*, 22(3): 71–92.

Derrida, J. (1978) *Writing and Difference*. London: Routledge & K. Paul.

Derrida, J. (1994) Spectres of Marx, *New Left Review*, 205: 31–31.

DiQuinzio, P. and Young, I.M. (1997) *Feminist Ethics and Social Policy*. Bloomington, IN: Indiana University Press (A Hypatia book).

Edwards, R. and Ribbens McCarthy, J. (1998) *Feminist Dilemmas in Qualitative Research: Public Knowledge and Private Lives*. London: Sage.

Ellison, D.R. (2001) *Ethics and Aesthetics in European Modernist Literature: From the Sublime to the Uncanny*. Cambridge: Cambridge University Press.

Foucault, M. and Faubion, J.D. (2000) *Essential Works of Foucault, 1954–1984*. London: Penguin.

Foucault, M. and Gordon, C. (1980) *Power/knowledge: Selected Interviews and Other Writings, 1972–1977*. Brighton: Harvester Press.

Foucault, M. et al. (1988) *Technologies of the Self: A Seminar with Michel Foucault*. Amherst: University of Massachusetts Press.

Gallacher L.-A. and Gallagher, M. (2008) 'Methodological immaturity in childhood research? Thinking through 'participatory methods', *Childhood*, 15(4) pp 499–561.

Gibbes, C. and Skop, E. (2020) The messiness of co-produced research with gatekeepers of resettled refugee communities, *Journal of Cultural Geography*, 37(3): 78–295.

Gordon, A.F. (2008) *Ghostly Matters: Haunting and the Sociological Imagination*. Minneapolis, MN: University of Minnesota Press.

Gordon, A.F. (2018) *Letters from the utopian margins. The Hawthorn archive*. New York: Fordham University Press.

Gordon, A.F. (2017) *The Hawthorn Archive: Letters from the Utopian Margins*. New York, NY: Fordham University Press.

Gordon, T., Holland, J. and Lahelma, E. (2001) Ethnographic research in educational settings, in P. Atkins et al. (eds) *Handbook of Ethnography*. London: Sage.

Hall, B.L. (2012) *Learning and Education for a Better World: The Role of Social Movements*. Rotterdam: SensePublishers (International issues in adult education, v. 10).

Hendrick, H. (1997) Constructions and reconstructions of British childhood: an interpretative survey, 1800 to present, in A. James, and A. Prout (eds) *Constructing and Reconstructing Childhood*. London: Falmer Press.

Humes, W. and Bryce, T. (2003) Post-structuralism and policy research in education, *Journal of Education Policy*, 18:175–188.

Horton, J. (2001) 'Do you get some funny looks when you tell people what you do? Mudlling through some angsts and ethics (of being male) researching with children,' *Ethics place and environment*. 4(2) pp 159–166.

Irigaray, L. (1977) *This Sex Which is Not One*. Ithaca, NY: Cornell University Press.

James, A. and Prout, A. (1997) *Constructing and Reconstructing Childhood: Contemporary Issues in the Sociological Study of Childhood*. London: Falmer Press.

Jones, K. (2016) *Education in Britain: 1944 to the Present* (2nd edn). Cambridge: Polity Press.

Jones, L., MacLure, M., Holmes, R. and McRae, C. (2012) Children and objects: affection and infection, *Early Years*, 32(1): 9–60.

Kellett, M. (2010) *Rethinking Children and Research: Attitudes in Contemporary Society*. New York, NY: Continuum International Pub. Group (New childhoods series).

Kettley, N.C. (2010) *Theory Building in Educational Research*. New York: Continuum International Pub. Group.

Lee, N. (2001) *Childhood and society, growing up in an age of uncertainty*. Buckingham: Open University Press.

Lyas, C. (1997) *Aesthetics*. London: UCL Press (Fundamentals of Philosophy).

Masny, D. (2013) "Rhizoanalytic Pathways in Qualitative Research," *Qualitative Inquiry*, 19(5), pp. 339–348. doi: 10.1177/1077800413479559.

MacLure, M. (2003) *Discourse in Education and Social Research*. Buckingham: Open University Press (Conducting Educational Research).

MacRae, C. (2011) Making Payton's Rocket: heterotopia and lines of flight, *International Journal of Art and Design Education*, 30(1): 102–112.

Mauthner, N. and Doucet, A. (1998) Reflections on a voice-centred relational method, in R. Edwards, R. and J. Ribbens McCarthy (eds) *Feminist Dilemmas in Qualitative Research: Public Knowledge and Private Lives*. London: Sage.

McGregor, D. (2021) Stories from history: more authentic ways of thinking through acting and talking about science, in P. White, J. Raphael and K. van Cuylenburg (eds) *Science and Drama: Contemporary and Creative Approaches to Teaching and Learning*. Switzerland AG: Springer Nature.

McNay, L. (1992) *Foucault and Feminism: Power, Gender and Self*. Cambridge: Polity (Power, Gender and the Self).

McNiff, J. (2010) *Action research for professional development*. Dorset: September Books.

McRobbie, A. (2004) Symbolic violence, and the cultural field. Notes on 'what not to wear' and post-feminist symbolic violence, in L. Adkins and B. Skeggs (eds) *Feminism after Bourdieu*. Oxford: Blackwell Pub (Sociological Review Monographs).

Meyer, R.E. (2009) *Institutions and Ideology* (1st edn). Bingley: Emerald Group (Research in the Sociology of Organizations, vol. 27).

Mills C.W. (1959/2000) *The Sociological Imagination*. Oxford: Oxford University Press.

O'Hanlon, C. (2003) *Educational inclusion as action research: an interpretive discourse*. Berkshire: Open University Press.

Palladino, M. (2018*) Ethics and Aesthetics in Toni Morrison's Fiction*. Leiden: Brill Rodopi (Costerus New Series, vol. 223).

Pascal, C. (1993) 'Capturing the quality of education provision for young children: A story of developing professionals and developing methodology', *European early childhood education research journal*, 1(1) pp 69–80.

Pinar, W. (1998) *Queer Theory in Education*. Mahwah, NJ: L. Erlbaum Associates (Studies in curriculum theory).

Pollner M. and Emerson R. (2001) Ethnomethodology and ethnography, in P. Atkinson, et al. (eds.). *Handbook of Ethnography*. London: Sage.

Preston, M. (2018) Queer Teachers, Identity, and Performativity, *Journal of LGBT youth*, 15(2): 145–147.

Rabinow P. (ed) (1997) *Ethics essential works of Foucault 1954–1984*. London: Penguin.

Raey, D. (2006) 'Spice girls', 'nice girls', girlies', and tomboys': gender discourses, 'girls' cultures and femininities in the primary classroom, in M. Arnot, and M. Mac an Ghaill, (eds) *The Routledge Falmer Reader in Gender and Education*. London: Routledge (Readers in Education).

Rikowski, G. and Mclaren, P. (1999) 'Postmodernism in educational theory. Postmodern excess' in Hill, D. et al (eds) Postmodernism in Educational Theory. Education and the politics of human resistance. London: The Tufnell Press, pp 1–9.

Rivers, D.J. and Zotzmann, K. (eds) (2017) *Isms in Language Education: Oppression, Intersectionality and Emancipation*. Boston: De Gruyter (Language and Social Life, v. 11).

Sarup, M. and Raja, T. (1996) *Identity, Culture and the Postmodern World*. Edinburgh: Edinburgh University Press.

Seidman, S. (1994) *The Postmodern Turn: New Perspectives on Social Theory*. Cambridge: Cambridge University Press.

Shaw, L. (2020) Play spaces as heterotopia: seeking new ways to trouble the discourses and enactments of playwork, *International Journal of Playwork Practice*, 1(1).

Shaw, L.J. and Manchester Metropolitan University (2017) *Heterotopia and Hauntings: Troubling the Spaces and Artefacts of Early Years' Education and Care in England*. Dissertation. Manchester Metropolitan University.

Shaw, L.J. (2021) Imagining playwork using sociological perspectives from Mills, Foucault and Gordon, in P. King and S. Newstead (eds) *Further Perspectives on Research Play from a Playwork Perspective: Process, Playfulness, Rights-Based and Critical Reflection*. Abingdon: Routledge (Advances in Playwork Research).

Silverman, H.J. (1989) *Derrida and Deconstruction*. New York: Routledge (Continental Philosophy, 2).

Silvers, A. (1997) Reconciling equality to difference: caring (F)or justice for people with disabilities, in P. DiQuinzio and I. M. Young (eds) *Feminist Ethics and Social Policy*. Bloomington, IN: Indiana University Press (A Hypatia book).

Spivak, G.C. (1993) *Outside in the Teaching Machine*. New York: Routledge.

Stephen, C. (2010) 'Pedagogy: the silent partner in early years learning' *Early Years*, 30(1) pp 15–28.

Tharp, R. and Gallimore, R.L. (1991) 'A theory of teaching as assisted performance', in Light P., Sheldon, S. and Gallimore, R. (eds) *Learning to think: child development in social context*. London: Routledge pp 42–61.

Tisdall, E.K.M., Davis, J.M. and Gallagher, M. (2009) *Researching with Children and Young People: Research Design, Methods and Analysis*. Los Angeles CA: Sage.

Tsantefski, M. and Connolly, M. (2013) Australia, in P. Welbourne and J.E. Dixon (eds) *Child Protection and Child Welfare: A Global Appraisal of Cultures, Policy and Practice*. London: Jessica Kingsley.

Weaver-Hightower, M. B. and Skelton, C. (eds) (2013) Leaders in gender and education: intellectual self-portraits. Rotterdam: SensePublishers (Leaders in Educational Studies, v. 4). doi: 10.1007/978-94-6209-305-8.

Woodhead, M. (1997) Psychology and the cultural construction of children's needs, in A. James, and A. Prout (eds) *Constructing and Reconstructing Childhood: Contemporary Issues in the Sociological Study of Childhood*. London: Falmer Press.

Zamudio, M., Russell, C., Rios, F. et al. (2010) *Critical Race Theory Matters: Education and Ideology*. Hoboken, NJ: Taylor and Francis.

XIII Conclusion: the Hidden Lives of Ethics: Beyond the Pragmatics

Mary Wild

It is one of the rare/few certainties of a researcher's academic life that ethical approval for projects will be required, and rightly so. On the face of it, ethics can be seen as cut-and-dried; a series of regulations, guidelines and protocols to be adhered to and arbitrated by ethics committees. In one sense, a series of non-negotiables, sometimes viewed by the academic as a series of obstacles to be overcome rather than an enabling process. However, this book was borne of multiple discussions between colleagues within one school of education and within one university, seeking to move beyond the back-and-forth of gaining project approvals and to engender deeper engagement and understanding of the research process. Our discussions proved productive, helping to hone individual projects along the way, but also served to illuminate the underlying ethical dilemmas and tensions that come into play as a project is conceived and which perpetuate and evolve throughout the lifecycle of the project and its subsequent dissemination. These dilemmas can be intensely pragmatic but also intensely philosophical and the purpose of this book has been to share these reflections more widely. Adopting the pragmatic/philosophical interplay throughout the book and as noted in the introduction (Chapter I), three key themes have emerged:

1 Researchers must always, first and foremost, engage with the ethical principles and guidance.
2 A careful balance must be struck between the needs of participants, increasing regulatory guidelines and the academic freedom of the educational researcher.
3 Ethical dilemmas do not exist in isolation and can be resolved as part of a community of researchers.

In highlighting these themes, this book sought to draw on perspectives from a range of differing research traditions. Educational research is a diverse discipline, even though it may be claimed that particular paradigms are privileged over others, as has been agued in various chapters. This book has not sought to presuppose any particular stance and it has also sought to cover the perspectives of researchers at differing points in their research trajectory from undergraduate level through to more established academics. Ethical dilemmas are pertinent at each and every stage of a research career and, as demonstrated in the earliest chapters of this book (see Chapters II and III), formal ethical regulations and expectations are themselves an evolving terrain. Therefore, this book could not offer prescriptive solutions to the dilemmas that its authors expose, but rather the various contributors offered insights and possible resolutions that they have found helpful in their own work.

Researchers must always, first and foremost, engage with the ethical principles and guidance

In the opening chapter, Brown documented the genesis of ethics codes in educational research and their subsequent development over the last half-century. Drawing on seminal underpinnings such as the Belmont Report in 1976 (DHEW 1979) and the United Nations Convention on the Rights of the Child (UNICEF 1989), this chapter elucidated some of the key principles enshrined across a range of relevant ethical codes. Education-specific guidelines produced by BERA (BERA 2018) were highlighted to demonstrate the differing responsibilities that individual researchers and the broader research community have. As would be expected, this list of responsibilities is led by the responsibility towards participants, but also accords ethical responsibilities towards sponsors, clients and stakeholders in research and towards the wider community in relation to the publication and dissemination of findings and for the wellbeing and development of researchers. One might raise a question about the order in which these are listed, but essentially the broad sweep and specificity of research responsibilities is well encapsulated in these guidelines and they are evoked and referenced throughout the chapters of this book alongside other regulatory codes pertinent to educational research, which are noted in a subsequent section of this conclusion. In doing so, the authors do not apply these guidelines without critical reflection. On the contrary, the contributors seek to probe some of the explicit and implicit tensions that can arise both in the empirical field and in the desk-based research environment. Some of the authors, most notably Patrick Alexander and Linda Shaw in Chapters XII and XI, seek to 'trouble' and interrogate some of the underlying assumptions of these various codes, which are based, as they claim, upon a predominantly individualist and modernist conception of the world and of research. These critiques, however, are positioned to unpick and further illuminate principles of ethical research. Throughout this book, contributors are committed to the pursuit of ethical research and finding ways to enact these principles in the practice of research.

It is significant to note the extent to which ethical codes are not static and unchanging. Though some of the principles may seem to be immutable, it is clear in many of the chapters that refer to the historicity of codes (see Chapters II, III and XI, for example) that ethical codes do not exist in a vacuum. Rather they are symptomatic of the times in which they are first developed and have been adapted as societal understandings and research contexts change. For example, the recent incorporation of GDPR Protection laws (GDPR 2018) and other concerns that have arisen as our societies are becoming ever more digitally dependent is noted in Chapters II and III and reprised in relation to research with existing and publicly available or longitudinal data sets (see Chapter VIII). These societal changes have also spawned a growing range of ethical dilemmas for the field-based educational researcher to address and accommodate within their projects as noted in Chapter X.

At a more critical, conceptual level, researcher understandings of participants – the bedrock of ethical guides – are changing, as for example in terms of the way children and childhood are now conceptualized as more agentive (see Capewell, Chapter VI). As Linda Shaw further argues in Chapter XII, there may need to be a further fundamental paradigmatic shift in conceptions of what constitutes research and the researched and the consequent role or position of the researcher. This echoes the redefinition of researcher position that is fundamental to the prism of research that focuses on the self, and the self in practice, as the researcher and the researched that is explored in Spiro's chapter (Chapter IX). Similarly, conceptions of legitimate study of culture and peoples across the globe may need to be re-orientated towards a more inclusive, respectful and more culturally relevant lens (Capewell, Chapter VI; Alexander, Chapter XI). It could be argued that these changing perceptions of research and the positionality of researcher and researched are not moving swiftly enough. However, this book does not contend that we should therefore eschew existing codes. Instead, we should seek to engage with debates and accelerate the signs of change that are emerging within key sector organizations, such as BERA, and to take this debate back to our own institutions and our individual practices.

A careful balance must be struck between the needs of participants, increasing regulatory guidelines and the academic freedom of the educational researcher

The preceding section focused mostly on BERA as the benchmark for the field of research with which this book is concerned, but throughout the book, authors have additionally drawn upon a range of diverse disciplinary or internationally specific ethical codes and frameworks. These have included codes in disciplines often allied to education, such as the British Psychological Society (BPS 2021) (Chapter II); the Education and Science Research Council (ESRC 2019) (Chapter IX) and the American Anthropological Association (Chapter XI). Other international codes have also been referenced, such as the American Educational Research Association (AERA 2011) (Chapter XI); the American Medical Association (AMA (2001) (Chapter IX); the International Visual Sociology Association (IVSA 2019) Code of Research Ethics (Chapter V); the Global Code of Conduct for Research in Resource Poor Settings (2018) in Chapter III; and, of course, the United Nations Convention on the Rights of the Child (UNICEF 1989).

Capewell in her chapter (VI) compares the national oversight of research ethics in Australia and Sweden. She draws an interesting contrast between Sweden, which adopts a relatively fluid approach wherein ethics committees are seen to provide a monitoring framework for researchers to develop their own ethical stance as part of their research practice, compared to Australia where research is guided by a national code. Even in the case of Australia though, she points out that this is a code not a law (Australian Government 2018), underscoring a similar point made by Quinton in Chapter III that ethics are frequently not enshrined as particular legislation but tend to be 'governed' by guidance or codes.

This does not mean that researchers are not bound by statutory regulation. As several authors point out, educational researchers must have due regard for a variety of legislation pertinent to working with children and young people. This includes safeguarding legislation https://www.gov.uk/government/organizations/disclosure-and-barring-service); the SEND code of practice,(Department for Education and Department of Health, 2014) and statutory guidance for organizations in the UK working with disabled CYP or special educational needs (Department for Education and Department of Health, 2014. Statutory requirements related to data collection, storage and dissemination are also applicable (GDPR (2018) as are regulations for accessing the UK data service. (https://www.ukdataservice.ac.uk/get-data/how-to-access/conditions.aspx). It is important to stress that this book does not set out to provide a definitive list of relevant legislation and all researchers should take responsibility to check via their own ethics committees and regulatory body/ethics codes for their disciplinary fields to ensure that their research plans are fully in accordance with relevant and current legislation at all times.

The plethora of disciplinary and jurisdictional codes provide powerful testament to the multifaceted and complex nature of the differing contexts that educational research spans. These encompass projects that have international reach as well as projects that necessarily interact with other facets of a complex social, economic and political environment.

Educational research is not confined to, nor always defined by, the school setting. As was noted in the introduction to this book, even where the primary focus is the school or other educational institution it is quite frequently necessary to engage with services and the community that extends beyond the school gates. The individual researcher therefore may be required to have recourse to a number of relevant but distinct frameworks, which, even when broadly similar in purpose and intent, may have nuances of emphasis and competing priorities. Throughout this book, authors have considered how the researcher can navigate this multiplicity of ethical responsibilities. This will start with gaining ethical approval for an intended project. Although it could be further argued that an ethical stance towards research should start in advance of the formal process in terms of reflection on what constitutes an ethical focus for a project. Linda Shaw, Carmel Capewell and Patrick Alexander reflect on this philosophically in their chapters. Other authors highlight the particular quandaries that face those for whom it is a requirement, or is otherwise expedient to conduct research, whether for their studies (See Pratt, Chapter IV), their careers (Wild and Frodsham, Chapter XIII; Wild and Brown, Chapter X) or their wider professional training or development (Jane Spiro, Chapter IX).

Notwithstanding this important caveat, formal engagement with the ethics committee is an integral and crucial part of research design and onward monitoring of projects. This was the focus of Sarah Quinton's chapter (III), in which she gave an invaluable insight into the responsibilities and objectives of such committees. Her chapter was honest and open about the ways in which ethics committees and researchers can come to view ethical approval as somewhat adversarial and find themselves 'lost in translation' when misconceptions of both the role of the committee and the imperatives are misunderstood and miscommunicated. From the perspective of those that sit on a university ethics committee, it was revealing to appreciate the extent to which external demands and pressures are multiple and often shifting. The ethics committee is accountable to a multitude of regulatory bodies and research funders and must be constantly mindful not only of the ultimate responsibility towards participants in research and for researcher wellbeing but also of the reputation of the institution that the committee represents. However, as custodians of these various responsibilities the ethics committee is not bound by a set of universal guidelines, rather, as noted by Carol Brown and Jane Spiro in their chapters (II and IX), the committee, like the researcher, must balance a range of differing codes as well as ensuring compliance to any statutory considerations such as safeguarding legislation.

Obtaining ethical approval from the ethics committee is but one, albeit extremely significant, step in conducting research to a high ethical standard. As many of the contributing authors to this book have demonstrated, the practicum of research will continue to yield ethical dilemmas no matter how well planned or thought out the research has been. Catherine Gilson (Chapter V) highlighted tensions that can arise between the procedural ethics in obtaining permission for a research project from the ethics committee and the subsequent and often myriad dilemmas that can arise in the field in the 'situated' context. She unveils several dilemmas she encountered in her own small-scale qualitative project, which involved interviews as well as video elicitation. She openly acknowledges that these dilemmas took her by surprise and in the momentary context she had no time to refer back to the ethics committee but needed to make immediate and sensitive decisions that reflected the in-the-moment responses and requests of her participants. In turn, this placed pressure on herself as the researcher, required to act and react using initiative and sensitivity to unexpected events in the field, a theme that is reiterated in Wild and Brown's chapter (X) on researcher wellbeing. Catharine Gilson shares how she resolved the dilemmas she encountered and explains how she sought to draw upon an ethical stance in her decision-making. In so doing, like other authors in this book, she does not suggest simplistic solutions but offers up strategies that she found useful as possible steers for others to consider.

Similarly, reflecting on a larger and classroom-based study, Sarah Frodsham and Deb McGregor consider some of the conundrums that they encountered when investigating creativity in the science classroom (Chapter VII). Although their methodology is very different to Catharine Gilson's, they too stress the centrality of an ethical stance in all the research decisions and choices they faced in the field. They make detailed reference back to the BERA guidelines, showing how such principles come to be enacted within a dynamic and fluid research environment. They also note the tensions that can exist for the researcher who is naturally keen to elicit new data, which must be necessarily balanced against the rights of the participants – in this case primary aged schoolchildren – to be agentive as well as fully respected by the adult researcher. The dilemmas may be implicit as well as explicit, since the underlying power differential between adults and children is not always easy to counteract. The dilemma caused by the drive to elicit new findings and to bring something new to the field of educational understanding is a pressure that is further explored in Wild and Brown's chapter in terms of its impact on the wellbeing of the researcher.

Specific forms of research throw up dilemmas that may not have been encompassed in some existing codes and in the established custom and practice of the regulatory bodies. Insider research and action research, for example, were specifically noted in Sarah Quinton's chapter. Such forms of research may be especially pertinent in areas of study like education wherein research is very often focused and led by professional and applied questions and imperatives. These forms of research are addressed directly by Jane Spiro. In her chapter, she argues powerfully that approaches such as action research, auto-ethnography and narrative enquiry are vital contributions to the field of educational research, conveying rich and unique insights for practice and for individuals who implement practice. One might say that she makes an ethically based case for such lenses of study and for insider-based methods. Nonetheless, drawing on her substantial experience of these modes of research, she charts some of the challenges that are unearthed when investigating a setting or practice with which one is personally involved or embedded within. Whilst the exigencies of the researcher/researched position are very different in these forms of research, Jane Spiro is committed to proactive engagement with ethical procedures and a self-aware and reflexive ethical stance on the part of the insider researcher. Once again, the chapter is replete with practical resolutions that have been adopted by insider researchers to mitigate the very particular ethical dilemmas they may experience.

The importance of adopting a self-reflexive stance towards ethical dilemmas in research is a recurring theme for contributing authors as a crucial way in which a balance can be struck between the sometimes competing needs of all participants and stakeholders. In Carmel Capewell's chapter, this is envisioned from the perspective of involving children as active and agentive stakeholders. Building explicitly on Brown's opening chapter, Capewell invokes the UNCRC (1989) with particular emphasis on Articles 12 (Right to provide their own views) and 23 (Rights of mentally or physically disabled child). She explores in detail the tension that can exist between a legitimate aim on the part of the ethics committee to ensure that participants are not harmed but problematizes the sometimes-unwitting assumption that children and young people are automatically positioned as vulnerable, which engenders negative interpretations of their competence. She argues that this can have deleterious connotations for their agency and sometimes expressed wish to be active and fully recognized participants in research.

Although she ponders some of these underlying presumptions of the ethics committee, she does not seek to disregard these processes. Indeed, she states the value of having an ethics committee overview to provide an independent view on a project and as a valuable means to ensure a clear focus on methods as well as the ultimate dissemination of findings. However, like Catharine Gilson, she recognizes the ways in which research is more complex and interactive in reality than can be presaged in advance. She highlights the importance of a researcher being guided by a 'moral compass', when the researcher encounters 'situations whereby a researcher could be within the ethical approval to continue with their research, but the situation may lead the researcher to question whether they should proceed'. Thus, she signals that research will often lead to a researcher needing to act beyond the parameters of what could be foreseen in order to ensure onward ethicality.

Turning to more vicarious engagement in research, Victoria Pratt reflects on the ethical dilemmas that redound not just to those who are actively conducting research, but also to those who are overseeing and guiding others in research. Although, as Pratt notes, undergraduate research is often perceived to be 'low stakes', it is in fact a very redolent position of responsibility for the supervisor who must guide the students, who are nearly always novice researchers. In such supervisory relationships, there are inherent power differentials and there are substantive pressures of time expediency. Paradoxically too there are very real 'high stakes' of securing a productive outcome to the research, which forms such a significant proportion of student assessment. Once again, there is resonance with the personal and professional pressures that researchers face at other stages in an academic career, as highlighted in Wild and Brown's chapter.

Desk-based research is suggested by Pratt as a possible alternative to empirical work that can potentially assuage some of the ethical dilemmas that challenge the undergraduate student. Pratt specifically considers the role of the supervisor of undergraduate research projects but some of the dilemmas that she points to might also be mirrored by those who oversee research teams but who do not themselves form part on the team on the ground who are collecting data. Both Pratt and Wild and Frodsham in their later chapter highlight an alternative set of ethical issues that can arise for those who focus on working with extant bodies of data. The latter chapter delves beneath the seemingly neutral figures in extant databases to consider the underlying basis of the original research from an ethical dimension. Probing the rationale for exploring and interpreting datasets requires attention to underlying assent and confers an ethical duty of faithfulness and integrity towards the original purpose, reliability and validity of the data that was generated. More philosophically, there are ethical reflections to ponder regarding the nature and genre of research that result in highly aggregated data. In considering the philosophical basis of numerically driven research, Wild and Frodsham discuss the increasing prevalence of marketized and neoliberal accounts of educational research. This theme is picked up in relation to the impact on researcher wellbeing and career development in Wild and Brown's chapter.

Wild and Frodsham return to the theme of reflexivity as a balancing force in research, arguing that reflection on ones' beliefs and assumptions is an ethical imperative for researchers. Shaw takes this argument further and calls for researchers to actively 'trouble' existing discourses of educational research. In a similar vein, Alexander, with his focus on research with Indigenous communities provides some graphic examples of how not troubling existing discourse can be highly problematic. These viewpoints will be important counterweights to be considered as we move to focus on the concluding theme of this book.

Before doing so, it is important to highlight one key thread that has run through the various accounts and perspectives that our authors have brought to the fore about balancing needs. All have revealed the complex and iterative challenges that make research undoubtedly interesting and stimulating to the researcher, but they have also at least hinted at and in many cases directly exposed the very real personal and professional challenges that the researcher faces. The wellbeing of the researcher is also included in codes such as BERA guidelines and is a key focus for those on the ethics committee too, as Carol Brown and then Sarah Quinton noted at the outset of this book. However as mentioned in our earlier chapter (Wild and Brown) we would suggest that in almost every instance of drawing together a research proposal or plan, the researcher is likely to be motivated principally by wanting to find out something they believe to be inherently worthwhile. They will also be rightly concerned to ensure that those with whom they will work with for the project will be protected. However, we would venture to suggest that they might not always fully focus on the potential impacts for themselves. Hence, we felt it essential to include a specific chapter on researcher wellbeing that considered some of the practical issues that may unfold in the field and some of the emotional challenge and risk that researchers experience. The importance of active self-reflection by the researcher was emphasized as a means by which socially sensitive research can be enacted and as a vital practice in helping to handle trauma to the researcher. That chapter also considered some of the implications of the wider working environment and culture that researchers find themselves within. This is a prevailing culture, which, like educational research, is seen to be increasingly driven by an agenda that focuses on outputs and measurable indicators of success. Which, albeit set squarely in the context of impact on the researcher, returns us to the philosophical contestations noted by Linda Shaw and Patrick Alexander and will be picked up in respect of the notion of a community of researchers.

Ethical dilemmas do not exist in isolation and can be resolved as part of a community of researchers

Our final theme invokes a sprit or community of research that it is suggested we could coalesce around. Our contributing authors have each alluded to this and it resonates with the repeated references that are to be found in the BERA (2018) guidelines to a 'community of education researchers' and is define explicitly in article 61 of the BERA guidelines as:

> 61 The 'community of educational researchers' is considered to mean all those engaged in educational research – including,... students following research-based programmes of study and independent researchers, as well as staff who conduct educational research in their employment within organizations such as universities, schools, local and national government, charities and commercial bodies. (BERA 2018: 28/29)

From the outset of this book, Brown and then Quinton drew attention to the complexity of the regulatory and contextual frames that inform and underpin educational research. Subsequent chapters provided many specific and detailed exemplars of this complex backdrop. The range of stakeholders was identified drawing on BERA guidance in Brown's chapter (II), and is echoed in their definition as noted above, as well as the multiplicity of settings in which educational research is conducted, which were elaborated upon in Quinton's chapter (III) and returned to in a variety of guises by authors throughout the book. Further dynamics were identified in term of the increasingly globalized and evolving nature of research and, although the UNCRC was seen as a widely adopted set of principles, the lack of a single definitive regulatory code of ethics was noted. Set against this complex portrayal, several questions arise. Is it indeed possible to refer to a community of researchers as if it were some readily identifiable and cohesive group? Is it possible to widen this group to include those involved in setting ethical parameters and how might this be accomplished? The contention of this book has been that whilst it may not be easy to resolve these questions, it is possible through critical self-reflection and dialogue to edge towards bridging some of these divides.

As is demonstrated in the differing contributions to this book, there is profound diversity in the conceptualization of educational research. This results in differing approaches to methodology, which surface quite distinct ethical dilemmas at the practical level that were considered in detail in the preceding section of this chapter. How these dilemmas were resolved in an ethical but iterative way was noted in various forms. It was evident that adopting a positive stance towards working with and through the ethics committee, beyond gaining institutional approval, was often integral in moving the research on in a productive way that remained respectful towards the involvement of all parties in the research. It was striking in these accounts that an ongoing communication with the ethics committee can be pivotal in building understanding that can transcend misconception and dispel divisive relationships between researchers and the ethics committee. Equally, there was recognition in Quinton's chapter that working together must work both ways, with a recognition from this former chair of an ethics committee that:

> ... a more explicit recognition by ethics committees that there is a wide diversity of research approaches and that within certain subject areas, such as education research, more ethically complex approaches ... may be appropriate. (this book p.71)

That is not to pretend that such dialogue will always be easy or uncontentious. As has been previously noted, some of the seemingly 'fundamental' principles of ethics in education, such as the focus on individual rights (Chapter XI), the construction of the child as non-adult (Chapter VI) or alternative definitions of educational truth (Chapter XII), are bound to be more contested when set against a systemic approach to ethics that is forged on a particular socio-historical anvil. Nevertheless, these authors are resolute in acknowledging the foundational importance of ethical guidance. In so doing, they echo the tenor of the BERA guidelines, which recognize the range of philosophical orientations to educational research and advocate that

> it is adherence to the spirit of the guidelines that we consider most vital to protect all who are involved in or affected by a piece of research. (BERA 2018: 2)

The coming together of researchers from differing perspectives and traditions within this book and the spirit of dialogue evoked by all contributors demonstrate that debate and differences can be the lifeblood, not the death knell, in forging common purpose and endeavour. Can this common endeavour extend to the ethics committee? Well, it was after all the former chair of an ethics committee who in this book suggested that 'progressing scholarship within education research is a shared priority' (this book p. 54).

A community of researchers does not necessitate nor imply homogeneity, but wrestling with ethical dilemmas and an unswerving ethical intent does unite all the authors in this book. This book is not intended to gloss over the points of difference and debate – the ethical dilemmas of our title – but that does not mean we cannot come together to discuss and share our perspectives whilst recognizing our differences. As the small sliver of the research community represented in this book shows we can find, and are finding, ways to work together and to learn from one another. The foundations of an ethical approach are of utmost importance to all involved in research and by offering up ethical dilemmas to discussion, it may be possible to forge a more united forward path. We hope this book will play a small part in that endeavour.

References

American Medical Association (AMA) (2001) *Council on Ethical and Judicial Affairs: Ethical Considerations in International Research.* Available at: https://www.ama-assn.org/delivering-care/ethics/code-medical-ethics-overview (accessed 20 December 2021).

American Educational Research Association (AERA) (2011) *Ethical Standards of the American Educational Research Association.* Available at: https://www.aera.net/About-AERA/AERA-Rules-Policies/Professional-Ethics (accessed 20 December 2021).

Australian Government (2018) *Australian Code for the Responsible Conduct of Research* https://www.nhmrc.gov.au/about-us/publications/australian-code-responsible-conduct-research-2018 (accessed 10 December 2021).

British Educational Research Association (2018) *Ethical Guidelines for Educational Research.* British Educational Research Association (BERA). Available at: https://www.bera.ac.uk/publication/ethical-guidelines-for-educational-research-2018 (accessed 10 July 2019).

British Psychological Society (BPS) (2021) Code of Human Research Ethics (2021). Available at: https://www.bps.org.uk/news-and-policy/bps-code-human-research-ethics (accessed 29 June 2022).

Department for Education and Department of Health:SEND (2014) *Special Education Needs and Disablity Code of Practice: 0-25 years*. Available at: from https://www.gov.uk/government/publications/send-code-of-practice-0-to-25 (accessed 21 November 2021).

Department for Education and Department of Health (2014) *Statutory Guidance for Organisations in the UK Working with Disabled CYP or Special Educational Needs*.

DHEW (1979) National Commission for the Protection of Human Subjects of Biomedical and Behavioral Research (NCPHSBBR) *The Belmont Report*. Government Printing Office.

ESRC Economic and Social Research Council (2019) Our Core Principles. Available at: https://esrc.ukri.org/funding/guidance-for-applicants/research-ethics/our-core-principles/ (accessed 2 August 2019).

GDPR (2018) *Guide to the General Data Protection Regulation (GDPR)*. Information Commissioner's Office. Available at: https://www.gov.uk/government/publications/guide-to-the-general-data-protection-regulation (accessed 29 June 2022).

Global Code of Conduct (2018) The Global Code of Conduct for Research in Resource Poor Settings Available at: www.glocalcodeofconduct.org (accessed 4 January 2022).

International Visual Sociology Association (IVSA) (2019) Code of Research Ethics Guidelines. Available at: https://visualsociology.org/?page_id=405 (accessed 21 December 2021).

United Nations Convention on the Rights of the Child (UNCRC) (1989) *United Nations Convention on the Rights of the Child*. Available at: https://www.unicef.org.uk/what-we-do/un-convention-child-rights/ (accessed 20 July 2021).

Index

Page numbers in italics are figures; with 't' are tables.

academic freedom 1, 7, 173, 175–80
academic life, and wellbeing 130–1
accountability
   and secondary data 96, 103, 107
   and wellbeing 131
action research 178
   and CYP 68
   and insider research 111, 112, 113, 117, 118, 122
aesthetics 163–4
agency
   children's 167
   and confidentiality 117
   and the creative classroom 76, 78
   see also cultural and historical activity theory (CHAT)
Alderson, P. 61
American Educational Research Association (AERA) 144
anonymity 113–14, 117–18
anthropology 144, 145, 147, 158
   and Indigenous communities 149
assent
   and CYP 64–6
   see also consent
audio data 28, 77, 80–3, 80t, 87, 88t, 89–90
   see also visual data
Australia 63–4, 69, 70, 98t, 130, 145, 166, 175–6
authorship 17–18
   undergraduate research dissertations 42

Babacan, A. 132, 133
Babacan, H. 132, 133
Balen, R. 63
Ball, S.J. 142, 148, 149, 157
   The Education Debate 164–5
Bauman, Zigmund 146
beings or becomings
   CYP as 61–4
Belmont Report 10
benchmark statements 35

beneficence, and insider research 112, 118–20
BERA *see* British Educational Research Association (BERA)
best interests 11, 14, 37, 79, 144
bias 29, 37, 115, 124
Biesta, G 94
Bloor, M. 128, 134, 137
Bourke, R. 65
Boyer Commission 33–4, 41, 45
Briganti, A. 122
British Educational Research Association (BERA) ethical guidelines 10, 12, 13–18, 102, 174, 175, 182
   and CHAT 78, 79, 80t, 83, 85
   and the community of educational researchers 180–1
   and CYP 70
   and Indigenous communities 144, 151
   researcher wellbeing 127–8, 129–30, 130, 138
   and undergraduate dissertations 33, 35–40, 41, 42–3
British Psychological Society (BPS) 10, 175
Bryce, T. 155
Buckley, P. 35, 41
Bulle, N. 97

Canada 98t, 143, 145
care, theory of 121–3
Cave, N. 107
Chamberlain, L. 66
CHAT *see* cultural and historical activity theory (CHAT)
child data protection act (CDPA) 83
childhood 166–7, 169, 175
children/young people (CYP) 61–2, 72, 178–9
   as beings or becomings 61–4
   as consulted or co-researchers 67–8
   and context 25–6

Index **185**

dependency issues 26–7
and research methods 68–70
and researchers' moral compasses 70–2
United Nations Convention of the Rights of the Child (UNCRC) 10–12
as a vulnerable group 28
Christensen, P. 65
clients, responsibilities to 16–17, 40, 174
codes/guidelines 12–18, 144–5, 173, 174–5, 181
see also British Educational Research Association (BERA) ethical guidelines
Cohen, L. 49, 95–6, 100
Collet-Sabe, J. 142, 148, 149
Collier, J. 52–3
common purpose 1, 21–3, 182
community of educational researchers 180–2
responsibilities to 17, 41
competency, and CYP 61–2
compliance, and ethics committees 21–2
confidentiality
and insider research 113–14, 117–18
see also privacy
consent 10, 14–15, 23
and children 11, 26–7, 64–6, 79, 80–3, 102
and insider research 113, 116–17
and interviews 51, 56–8
consequentialist/non-consequentialist approaches 54–5
context 24–6
cultural 55–6
Costley, C. 121
creativity in the classroom 76–8, 89–90, 164, 177–8
and cultural and historical activity theory (CHAT) 78–89, *78*, 80t, *85*, *87*, 88t
cultural and historical activity theory (CHAT) 78–83, *78*, 80t
and creativity 84–9, *85*, *87*, 88t
culture 25, 175, 180
and interviewing 55–6
and socially sensitive research 132
see also ethnography
CYP *see* children/young people

Dahlberg, G. 165
data *see* audio data; visual data
Data Protection 16, 107, 176
data storage 16, 40
decolonization 143, 147, 149–50
see also post-colonialism
Demirbag, J.R. 121
dependency issues 26–7
Derrida, J. 158
desk-based research *see* numerical data
Dhillon, J.K. 120, 121
DiQuinzio, P. 156–7
disabled children/young people 61, 62, 65, 67–8
disclosure 16, 40
dissemination of research 17–18, 41–2, 45
dissertations 33–5
distress *see* harm
Doyle, E. 35, 41
Durham Commission 77

Ethical Research Involving Children (ERIC) 36, 37
ethical review 64, 71
ethics in action *see* situated ethics
ethics of care 121–3
ethics committees 21, 177, 179
common purpose and misunderstandings 21–3
and CYP 70–1
and good practice 29–30
and insider research 123–4
and researchers' wellbeing 136
and socially sensitive research 132–3
specific sensitivities 24–9
and technology 23–4
ethnographic stance 149–50
ethnography 158–63, 178
ethnomethodology 160, 162–3
Être et Avoir (documentary film) 53

Fenge, L, 134–5, 136
field research 128–30
film elicitation interviews 52–5
Foucault, M. 160–1, 163–4
freedom of expression 11–12

Gallagher, C. 38, 41
gatekeepers 14

ethics committees as 119, 124
parents/carers as 62, 69
gender 156–7
Gibbs, C. 121
Global Code of Conduct for Research in Resource Poor Settings 25, 175
good practice, and ethics committees 29–30
Gordon, A.F. 164, 167
Ghostly Matters 166
guidelines *see* ethical codes/guidelines

Hack, C.J. 38, 44–5
Harcourt, D. 63
harm 15–16, 18, 144, 148
 and CYP 61
 and interviewing 51–2
 and undergraduate dissertations 39
Healey, M.J. 38, 42–3
historical context 9–10
 and Indigenous communities 144–8
Humes, W. 155
Hunt, S. 147

imagination 164–8
Implementation Handbook for the Convention of the Rights of the Child (UNICEF) 11
incentives 39
India 145
Indigenous communities 142–3, 151–2
 decolonizing research 147, 149–50
 defining 143
 historical context 144–8
 and school 148–9
individualism 148, 151
informed consent *see* consent
insider research 28–9, 111–12, 134
 and anthropology 158–9
 core ethical values 112–15
 and ethics committees 123–4
 and Indigenous communities 150
 process and principles 120–3
 response to ethical questions 116–20
insider-outsider partnerships 120–2, 124
international data 96–7, 98–100t, 100, *101*
International Early Learning Study (IELS) 94–5
International Visual Sociology Association (IVSA) 53
internet 23, 37–8, 70

intersectionality 128, 155, 157
interviews, as research method 50–9
Isham, L. 133, 135

Jenkins, A. 38
Jones, F. 130
justice 112, 115, 157

Kettley, N.C. 165–6
Kinman, G. 130
Klykken, F. 65

Lawthom, R. 69, 70
Lewis, A. 67
Lighthouse Keeper's Son lessons 84–7, *85*, *87*
Löfström, E. 41, 45
Loveridge, J. 65

McCosker, H. 136
MacDonald, A. 68
McLaren, P. 157–8
Mannay, D. 87
Miles, S. 69, 70
Milgram, Stanley 10
Milligan, L. 120, 121
Mills, C.W. 166
moral compasses 70–2, 179
Morrow, V. 61
Moss, Peter 94

naming 113–14
New Zealand 97, 98t, 100, *101*
non-maleficence *see* harm
Norway 65, 98t
numerical data 93, 179
 evaluating experience of the participants 103–4
 hidden dilemmas 104–7
 secondary data 107–8
  international 96–7, 98–100t, 100, *101*, 102–5
  local 102
 what works research 93–5
Nuremberg Code 9–10

ontological turn 147
open access 17
O'Reilly, M. 129
Organization for Economic Co-operation and Development 96–7

International Early Learning Study (IELS) 94–5
Ortner, S.B. 149
ownership of data 118

Palaiologou, I. 122–3
Parker, N. 129
participant action research (PAR) 160
  see also action research
participants
  and PISA 103–4
  respect for 112–15
  responsibilities to 14–16, 35–40, 106, 174
  rights 178
personhood 147, 148, 151, 155
photos
  use of 69–70, 83
  see also visual data
Photovoice 69
Pillay, J. 63, 71
plagiarism 17, 41
politics 165
positionality 95, 106, 134–5, 135, 137, 149, 175
post-colonialism 155, 156
post-feminism 155, 156–7
post-modernism 155–8, 166
post-paradigms 154–5, 168–9
  aesthetics 163–4
  ethnography and ethno-methodology 158–63
  imagination/sociological imagination 164–8
  post-modern classrooms 155–8
post-structuralism 154–5, 159–61, 163–4, 168–9
power, and research of self 115
privacy 2, 12, 16, 23, 28
  and CHAT 81, 83
  GDPR 107, 176
  and undergraduate dissertations 40
procedural ethics 3, 49–50
Programme for International Student Assessment (PISA) 89, 94, 95, 96–7, 98–100t, 100, *101*, 103
Prout, A. 65
publication 17–18, 41–2, 45

Quennerstadt, A. 63

regulation see ethical codes/guidelines
religious context 26
research ethics committees see ethics committees
respect for persons/participants 112–15
rights see freedom of expression; participants; privacy; withdrawal
Rikowski, G. 157–8
risk
  and CYP 64, 102
  for researchers' wellbeing 128–30
Rose, G. 56
Rose, Jacqueline 56

school, and Indigenous communities 148–9
scope and format, undergraduate research dissertations 42
second generation activity theory see cultural and historical activity theory (CHAT)
secondary data 96–7, 98–100t, 100, *101*, 102, 104–5, 107–8
secondary trauma 133–5
self, research see insider research
self-reflection 131, 135, 136, 180
Shapiro, J. 121
Sieber, J.E. 132, 133
Sikic Micanovic, L. 136, 137
Simons, Helen 58–9
situated ethics 49–50
social context 26
social haunting 164
socially sensitive research 132–3
  and secondary trauma 133–5
sociological imagination 166
South Africa, and CYP 63
sponsors 15, 16–17, 40, 174
stakeholders, responsibilities to 16–17, 40, 174
Stanley, B. 132, 133
statutory regulation 16, 28, 176
  and CYP 65, 176
  see also ethical codes/guidelines
storytelling 150
students as researchers approach 45
summative assessment tests (SATs) 103
supervision, undergraduate research dissertations 32–46
Sweden 63–4, 70, 98t, 175–6

technologies 129
  internet 23, 37–8, 70
  see also audio data; visual data
theory in education 158, 165–6
Thomas, G. 96, 102, 106
Thomas, N. 120, 121
Todd, M. 44, 147
Traianou, A. 50
training, for supervisors 44
transparency 15, 38–9
trauma, secondary 133–5
Tuhiwai Smith, Linda 143, 145, 146–7, 147–8, 149–50

UK data service 107–8
undergraduate research dissertations 32–46, 43–5, 179
UNICEF 11–12, 28
  Ethical Research Involving Children (ERIC) 36, 37
United Kingdom 97, 98t, *101*, 157
United Nations Convention of the Rights of the Child (UNCRC) 10–12, 174, 178
  and Indigenous communities 144
  on participation in research 61, 64–5, 67
  on school 148
United States 33–4, 98t, 143, 145, 165
universality 148, 156, 157
Urban, Matthias 94

van Stumm, S. 107
video data *see* visual data

visual data 16, 51, 52–5, 56
  and CHAT 81–3
  and CYP 68
  see also audio data
Vivieros de Castro, E. 147
voluntary involvement, and insider research 114–15, 118–20
Vostal, F. 130
vulnerable groups, children 28

wellbeing
  researchers' 18, 21, 25, 127–8, 137–8, 177, 180
    preparedness 135–7
    reflective issues 131
    risk and dilemmas 128–31
    secondary trauma 133–5
    socially sensitive research 132–3
  and undergraduate dissertations 42–3
what works research 93–5
Wilson, M. 80, 97
withdrawal, right 15, 39, 79, 81, 82
Woodhead, M. 166–7
workplace, and researchers' wellbeing 130–1
writing research 168, 169

Young, M. 156–7
young people's advisory groups (YPAGs) 67

Zimbabwe 66
Zimbardo, Philip 10